Praise for *Motivation and Performance*

'Few topics are as important, yet poorly understood, as workplace motivation. This book provides an authoritative guide for leaders and professionals interested in leveraging the science of motivation to enhance individual, team and organizational performance. A must-read if you care about evidence-based management and understand the limits of intuition.'
Tomas Chamorro-Premuzic, CEO, Hogan Assessments, and Professor of Business Psychology, University College London and Columbia University

'Everyone knows that an engaged workforce is more productive and profitable, yet so many try to achieve this with a singular "silver bullet" solution that often harms as much as it helps. *Motivation and Performance* gives balance to the complex factors at play, shows leaders where to look and guides their judgement. It clearly shows just what startling results can be achieved by getting it right and how dire the consequences of getting it wrong. Leaders of any size of organization can learn and profit from this book.'
Group Captain John Jupp PhD OBE

'This book is an extremely valuable resource for leaders of businesses of all sizes and anyone working in HR. It contains great practical tools, such as templates and guidelines for best practice. The anecdotes and case studies bring the academically informed points to life, articulately making them relevant and accessible to readers.'
Paul Rein, Principal Consultant Psychologist, Thomas International

Motivation and Performance

A guide to motivating a diverse workforce

Ian MacRae

Adrian Furnham

KoganPage

First published in Great Britain and the United States in 2017 by Kogan Page Limited

2nd Floor, 45 Gee Street	c/o Martin P Hill Consulting	4737/23 Ansari Road
London EC1V 3RS	122 W 27th St, 10th Floor	Daryaganj
United Kingdom	New York NY 10001	New Delhi 110002
	USA	India

www.koganpage.com

© Ian MacRae and Adrian Furnham, 2017

ISBN   978 0 7494 7813 1
E-ISBN   978 0 7494 7814 8

British Library Cataloguing-in-Publication Data

A CIP record for this book is available from the British Library.

Library of Congress Cataloging-in-Publication Data

Names: MacRae, Ian, author. | Furnham, Adrian, author.
Title: Motivation and performance : a guide to motivating a diverse workforce
   / Ian MacRae, Adrian Furnham.
Description: 1st Edition. | New York : Kogan Page Ltd, [2017] | Includes
   bibliographical references and index.
Identifiers: LCCN 2016048910 (print) | LCCN 2016057722 (ebook) | ISBN
   9780749478131 (alk. paper) | ISBN 9780749478148 (ebook)
Subjects: LCSH: Employee motivation. | Diversity in the workplace. |
   Organizational change.
Classification: LCC HF5549.5.M63 M327 2017 (print) | LCC HF5549.5.M63 (ebook)
   | DDC 658.3/14–dc23

Typeset by Integra Software Services, Pondicherry
Print production managed by Jellyfish
Printed and bound by CPI Group (UK) Ltd, Croydon, CR0 4YY

CONTENTS

ACKNOWLEDGEMENTS

We would like to thank everyone who contributed to, or supported us, in writing this book in a number of different ways. Thanks to Rachel Casper, Lloyd Craig, Heather Craig, Shonagh Doherty, Delta Emerson, Karen Fox, Sean Graham, Marcus Gee, Matthew Griffiths, Alison Grenier, Lara Kotobi, Kody Krogh, Brendan MacRae, Diana MacRae, Duncan MacRae, Cherie Mandoli, Celeste McFarland, Kyleen Myrah, Michael Orwick, Damita Pressl, Martin Reid, Paul Rein, Roberta Sawatzky, Heather Stewart, John Taylor, Alexandra Theodorescu, Isobel Thomson, Katherine Thornton, Skye Trubov, Laura Weis, Ken Whittall, Jessica Weaving, Jian Xu and anyone else who may have inspired content in this book. And particular thanks to Alixe Lay who has made significant contributions to the research and content throughout much of this book.

Special thanks also go to the editorial team: Lucy Carter, Katy Hamilton, Amy Minshull, Philippa Fiszzon, Amanda Dackombe, Anita Clark and Sarah Hilton. Their hard work and excellent advice has greatly improved the book.

To the memory of Ruth Stewart.
And to Alison and Benedict Furnham.

Nothing bolsters the motivation to strive for success and risk failure like knowing there are always people who will love you no matter what.

Introduction 01

Motivation is the difference between action and inaction. It is the difference between *thinking* about doing something and getting it done. It is the difference between average and excellent performance. Without motivation, there is nothing.

Demotivated employees are more likely to leave their current organization to find a more motivating job. Failures in employee retention are estimated by PricewaterhouseCoopers to cost the UK economy £42 billion annually. They estimated that every 1 per cent reduction in turnover would save the UK economy £8 billion (Thomas, 2010). Bond and Bunce (2001) found that a well-being intervention reduced sick days by 1.4 days per employee per year. Sick days are estimated to cost the UK another £16 billion annually (Personnel Today, 2015). Sometimes people get sick, but there is clear evidence (Consiglio *et al*, 2013; Schaufeli, Bakker and van Rhenen, 2009; van Rhenen *et al*, 2007; de Boer *et al*, 2002) that better working conditions and work engagement can reduce sickness absenteeism. Bond, Flaxman and Bunce (2008) reported £105,164 savings at a call centre from a well-being intervention reducing short-term absences with an average of five fewer days absent per employee over a 14-month period. Another study (Wall, Jackson and Davids, 1992) found that relatively minor improvements to human resource policy on an assembly line led to a productivity gain of US $2,400 per week.

Fields such as management, human resources and psychology are not immune to trends and fads. Different theories of motivation rise and fall, while different techniques to motivate employees are constantly emerging. In each of the subsequent chapters we present practical tools and recommendations for improving motivation and hence productivity at work. And throughout we provide examples of actual people and companies to illustrate the concepts, successes and opportunities.

The usefulness of the trends varies. Some trends are little better than snake oil, a brief (but expensive) workshop with an impressive-sounding name. Often the previous methods or approaches are discarded for newer, slicker methods. In some cases, this means the lessons learned from previous methods are also discarded.

The generational differences example

It is inevitable that each new generation differs from the previous one – new values, new motivation and reinvigorated ideas. Each generation has much more in common with people their own age than with their parents or grandparents. Correct? Actually, it's not. Much has been written on categorizing, classifying and constructing specific generations to compare their differences at work (described in Chapter 3). Myths about generational differences are an easy target, mostly because the scientific evidence lends little support to theories of generational differences. Yet it's a useful target for initiating the discussion about motivation and performance at work. It's one of the fads that at best is incorrect but at worst causes poor decision making in organizations based on incorrect assumptions.

There is something amiss with generational difference myths; there is an implicit agreement, rarely discussed, in any conversation about generational differences: we assume that generational differences exist. And they can in a historical sense. Of course the new millennium is profoundly different from the 1970s or 1870s. Labour laws 150 years ago, or even 50 years ago, have been largely moving towards being more favourable to workers. The nature of work and workplaces are always changing. We mention the historical changes, and then, in Chapter 12, describe in detail the shift to contracting and outsourcing work.

But what of the people in those time periods? How much can we infer about any individual based on their year of birth? The fact is, there are almost no valid psychological predictions we can make based on the year of birth. This may sound controversial. Everyone will be able to think of substantial differences between themselves and someone else who is significantly older or younger. Chapter 10 explains this through the motivational profiles of two individuals in similar careers from different generations.

We will be returning to the question of generational differences throughout our discussion of motivation, highlighted by some of the misconceptions that stem from theories about generational differences. The reason this is a useful discussion, more constructive than just examining motivation alone, is because many of the misconceptions and misinformation about generational differences highlight the greatest improvements that can still be made in the way we work and work to motivate. These improvements can also be made in areas such as in performance management systems (Chapters 5 and 6), work engagement and organizational culture (Chapter 8), compensation structures (Chapter 9) and succession planning (Chapter 10).

If you are looking to know '*are there generational differences?*' you can get a quick answer by plugging that question into a search engine. You will almost certainly get millions of results arguing both sides. Most results miss the most important point.

The important question in the workplace – and in this book – is: *are there generational differences that have meaningful implications for managers, leaders, human resources, or anyone involved in motivation in the workplace?* The question can be extended to other differences such as gender or ethnicity (and the benefits of employment equity are discussed in Chapter 5). The short answer is no, there are no meaningful generational differences. Most generational differences are superficial or irrelevant to the workplace (we discuss this in more detail in Chapter 3). The differences that have the most profound implications for the workplace are the differences between people instead of the differences between groups. Of course people of different ages exist and, yes, people can have different experiences depending on when they were born and what is happening in the world at that time, but these factors have very limited effects on organizational concerns like motivation and performance.

Furthermore, when generational differences exist, there is often a secondary explanation. For example, in Chapter 9 we discuss findings about generational differences, and valuing pay. Surprisingly, younger workers value pay more than their colleagues in older generations. Yet when we considered income levels, the real conclusion was obvious. Income levels explain the differences in motivation. Younger people, it turns out, often tend to earn much less money. Those who do not earn enough (or in some cases too much) money value it more. We explain the reason behind this in Chapter 9.

Often, in everyday conversation and discourse, generational differences are discussed in the context of a particular case study or individual example. Stories should be used cautiously, and not to prove a particular point. If you catch yourself thinking, at any time, during this book '*Well, I know someone who...*', stop yourself. Individual stories are poor evidence (and we explain why in Chapter 5, along with when they are useful). Stories are good for illustrating facts, but should not be used as a supplement for strong evidence. Throughout this book we will present the evidence, along with practical steps to use the research in the workplace. The book concludes (Chapter 14) with three case studies that highlight best practice in relation to motivation and performance: two case studies of impressive success and one of extreme failure. To illustrate the importance of motivation, let's first look at some of the more extreme examples of how systems can shape motivation.

Two illustrative examples of motivation and performance

There are countless stories from the Soviet Union with centrally planned factories and specific targets, tied to five-year plans: for example, required to build a set number of tractors or airplanes. Even if apocryphal these stories are instructive. Ambitious plans were set out, with a specific output target for each factory. This is not unlike many performance management systems that set output targets. Some production targets in these Soviet factories may have been entirely unrealistic, but the consequences of failing to meet targets were extremely severe. Anyone who says punishment does not work has probably never been threatened with 20 years in Siberia. Of course, Soviet-style motivation, and severe consequences, have their own rather severe drawbacks. In *The Gulag Archipelago*, Aleksander Solzhenitsyn (2003) describes how terrified audiences would applaud for achingly long periods of time in tribute to their Comrade Stalin. The first person to cease clapping was likely to get shot. Heavy-handed approaches may superficially lead to the desired effect, but they come with severe consequences, which we discuss in detail in Chapter 6, along with discussing how to effectively work motivation into performance management frameworks.

In a system of centrally mandated tractor targets, for example, those in the factory would find creative ways to meet the targets, often undermining the actual purpose of the factory. Delegates, visitors and foreign dignitaries would be paraded around the factory, showing the hundreds of new, gleaming tractors. Just one problem. No engines. The tractors were little better than props to meet the targets.

Take a similar example from a multinational high-street coffee chain. With hundreds of thousands of staff in tens of thousands of locations, one would think they would be a model of best practice instead of a cautionary tale. But, such a large organization necessarily has various levels of management with reporting requirements and inspections. These include delegate inspections that are announced days or weeks ahead of time to the storefront location; everyone on site knows the drill. The shop is polished top to bottom, as are the staff. Stock is restocked and overstocked to give an impression of plentiful supply and customer demand. The best employees are put out front and told to be on their best behaviour. The local, regional or international delegates are paraded past smiling staff and gleaming counters to show how the store is a model of performance.

It is, of course, a farce. The shop is never that clean and the overstocked food will be thrown out at the end of the day. The staff are *not* happy about their participation in this masquerade but they have no choice. It is not far from those shiny tractors without engines. Worse still, these kind of experiences can gut the engines of motivation from previously hard-working staff. Inspections can be either motivating or demotivating experiences, depending on how they are conducted. Chapter 6 uses this example in greater detail and includes a framework for getting the 'inspection' right. This raises the question beyond current profitability, or whether employees are sufficiently motivated to do their job. But *how could it be improved*?

Another important issue is exemplified by these retail inspections: even hugely successful companies that bring in billions still have room for improvement. Potential improvements can be incredibly simple changes while others are much more complex. For example, in Chapter 11 we talk to an ex-MI6 agent who was active through most of the Cold War to illustrate how much damage can be done by one disgruntled or demotivated person; Chapters 10 and 11 have examples from young people early in their careers; and Chapters 8 and 14 discuss a company that has moved to entirely flexible work schedules, including how people react when they never again have to go into the office or brave their commute.

Throughout many of the chapters we revisit the issues surrounding generational differences and give advice for multigenerational workforces. Generational differences are discussed in detail in Chapter 3, but will be an enduring theme throughout many of the chapters.

Conclusion

The content in this book is intended to be interesting, engaging, motivating and in some places even amusing. Above all, it is written to be useful. If you are in the business of managing and motivating people, there will be many practical components you can use. Each chapter is written using scientific evidence and academic research, but will not require any specialized knowledge to read.

Alongside stories of success, failure, defection, whistle blowing, incompetence, wickedness, and problems currently in workplaces, this book has two consistent and positive messages:

1 **People can get better**: individual performance can improve, and there are many ways to spark motivation and improve performance.

2 **Work can get better**: despite substantial and continual improvements to workplaces, there are still opportunities to make work better, more effective, more productive, more profitable and better for those within them as well as for the company.

There are dramatic improvements that can still be made in workplaces to improve performance and productivity. Equally important is making workplaces a better place to work for the people inside the organization. Although tremendous progress has already been made in that area, there is still much that can be done. The evidence from research and practice clearly demonstrates how motivation links to performance in the workplace. Each chapter in this book highlights a different opportunity for improving motivation and performance – and that will benefit organizations and employees.

Importantly, this is not a trade-off between company success and employee well-being. The resounding evidence (see Chapter 8) is that happier, healthier people are more productive. Healthy workplaces produce better results. It should not be seen as a trade-off between what is best for the company or what is best for the employee. It is not about tricks: a manager and the HR team are not some sort of puppeteers, engineering a dystopian workplace where employees are tricked into working harder against their own interests or at the expense of their well-being. Getting the balance right improves the outcomes for everyone involved. There is a case to be made for the bottom line in combination with employee well-being.

Using case studies, practical examples, individual and company stories we will illustrate all the points made in order to provide a greater depth of information about how the theories, research and recommendations can be used successfully in any organization.

In Chapter 2 we present a model of workplace motivation and in Chapter 3 discuss the myths surrounding generational differences and their relationship to motivation and performance at work.

Further resources

We would encourage you to go beyond the information in this book. We will be adding additional resources online, including short online tests to measure some of the topics under discussion. What motivates you? Which generational stereotype do you most resemble? What kind of culture does your organization have? Do you want more specific resources, such as a sample performance management framework using everything discussed in subsequent chapters? Go to www.highpotentialpsych.co.uk/motivperformance.

References

Bond, F and Bunce, D (2001) [accessed 10 October 2016] Reducing Stress and Improving Performance Through Work Reorganisation, Final Progress Report for the British Occupational Health Research Foundation [Online] http://www.bohrf.org.uk/downloads/job_ctrl.pdf

Bond, FW, Flaxman, P and Bunce, D (2008) The influence of psychological flexibility on work redesign: mediation and moderation of a work reorganization intervention, *Journal of Applied Psychology*, 93 (3), pp 645–54

Consiglio, C, Borgogni, L, Alessandri, G and Schaufeli, WB (2013) Does self-efficacy matter for burnout and sickness absenteeism? The mediating role of demands and resources at the individual and team levels, *Work and Stress: An international journal of work, health and organisations*, 27 (1), pp 22–42

de Boer, EM, Bakker, AB, Syroit, JE and Schaufeli, WB (2002) Unfairness at work as a predictor of absenteeism, *Journal of Organizational Behavior*, 23, pp 181–97

Personnel Today (2015) [accessed 10 October 2016] Sickness Absence Rates and Costs Revealed in UK's Largest Survey [Online] http://www.personneltoday.com/hr/sickness-absence-rates-and-costs-revealed-in-uks-largest-survey/

Schaufeli, WB, Bakker, AB and van Rhenen, W (2009) How changes in job demands and resources predict burnout, work engagement and sickness absenteeism, *Journal of Organizational Behavior*, 30 (7), pp 893–917

Solzhenitsyn, A (2003) *The Gulag Archipelago 1918–56*, Harvill Press, London

Thomas, D (2010) [accessed 10 October 2016] Failure To Retain Talent Costs UK Firms £42 Billion, Says PwC, *Personnel Today* [Online] http://www.personneltoday.com/hr/failure-to-retain-talent-costs-uk-firms-42-billion-says-pwc/

van Rhenen, W, Blonk, RWB, Schaufeli, WB and van Dijk, FJH (2007) Can sickness absence rates be reduced by stress reduction programs: on the effectiveness of two approaches, *International Archives of Occupational and Environmental Health*, 80, pp 505–15

Wall, TD, Jackson, P and Davids, K (1992) Operator work design and robotics system performance: a serendipitous field study, *Journal of Applied Psychology*, 77 (3), pp 353–62

A model
of motivation

02

Introduction

Why do two people, faced with the same decision, make different choices? What about two people with the same opportunities? Why does one seize the opportunity and thrive while the other languishes? In exactly the same situation, two people with similar backgrounds and experiences may behave in very different ways. What about at work – why does one person seek to be promoted and recognized, while a colleague in a similar position just wants to get their job done with no desire for the spotlight or career advancement?

Two equally qualified, knowledgeable and capable people in the same position might behave in very different ways. Why? That's the question. Motivation is the explanation.

This chapter explains how all research on the topic finds that motivation can be distilled into essentially two categories. Then we present a more nuanced model of motivation using our research to explain how to understand and measure motivation in the workplace. Asking the question of what motivates people can help to explain *why* individuals work in certain ways and perform at certain levels. Consider a common workplace expression: 'So-and-so is extremely ambitious'. It implies drive and focus, but begs the question: ambition to do what? We revisit this question in Chapter 13 in explaining why people derail and fail, but first it is essential to discuss it in the context of success.

Break down the concept of 'ambition' – asking the question 'ambition to do what?' – and the importance of that nuance becomes very clear. When someone is described as ambitious, does that ambition stretch to:

- fame;
- fortune;
- freedom;

- philanthropy;
- or something else?

This is not to say that any of these are mutually exclusive. Non-profit does not mean a company that does not make any money, just a company that reinvests its profits. A successful non-profit company may have a philanthropic focus, but that does not preclude financial motivations. Any combination of motivations are possible – it is rare that anyone is motivated by just one thing to the exclusion of all others.

This chapter describes the most compelling and well-proven two-factor model of motivation. Then it continues with our model of motivation, which has been specifically designed and validated for a workplace context. Our model will be used throughout this book, including in case studies and individual profiles of motivation to discuss motivation in a practical context using real-world examples.

Two-factor theory

Motivation is an 'energizing force that induces action' (Parks and Guay, 2009). Motivation is closely related to goals, or objectives. Mitchell (1997) describes four key aspects of motivation:

1 **Arousal**: the interest in a particular goal (eg wanting to read a good book, wanting to get a promotion).

2 **Direction**: focus on a particular goal (eg I would rather spend more time working to earn that promotion than read that book).

3 **Intensity**: the degree of effort expended in pursuing a particular goal (eg I am only prepared to work one extra hour per day to get that promotion).

4 **Persistence**: continuing to pursue the goal in spite of difficulties, challenges or barriers (eg even though my colleagues are highly qualified for that promotion, I'm still going to work for it).

Over 60 years ago a group of psychologists led by Frederick Herzberg developed the most important theory of motivation, which is still relevant today. Take the example of an extraordinarily successful entrepreneur, leading a medium-sized and rapidly growing company. Our entrepreneur is constantly busy with various elements across the company. Growing the business and enjoying the rapid expansion may be time-consuming, but it is also incredibly satisfying. But what happens if, after years of rapid growth, profits decrease during a financial quarter, or even for a year?

Our entrepreneur may be extremely dissatisfied with a decrease in profits after so much success. But the job responsibilities can still be exciting and motivating, focusing on opportunities to continue growing the business. In some ways, that drive to return to profitability and to find new opportunities may be incredibly motivating even while the financial situation creates a level of dissatisfaction. In some ways that dissatisfaction can even be a useful tool if it is directed appropriately into improvement. But the most important point is that one can be satisfied with certain aspects of the work, such as the challenge and opportunity, while at the same time being dissatisfied with other aspects of the work.

Herzberg's two-factor theory (Herzberg, Mausner and Snyderman, 1959) states that there are certain factors in the workplace that cause job satisfaction, while a separate set of factors cause dissatisfaction. The researchers found that job characteristics related to what an individual does at work have the capacity to gratify specific needs such as achievement, competency and personal worth, leading to happiness and satisfaction. However, the absence of such specific job characteristics did not appear to lead to unhappiness and dissatisfaction – this resulted from other very specific factors such as company policies, supervision, salary, interpersonal relations on the job and working conditions.

Two-factor theory then distinguishes between:

- **Motivating factors** such as challenging work, recognition for one's achievement, being given responsibility, opportunity to do something meaningful, involvement in decision making, sense of importance to an organization. These together give positive satisfaction, arising from intrinsic conditions of the job itself, such as recognition, achievement or personal growth. These factors are now more commonly referred to as intrinsic motivation.

- **Hygiene factors** such as job security, salary, fringe benefits, work conditions, good pay, paid insurance and vacations do not, paradoxically, give positive satisfaction or motivation, though dissatisfaction results from their absence. The term 'hygiene' is used in the sense that these are maintenance factors. These are extrinsic to the work itself, and include aspects such as company policies, supervisory practices or wages/salary. These factors are now more commonly referred to as extrinsic motivation.

According to Herzberg, hygiene factors (extrinsic) are what cause dissatisfaction among employees in a workplace. In order to remove dissatisfaction in a work environment these demotivating factors must be eliminated. There are several ways that this can be done but some of the most important ways to decrease dissatisfaction would be to pay reasonable wages, provide appropriate levels of job security and to create a positive culture in the workplace. Herzberg and his team rank-ordered the following hygiene factors from highest to lowest importance: company policy, supervision, employee's

Table 2.1   Possible combinations of intrinsic and extrinsic motivating factors

| | | **Motivating Factors (Intrinsic)** | |
		High	**Low**
Hygiene Factors (Extrinsic)	**High**	Employees are motivated and satisfied. This is the ideal situation, where the employees are both motivated and happy. They are paid enough to be satisfied, but not overpaid to the point of entitlement or greed. They work hard and enjoy doing their job. Think thriving entrepreneurs and successful non-profits.	Employees are not motivated, but are satisfied. This often occurs when the job is relatively well paid, compensation is equitable and perks match needs and expectations. Employees have no major complaints, but no drive, passion or excitement in their work. Think civil service ennui or bored accountants.
	Low	Employees are motivated but dissatisfied. This is an unusual situation, which can potentially be very destructive, depending on who the employee blames for their dissatisfaction. It also raises the question, *Motivated to do what?* Employees who are dissatisfied with their work but highly motivated may become saboteurs, thieves or whistleblowers (see Chapter 11). Think highly skilled, but badly managed or poorly treated professionals.	Employees are both unmotivated and dissatisfied. This is the most undesirable situation and can be the most difficult to remedy. Often these people are in jobs they do not enjoy and are poorly compensated for their effort. Or, they may be highly paid professionals doing a job that they dislike for rewards that may be high, but still feel too low compared with their colleagues or leaders. Think unhappy, underpaid retail staff or overworked investment bankers, unsatisfied with the latest bonus.

relationship with their boss, work conditions, salary and relationships with peers.

Herzberg distinguished between work-related action because you *have to*, which is classed as 'movement', versus if you perform a work-related action because you *want to*, which is classed as 'motivation'.

Most importantly, Herzberg thought it was important to eliminate job dissatisfaction before going on to creating conditions for job satisfaction, because the two dimensions can work against each other.

According to the two-factory theory there are four possible combinations, as set out in Table 2.1.

The two main factors and the HPMI motivation test

The most enduring model of motivation is based on two factors. Although this has been tested, tweaked and honed over the past decades, it is remarkably similar to its initial conception. Findings consistently demonstrate two main motivational factors. Like all good science, the theory has endured because research findings consistently demonstrate that the two-factor model works. This research is discussed further in Chapter 7.

Thus, in the most basic sense, there are two different types of motivation:

- **Intrinsic factors** that are internal to the person such as challenging work, recognition for one's achievement, being given responsibility, opportunity to do something meaningful, involvement in decision making, sense of importance to an organization.

- **Extrinsic factors** that are external to the person such as job security, salary, fringe benefits, work conditions, good pay, paid insurance, vacations.

We set out to develop a model of motivation and an accompanying test specifically designed for use in the workplace, which was initially developed by Furnham and colleagues (2009): the High-Potential Motivation Indicator (HPMI).

Our research with over 1,000 participants confirms that the two main factors hold up and largely fit the internal–external dimensions. Furthermore, we found in this workplace measure of motivation that each main factor can be divided into three facets. The HPMI is a short questionnaire with 30 items to measure the two main factors and six facets. It only takes a few minutes, and is statistically very robust.

We also find six factors that are related at the intrinsic/extrinsic level, but are distinct facets within the model. The three facets of intrinsic motivation are:

- **Autonomy:** this means a focus on engagement, active participation and stimulation and personal development. Those who are motivated by autonomy want a job that is consistent with their own passions, career development or self-expression.

- **Accomplishment:** this means being motivated by achievement, advancement and visible success. It often is related to a desire for promotion, power, status and recognition. People who highly value this want to be known either publicly, within the company or within their team for their accomplishments at work.

- **Affiliation:** this means social responsibility, passing on knowledge, teaching and instruction and working with others. Those who value affiliation prefer to work with others, to pass on their knowledge and experience, and they value the social aspects of work.

The three extrinsic facets are:

- **Security** involves job security, personal safety as well as consistency and regularity. This could mean a job in a company or profession with a long-established history, consistent reputation or clear organizational culture. Valuing security is a focus on stability, consistency and reliability.

- **Compensation** includes material rewards such as pay, insurance, bonuses and job perks that are easily measurable, counted and defined. It may also include other perks or advantages that make work life a bit easier: a convenient location, a nicer office or a more desirable working schedule.

- **Conditions** include elements of safety and security and personal convenience. Conditions require that a job fits within the person's lifestyle, and provides an environment conducive to their needs and comfort.

Workplace context

The HPMI was specifically designed for use in the workplace. This is important for the three key elements of tests and all research (discussed in more detail in Chapter 5):

- **Reliability:** the ability for a test to deliver consistent results. The test consistently delivers results that reflect a person's actual motivation at the current time. The questions are clear, easy to understand and people are unlikely to try to trick the test, because there is no 'right' answer.

- **Validity:** the ability of a test to measure what it says it measures. The test aligns with the extensive scientific theory and historical research in this area while honing the test to focus on a workplace context. This is important because motivation at work can be very different from a person's motivation at home or in a social context.

- **Utility:** the usefulness of a test in the context it is being used. The test was specifically tested to be fast and easy to take, because time is an important factor in workplace testing. The test only takes a few minutes of time, so is easy to fit into busy schedules. It was specifically designed for use in the workplace, without compromising validity for the scale of practicality.

So, how to use it specifically in the workplace. There are many potential uses and we will discuss some specific examples in upcoming blogs (see www.highpotentialpsych.co.uk/motivperformance) about three main areas of the HR department's remit: selection, development and retention.

The Hierarchy of Needs

In 1943 Abraham Maslow published his theory of motivation, in which he set out what is probably one of the most well-known psychological theories today.

The basic idea answers the question of the relative importance of different motivators. His idea was that some motivating factors are absolutely fundamental, and if they are not met they preoccupy the individual's attention, thwarting any motivation on factors 'higher' up the pyramid. Basic survival and physiological well-being needs are at the bottom of the pyramid, while more abstract, complex or idealistic needs are higher at the top. In Maslow's words: 'This means that the most prepotent goal will monopolize consciousness and will tend of itself to organize the recruitment of the various capacities of the organism. The less prepotent needs are minimized, even forgotten or denied. But when a need is fairly well satisfied, the next prepotent ("higher") need emerges, in turn to dominate the conscious life and to serve as the centre of organization of behaviour, since gratified needs are not active motivators' (Maslow, 1943: 395). No one cares about self-esteem when they are caught up in a natural disaster or threat to their safety and well-being.

Although there has been some criticism of this research, particularly the hierarchical structure, this pyramid of needs can be a useful guideline for motivating employees:

- **Physiological needs:** these are basic survival needs; they are not directly threatened in most workplaces, but needs like hunger can affect performance.

- **Safety needs:** job security and financial security factor in and can be powerful demotivators if they are not met.

- **Belonging needs:** these are the desire to feel included, like one is part of the organization and is making meaningful contributions to the team.

- **Esteem needs:** the need to feel respected and for contributions to be acknowledged.

- **Self-actualization needs:** the need to fulfil one's potential.

Figure 2.1 shows the five needs, redefined from a workplace perspective using the HPMI facets. There are three important points that should be highlighted:

1 These five needs largely resemble the intrinsic–extrinsic dimensions of our model, with the bottom portion of the pyramid as extrinsic motivators, and the top portion as intrinsic motivations. This suggests that extrinsic motivation can be a barrier to remove, while intrinsic motivators are an opportunity to improve.

Figure 2.1   HPMI facets mapped onto Maslow's pyramid

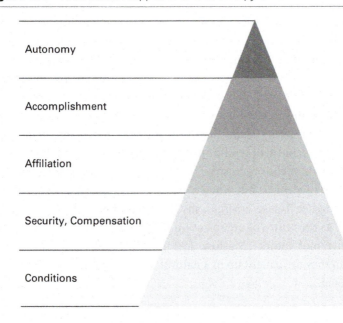

Autonomy

Accomplishment

Affiliation

Security, Compensation

Conditions

2 Security in the workplace encompasses safety from bullying, harassment, and elements of mental health and psychological well-being (the topic of Chapter 4). Without removing this barrier it is difficult to improve potential and performance in the workplace.

3 Although the intrinsic motivators at the top of the pyramid are generally seen as the most desirable, they may not be equally important to everyone. Some people pursue their 'self-actualization' goals outside of work, and do not see work as a focus of their personal development. That is not to say these types of people cannot be or are not effective workers. Every workplace needs a core group of people who do their job, do it well, and that's that. They do not want a leadership role, or a stretch assignment or to attend the company picnic. Recognizing this motivational profile and this type of potential to be a strong, stable, unambitious worker can be a huge asset in the right role (MacRae and Furnham, 2014). If well positioned, and their motivations understood, respected and applied effectively, the people who quietly keep the company running efficiently often go unnoticed, but their contribution is invaluable.

The evidence shows that this is not necessarily a pyramid in a strict sense, because various needs can exist at one time, acting on both satisfaction and dissatisfaction. But the base of the pyramid does highlight the importance of some foundational needs. Without financial security it may become more difficult to pursue those 'high-level' goals, and this may lead to sacrificing time pursuing esteem or career goals when money is a greater priority.

The floor and ceiling effects of motivation

Think of it as potential floors and ceilings of motivation. They are not mutually exclusive, both have important but differing effects. Extrinsic motivation determines the floor of performance while intrinsic defines the ceiling of potential performance. A minimum level of extrinsic motivation is an essential foundation but does not create benefits when it exceeds basic needs (see Chapter 9). Intrinsic motivation (Chapter 7) is a ceiling that can be raised high above the floor and can greatly improve performance to much greater levels.

Conclusion

Motivation can largely be described within a two-factor framework, and there are facets within each of the major factors that provide a more nuanced model of motivation. It can be measured relatively quickly and easily with a very short measure of motivation. These factors align closely with the scientific findings about the concept of motivation and how it affects individuals and teams at work. This model will be used throughout this book, first to look at how it is related to the popular (and often misinformed) public discourse on generational differences in motivation in the workplace (Chapter 3). Subsequent chapters explain each motivation facet in greater detail and describe how those facets are linked with performance, profitability and employee well-being. As we will see, it should not be underestimated how many opportunities there still are for companies to use this information to improve profitability, performance and employee well-being.

References

Furnham, A, Eracleous, A and Chamorro-Premuzic, T (2009) Personality, motivation and job satisfaction: Herzberg meets the Big Five, *Journal of Managerial Psychology*, **24** (8), pp 765–79

Herzberg, F, Mausner, B and Snyderman, BB (1959) *The Motivation to Work*, John Wiley & Sons, New Jersey

MacRae, IS and Furnham, A (2014) *High Potential: How to spot, manage and develop talented people at work*, Bloomsbury, London

Maslow, A (1943) A theory of human motivation, *Psychological Review*, **50**, pp 370–96

Mitchell, TR (1997) Matching motivational strategies with organizational contexts, in BM Staw and LL Cummings (eds) *Research in Organizational Behavior*, vol. 19, pp 57–149, JAI Press, Greenwich CT

Parks, L and Guay, RP (2009) Personality, values, and motivation, *Personality and Individual Differences*, **47**, pp 675–84

Generational differences

03

Introduction

There is much written on generational differences. The Google ngram in Figure 3.1 displays the frequency of the term *generational differences* within the Google library. While there is a growing number of publications on generational differences, much is incorrect or misleading.

Typically the misinformation falls into one of two categories:

1 First, widely generalizable statements that would apply to any generation, or advice that would be useful for any age group. This is often a marketing exercise, where 'Top 8 HR Tips' gets more attention if the title is 'Top 8 Tips for Managing Millennials in the Workplace'. Take a few examples from Lancaster and Stillman (2010), who clearly had difficulty settling on a title: *The M-factor: How the millennial generation is rocking the workplace – 7 trends you need to know to survive and thrive*. They suggest that millennials 'are hardwired to want to do almost everything faster' and 'not only is dues-paying dialogue troublesome, it's literally a foreign language'. The suggestion is then essentially to discuss expectations and clearly communicate job requirements and opportunities – fairly good advice as standard when working with people of any age. *Forbes* has a similar approach in their article '7 surprising ways to motivate millennials' (Goudreau, 2013). Tips like 'Explain the Company Vision' and 'Provide Education and Professional Development' are neither surprising, nor unique to millennials.

2 Second, are the more harmful and often untrue statements. They make assertions of fact with little to no supporting evidence. The *Forbes* article (Goudreau, 2013) goes on to say that millennials are: 'notorious job-hoppers who dislike bureaucracy and distrust traditional hierarchies', but without providing any evidence to support the claim. Small surveys

Figure 3.1   History of generational differences in publications

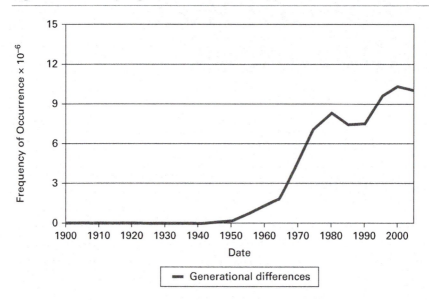

- ■ Generational differences

that are not representative of the population, or specific examples, may be used to present generational differences as fact. For example, one *Daily Mail* article describes 'the wasted generation' and 'even millennials think they are self-absorbed and lazy' (Zolfagharifard, 2015). These types of statements usually favour the use of polls over the large amount of strong scientific evidence that is available.

The first is less harmful when the advice is generally good, but can be counterproductive when stereotyping groups of workers makes some members of the group feel alienated or misunderstood. The second is more harmful because poor information can lead to poor decision making (Costanza and Finkelstein, 2015). However, the appeal of generational differences endures.

The concept of generational differences can be appealing because, if generational differences exist, it makes policymaking simpler. If there are a few handy attributes that are exclusively true of all members of a workforce segment, they can all be managed in the same way. It is a useful rule of thumb that helps one automatically understand something about an individual based on their age/generation. The problem is that this is stereotyping, and often incorrect.

It is unusual for management manuals to be founded on a stereotype, but millennials are the exception. Many examples, such as *Managing Millennials* (Espinoza, Ukleja and Rusch, 2010), recommend management and HR policies based on a stereotype. It is surprising that this is one stereotype that is acceptable – it would be wildly inappropriate to have similar guides for other stereotypes, such as 'Leadership with Lithuanians', 'Business Strategies for Blondes' or 'HR for Homosexuals'. In Chapter 5 we discuss how the legal consequences could be the same as for other types of discrimination. So where do these pervasive generational differences myths come from?

A case study

To explore the topic of generational differences, let's start with an example of events unique to a particular generation.

A group of young men had been protesting the lack of available housing for months. They were frustrated with lack of housing, few job opportunities and uncertain prospects. Many in the group were unemployed and looking for work, some were students. The group, and many of their peers, had been struggling to settle into independence in their city. Some had moved back home to live with their parents, and sleep on couches.

Some of these young men had protested and staged demonstrations. They continued to protest, to lobby government and to look for a solution to the housing crisis. A group of them were in negotiations to turn an abandoned hotel into temporary accommodation. Over months of lobbying and negotiation, nothing happened. Various levels of government and the owner of the hotel were locked into unending and unproductive negotiations.

On a snowy January day, after a meeting of contemporaries, 35 of these young men marched to the hotel in question and told the guard at the gate that they would be going in. The group took over the hotel and put up a 15-foot tall banner saying, 'Action at Last! Rooms for you. Come and Get Them' (Cornwall, 2006). That night they hosted a party in the hotel's ballroom to celebrate their success: they had accommodation for 100 of their peers. The following day, 700 people had 'registered' for accommodation, which was provided in the occupied hotel.

Without context, consider your opinion of this group. Are they valiant activists? Entitled scroungers? What do their actions say about their generation? Are their actions representative of their generation?

Here is where the context matters. This was a group of Second World War veterans in Vancouver, in 1946. After they returned to Canada from fighting in Europe there was little or no housing available. A flood of veterans were returning home to cities across the country that had little housing capacity. The soldiers were promised veteran accommodation, but the promised support was not materializing.

This example from 1946 could be compared with the actions of the more recent 'Occupy' movement. For example, in 2011 in London, a group took over an abandoned building that was owned by UBS bank (Alleyne, 2011). These events were in different countries and 65 years apart, but the actions by a group of young people were remarkably similar. Yet public reactions to these events were very different and the Occupy movement is often used to caricature millennials (for example Hansen and Spaeth, 2013).

When the veteran soldiers occupied the Vancouver hotel in 1946 public support was largely sympathetic. Politicians quickly jumped on board. The local MP said, 'You did right. You waited until all negotiations had failed, then you took the bull by the horns and moved in' (Cornwall, 2006).

Of course, it was a different generation in 1946; a different time and different circumstances. But stereotyping any generation, or making assumptions about any group or individual based on a story, is an error. Making those mistakes in the workplace will lead to mistakes hiring, developing, retaining and motivating people at work. Assuming anyone in the workplace has particular political beliefs, personal values or motivations is a mistake. Imagine incentivizing workers with a company-wide charitable donation to a left-leaning charity, only to learn that a large number of employees have right-wing political beliefs.

Generational difference theories

One of the most well-known generational categories emerges from Strauss and Howe's (1991) influential book *Generations: The history of America's future*. The book traces back generational trends and the distinguishing features of US society over hundreds of years. The theory suggests that the effects of each generation trigger certain conditions that naturally lead to reactions in successive generations. The generational changes reflect a constant tension between the power of institutions versus individuals. Successive generations react by drawing away from the previous generation's power structures. Their model is suggested to be a large cycle spanning approximately a century, with four sub-cycles in each cycle.

The Strauss–Howe model attempts to be prophetic in predicting some features of the next generation. As with most prophesying it is vague enough to be plausible, simple enough to be memorable, and optimistic enough to be appealing. There may be defining events and prevailing attitudes during a time period. However, it becomes less useful for describing any particular individual. It describes historical trends, but has no real predictive ability.

It should also be noted that not all stereotypes are negative. Carroll and Tober's (2004) *The Indigo Children* paints their next generations as an almost messianic force for good. Slightly more optimistic, but again suffering from the same fatal flaw of being an inaccurate overgeneralization.

Anyone interested in finding or developing the potential in others must consider the value of any theory, starting with the question: *what does this tell me about any particular individual*? Upon examination of categories, the Strauss–Howe theory is really a description of US cultural attitudes and power structures. This may be an interesting discussion for historians or political scientists looking at long-term trends, but it does nothing to explain individual differences that exist within the population. The theory does not explain anything about an individual's performance, potential or preferences.

The problem is not that discussions about generations can *never* be applied to people. Any particular stereotype may be descriptive of some people, it might even describe a majority. Certainly, terms like 'the greatest generation' or the 'baby boom generation' may neatly sum up cultural attitudes about those who grew up in the United States during that time. The 'greatest generation' lived through a major recession and went on to fight in the Second World War. The 'baby boomers' is a shorthand term for the demographic bulge that appeared after the Second World War. It is an observable population trend. It usually implies a time of economic prosperity as well as a boom in the number of children.

Many business commentators and writers have tried to explain generational differences in the workplace. In *Millennials Rising: The next great generation*, Howe and Strauss (2000) suggest that 'millennials are unlike any other youth generation in living memory' and 'over the next decade, the millennial generation will entirely recast the image of youth from downbeat and alienated to upbeat and engaged'. A decade later, the stereotypes have changed little. Popular press coverage casts millennials as 'the anxious generation' – a problem that apparently 'shouldn't be confused with their omg! lol! I can't even social ineptitude' (Markowicz, 2016).

The limitation with generational differences is in drawing any meaningful conclusions about an individual based on the year they were born. Take the following five facts about an individual applying for a chief executive officer (CEO) position. Which do you think would give the best indication towards their potential performance (either positive or negative)? If you could only choose one, which would be the most useful?

- highly intelligent;
- lied during interview;
- emotionally stable;
- born in 1959;
- attended top-ranked university.

The date of birth is, in fact, the least useful. In order from most to least useful these factors (MacRae and Furnham, 2014) are:

1 highly intelligent;

2 emotionally stable;

3 lied during interview;

4 attended top-ranked university;

5 born in 1959.

Not only are generational stereotypes useless in the workplace, there are significant flaws in the concept.

Problems with generational myths

One of the constant challenges in psychological research is separating what effects are caused by age, and which could be generational differences. Parry and Urwin (2011) provide an excellent review of generational differences research and show that generational differences in values are not confirmed by the scientific research. They discuss six key problems:

- Definitions are poorly or inconsistently defined. Many studies and publications use different age ranges or time periods for generational categories. There is no real overlap in what different authors mean by a 'millennial'.

- **Age effects** can be challenging to disentangle. Studies need to consider both age and date of birth. Age differences are often responsible for what many studies present as generational differences.

- **Generational experiences** do not always reflect individual experiences. Not everyone within a generation directly participated in an event and some will be detractors. Schuman and Scott (1989) found that when asked about events over a 50-year period, such as the Vietnam War or the Second World War, Americans remembered many of the same events but their memories tended to be unhelpful or superficial unless they directly experienced the event.

- **National culture** is important and there are national biases in much of the research. A majority of the research is based on theories based on US generations (for example, Strauss and Howe). Even though some events may have worldwide impacts, national and cultural differences can vary substantially.

- **Marketing influences** play heavily into generational differences. Advertisers use generational stereotypes to appeal to the target demographic. Much popular writing uses generational stereotypes as a positioning tool. 'Managing millennials'-type publications are likely targeted to an older readership.

- **Developmental differences** can affect research results because there are many psychological differences between young adults (late teens and early twenties) that have well-established biological and psychological causes.

Developmental differences pose a particular challenge when comparing younger people with older, because the human brain does not finish developing until the mid-twenties (Geidd, 2008; Pujol *et al*, 1993). Unfortunately, one of the last parts of the brain to develop is the prefrontal cortex. This region of the brain is responsible for desirable capabilities such as long-term planning, emotional regulation and impulse control. It will not come as a surprise to most in pointing out that teens can be risky and impulsive. That is not just a product of culture or environment; young brains still need time to fully develop.

This may help to explain the persistency of descriptions of the next/younger generation as less responsible or more narcissistic. Any employer taking on new employees at 16, 18 or 23 years old should be aware that those young brains are still growing. Rates of development differ, but brain development continues into the mid to late twenties (Pujol *et al*, 1993). As a general rule, working with young people will come with significant differences compared to working with adults. In Chapter 10 we present two very similar motivational profiles of teachers from different generations and provide practical suggestions for motivating younger individuals and groups.

Of course, there are exceptions. Some people mature extraordinarily early while a few others never seem to grow up. Another inconsistent truth about development is that it happens at varying rates. As a rule of thumb, most brains are fully developed in the mid-to-late twenties. But some people develop much more quickly than others, psychologically as well as physically.

Psychologists refer to the 'concept of maturation' to describe how psychological development tends to happen in socially desirable directions at all ages. People tend to develop in a direction that is more socially desirable and, hence, more useful in the workplace. In other words, people tend to get more hardworking, more motivated and improve their capacity to deal with stress as they get older. This is true within younger groups, but that trend continues throughout the lifespan (Roberts, Walton and Viechtbauer, 2006).

One of the key lessons from these findings is the importance of development. Developing people at work is a substantial opportunity to improve performance. Chapter 6 discusses some best practices for motivation and development. And in Chapter 4 we will use a case study along with the evidence to show how getting it right with younger employees has the potential to build long-term company loyalty.

Hiring young people should not be seen as a burden. Get it right, and younger employees have substantial potential.

Older workers

While much of the discussion on generational differences centres around younger generations and new workers, older workers can also face a different set of prejudices and assumptions. Ng and Feldman (2012) studied six common stereotypes about older workers in a meta-analysis that included over 200,000 participants:

1 **Less motivated**: some assume that older workers are less motivated because they could be nearing the end of their career and do not have the same level of career ambitions as younger workers. This creates the perception that older workers are no longer motivated workers.

2 **Lower participation in training and development**: trained experts, experienced professionals and dab hands with long careers will see less benefit from training if they are near retirement. This means that older workers are offered training and development places less often than their younger colleagues.

3 **Less willing and able to change**: the 'can't teach an old dog new tricks' stereotype assumes that older workers are set in their ways and unable or uninterested in learning new approaches, adapting to new technology

and are less adaptable. This can lead to discrimination in selection, development and retention decisions.

4 **Less trusting**: another stereotype is that older workers are less trusting of their colleagues at work and are consequently more lonely. This often means that older workers' interpersonal skills are rated as poorer than their younger colleagues.

5 **Poorer health**: the assumption is that age necessarily comes with health concerns, and older workers are often rejected based on health concerns from the employer, even when no health condition exists. Older workers may also be overlooked for physically or psychologically demanding positions.

6 **Greater work–family imbalance**: unlike younger workers, who may be thought to have less demands from family life, older workers are often perceived to need more 'family time'. Some perceive older workers as more suited to family and community activities than the workplace.

Their findings showed mixed to weak evidence for the first two stereotypes. Older workers reported slightly lower levels of motivation and slightly lower motivation to learn and participate in training. These findings are modest, and should certainly not be generalized to all older workers.

For the third stereotype, the evidence showed the opposite effect to the stereotype of older workers being less willing to change. Older workers were actually much more likely to participate in change-related behaviours at work. There was no relationship between age and factors such as attitudes to organizational change, risk taking and innovative behaviours.

There was no support for the fourth stereotype. Age was not significantly related to any trust factors such as interpersonal trust, interpersonal conflict, trust in co-workers or trust in supervisors.

Some support for the fifth stereotype of health concerns was found. Older workers were found to have modestly higher blood pressure and cholesterol levels, a very slight increase in mental health concerns in older workers but no significant differences in overall physical health or perceptions of health.

There was some evidence that aligned with the sixth stereotype of older workers having different work–family imbalance. However, the evidence showed that older workers actually have slightly less work–family conflict and was unrelated to work–family balance.

These findings and previous work do indicate that older workers face discrimination (Ng and Feldman, 2012), but that is often overlooked (Bendick, Brown and Wall, 2008). It is ironic that discrimination exists, in different ways, for all generations. These stereotypes and assumptions about motivation based on age must be overcome in order to motivate the entire workforce, and make the most of different strengths and capabilities of all employees irrespective of age. James *et al* (2012) confirmed that discrimination against older workers was often unintentional but significantly decreased work engagement amongst those workers.

Looking further back

Stereotyping the next, younger, generation is not a recent phenomenon. There are examples of similar statements going back hundreds of years and in different countries.

General statements are fairly easy to believe. Consider the following list of attributes. How accurate do you think these are of millennials?

- ability to understand and absorb other people's emotions and feelings;
- mind is full of ideas and creative thoughts, so are often indecisive;
- dislike repetition and need to be constantly inspired;
- have difficulties resolving interpersonal conflict;
- prefer social activities, like being around others;
- idealists who may not always understand practicality;
- tend to have many relationships, fear commitment.

These may be some of the common traits ascribed to millennials, but these are actually adapted descriptions from a Pisces horoscope. A large body of evidence suggests that generational differences are no better than horoscopes. It would, though, be a clever PR trick to turn a single 'horoscope-based management' book into a 12-book series.

Examples from historical publications and literature paint a similar picture of stereotypes. In *The Brothers Karamazov* published in 1880, Dostoyevsky notes that young children, 'are fond of talking among themselves, and even aloud, of things, pictures, and images of which even soldiers would sometimes hesitate to speak'. He goes on to say, 'More than that, much that soldiers have no knowledge or conception is familiar to quite young children of our intellectual and higher classes.' It is disappointing that Dostoyevsky does not go into detail about what would have been unspeakably coarse to late 19th-century Russian soldiers. The capacity for young people to shock older generations is timeless.

In 1906, psychologist Granville Stanley Hall said:

Never has youth been exposed to such dangers of both perversion and arrest as in our own land and day. Increasing urban life with its temptations, prematurities, sedentary occupations, and passive stimuli just when an active life is most needed, early emancipation and a lessening sense for both duty and discipline, the haste to know and do all befitting man's estate before its time, the mad rush for sudden wealth and the reckless fashions set by its gilded youth – all these lack some of the regulatives they still have in older lands with more conservative conditions.

That is the generation that would have gone on to fight in the First World War.

In an amusing warning about a newly popular game, chess, an 1859 article in the *Scientific American* said:

A pernicious excitement to learn and play chess has spread all over the country, and numerous clubs for practising this game have been formed in cities and villages… chess is a mere amusement of a very inferior character, which robs the mind of valuable time that might be devoted to nobler acquirements, while it affords no benefit whatever to the body. Chess has acquired a high reputation as being a means to discipline the mind, but persons engaged in sedentary occupations should never practise this cheerless game; they require outdoor exercises – not this sort of mental gladiatorship.

(Schlenoff, 2009)

The parallels with contemporary concerns about young people and video games should be noted.

The myths about generational differences and concerns about the younger generations is nothing new. The content, does of course, depend on the context.

Context and environment

Let us return to the question of shared experiences within generations. Howe and Strauss continue to argue in 2007 that generations are shaped by 'events or circumstances'. They go on to suggest: 'Generations are formed by the way historical events and moods shape their members' lives – and by the fact that these events and moods affect people very differently depending on the phase of life they occupy at the time.' This statement is accurate in that people's experiences shape their development.

Of course, people can be shaped by their shared cultural or historical experiences. But what makes for a shared experience? Does a child growing up in Buckinghamshire have a shared cultural experience with one in Barnsley or Battersea? Does someone who went to the best school in the country have very much shared experience with someone who went to the worst? What about people who grew up in agriculture, military, mining or political families? Are a man and a woman born in the 1946 baby boomer generation likely to have the same experiences, opportunities and shared cultural experiences? Why do politicians of similar ages, who go to the same schools, study the same subjects, and have similar career trajectories end up with different political beliefs? Despite a similar age could one really say that Margaret Thatcher and Arthur Scargill were shaped by shared cultural experience?

The findings are clear. The science on generational differences provides no evidence to support differences between generations. Costanza *et al* (2012) conducted a meta-analysis of nearly 600 articles, including 329 scientific studies, and found no strong evidence for generational differences. They concluded that 'relationships between generational membership and work-related outcomes are moderate to small, essentially zero in many cases'. Another study by Gardiner (2008) of 3,535 managers and professionals concluded, 'in practical terms these [generational] differences are almost negligible'. In a review of the generational differences literature, Parry and Urwin (2011) suggested the research had found more areas of similarity than differences between generations. In an even more recent study, Costanza and Finkelstein (2015) reinforced that there was 'little solid evidence' supporting generational differences and 'almost no theory behind why such differences should exist'.

There are more differences within generations than between (Gardiner, 2008; Parry and Urwin, 2011; Cadiz, Truxillo and Fraccaroli, 2015; Costanza and Finkelstein, 2015; Moore, Gunberg and Krause, 2015). But this confusion is sometimes interpreted as more evidence against the younger generations. A recent article in the *Atlantic* titled 'Millennials' political views don't make any sense' (Thompson, 2014) suggested that the generation's views were completely contradictory. The article presents findings from political polls suggesting, for example, that US millennials are least likely to approve of single parents, but most likely to *be* single parents. The alternative explanation could be that the people who are single parents are different individuals from those who disapprove of single parents.

A diversity of opinions within a generation is not an inherent paradox, inexplicable to rational adults. A diverse group within a generation should not be expected to present a firm and consistent set of beliefs like a political party. There are different people, and they are bound to have different opinions. Amusingly, the *Atlantic* article carries on to suggest that as millennials' incomes increase they tend to become more conservative. Again, this could be understood not as an inherent contradiction, just an indication that as one's circumstances change, often their values follow. It is true that income affects motivation and values, as is explained in Chapters 7 and 9.

It should be clear that individual differences are far more useful in the workplace than any sort of 'generational effect'. This should be taken as a profoundly encouraging fact for anyone interested in hiring, training and employing anyone. The upcoming pool of talent is not at an inherent disadvantage, employers just need to know how to select and develop appropriately. The evidence from decades of research in psychology shows there are attributes that are related to a wide range of desirable workplace outcomes, from health and absentee rates to work engagement and organizational commitment, turnover intention, performance and potential.

On all meaningful dimensions, generational differences are a myth.

HPMI evidence of generational differences

To explore the generational differences argument we explored potential generational differences in our data from over 1,000 participants. The initial finding was of minor generational differences, but not in the direction that many would expect. Many expect younger workers to be more motivated by independence and achievement and less by job security and money than previous generations. However, the results do not support these assumptions. The older workers reported being less motivated by intrinsic factors, while on average the younger generation said that extrinsic factors, particularly financial motivators, were more important. Figure 3.2 and Table 3.1 show the differences in each motivational facet between the generations.

Any differences are modest at best. All three intrinsic factors are not statistically significant, meaning they are no different than the differences we would expect to see between any groups by chance. Superficially, the millennials do appear to be more motivated by the three extrinsic factors of security, compensation and conditions. Upon further examination, it was very clear there was a very simple explanation for this. Income levels among generation X and baby boomer categories were more than double that of the millennial group. When we included pay in the analysis, income levels removed all significant generational differences in motivation. When

Figure 3.2   Generational differences in motivation scores

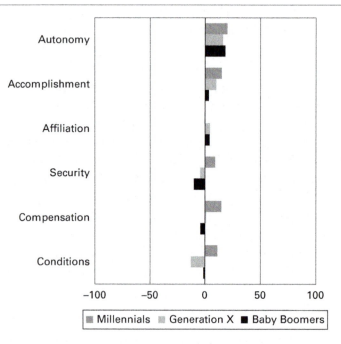

Table 3.1   Generational difference in motivation scores

Motivator	Millennials Born 1982–2005	Generation X Born 1961–1981	Baby Boomers Born 1943–1960
Autonomy	20.2	16.2	18.4
Accomplishment	15.1	10.1	3.5
Affiliation	−0.5	4.5	4.1
Security*	9.2	−4.5	−10.3
Compensation*	14.8	1.0	−4.2
Conditions*	11.3	−13.0	−1.1

* Indicates statistically significant differences between groups, using Strauss and Howe's definitions of generational categories

considering income levels, income accounted for 35 per cent of the variance in compensation and age was not a statistically significant predictor of compensation motivators (MacRae, 2015). The implication is quite clear: factors like income levels explain the modest generational differences in extrinsic motivation. Thus, these are not real generational differences, they are a product of individual circumstance.

The explanation for this is unsurprising, and the reasons, along with the impact of pay on motivation, is discussed in Chapter 7 in greater detail. Those who make less money tend to say that money is more important for them. This is true across the generations – younger and older workers alike, on lower salaries, say that compensation is more important to them at work.

Conclusion

Much of the discussion in this chapter was intended to debunk popular misconceptions about generational differences in the workplace. Overall, the evidence clearly shows there are little to no actual generational differences, and any generational differences have a much greater range within any particular generation than between any generations.

It was mentioned in Chapter 2 that there are no 'right' answers for the motivation test, there are no 'good' or 'bad' results, people are just motivated by different things. Generations, too, should not be painted broadly with the same brush when explaining motivational factors. Understanding individual motivation is a much more powerful tool than managing based on group stereotypes. Furthermore, managing based on stereotypes can be counter-productive. It is also necessary to understand motivation without judging particular motivators as essentially good or bad. While some types of motivation, like autonomy, are celebrated, it is not inherently a bad thing to be motivated by money at work (in Chapter 14 we provide an example of when it can be terribly bad, but this does not mean it is always a problem). Returning to our initial themes of the book, consider the following:

1 **People can get better.** The biggest issues regarding motivation in the workplace are gaps between what motivates people and what they get from their work (Chapter 11). But improving individual performance requires an individual approach. A significant area of improvement is finding those gaps where they exist, and finding the best way to improve them.

2 **Work can get better.** There is not always a simple way for improving profit and probability while improving workplaces. And an individualized approach is not always possible or feasible. But genuine policies can make work better (we provide excellent best-practice examples in Chapter 14).

The motivational gap will be discussed throughout the book – the main answer to the question 'which type of motivation is best' being that (annoyingly) psychologists answer 'it depends'. However, instead of asking the question of the best, a clearer rule-of-thumb answer can be provided to the question of which is most *important*.

References

Alleyne, R (2011) Occupy London campaigners take over derelict building, *The Telegraph*, 18 November

Bendick, M, Brown, LE and Wall, K (2008) No foot in the door: an experimental study of employment discrimination against older workers, *Journal of Aging and Social Policy*, **10** (4), pp 5–23

Cadiz, DM, Truxillo, DM and Fraccaroli, F (2015) What are the benefits of focusing on generation-based differences and at what cost?, *Industrial and Organisational Psychology*, **8** (3), pp 356–62

Carroll, L and Tober, J (2004) *The Indigo Children: The new kids have arrived*, Hay House, London

Costanza, DP, Badger, JM, Fraser, RL, Severt, JB and Gade, PA (2012) Generational differences in work-related attitudes: a meta-analysis, *Journal of Business Psychology*, **27**, pp 375–94

Costanza, DP and Finkelstein, LM (2015) Generationally based differences in the workplace: is there a *there* there?, *Industrial and Organisational Psychology*, **8** (3), pp 308–23

Cornwall, C (2006) The night war vets seized the Vancouver Hotel, *The Tyee*, 13 November

Espinoza, C, Ukleja, M and Rusch, C (2010) *Managing Millennials: Discover the core competencies for managing today's workforce*, John Wiley and Sons, New Jersey

Gardiner, E (2008) Generational differences in personality and motivation: do they exist and what are the implications for the workplace?, *Journal of Managerial Psychology*, **23** (8), pp 878–90

Geidd, JN (2008) The teen brain: insights from neuroimaging, *Journal of Adolescent Health*, **42**, pp 335–43

Goudreau, J (2013) [accessed 10 October 2016] 7 Surprising Ways to Motivate Millennial Workers, *Forbes* [Online] http://www.darley.com/documents/inside_darley/seven_ways_to_motivate_millenials.pdf

Hansen, L and Spaeth, R (2013) Narcissistic, broke and 7 other ways to describe the millennial generation, *The Week*, 18 April

Howe, N and Strauss, W (2000) *Millennials Rising: The next great generation*, Vintage Books, New York

Howe, N and Strauss, W (2007) The next 20 years: how customer and workforce attitudes will evolve, *Harvard Business Review*, July–August

James, JB, McKechnie, S, Swanberg, J and Besen, E (2012) Exploring the workplace impact of intentional/unintentional age discrimination, *Journal of Managerial Psychology*, **28** (7/8), pp 907–27

Lancaster, LC and Stillman, D (2010) *The M-Factor: How the millennial generation is rocking the workplace*, HarperCollins, New York

MacRae, I (2015) [accessed 10 October 2016] Are There Really Generational Differences in Workplace Values? *High Potential Psychology* [Online] https://highpotentialpsych.co.uk/articles/are-there-really-generational-differences-workplace-values

MacRae, IS and Furnham, A (2014) *High Potential: How to spot, manage and develop talented people at work*, Bloomsbury, London

Markowicz, K (2016) 'They can't even': why millennials are the 'anxious generation', *New York Post*, 20 March

Moore, S, Gunberg, L and Krause, AJ (2015) Generational differences in workplace expectations: a comparison of production and professional workers, *Current Psychology*, **34**, pp 346–62

Ng, TWH and Feldman, DC (2012) Evaluating six common stereotypes about older workers with meta-analytical data, *Personnel Psychology*, **65** (4), pp 821–58

Parry, E and Urwin, P (2011) Generational differences in work values: a review of theory and evidence, *International Journal of Management Reviews*, **13**, pp 79–96

Pujol, J, Vendrell, P, Junque, C, Marti-Vilalta, JL and Capdevila, A (1993) When does human brain development end? Evidence of corpus callosum growth up to adulthood, *Annals of Neurology*, **34** (1), pp 71–75

Roberts, BW, Walton, KE and Viechtbauer, W (2006) Patterns of mean-level change in personality traits across the life course: a meta-analysis of longitudinal studies, *Psychological Bulletin*, **132** (1), pp 1–25

Schlenoff, DC (2009) 100 years ago: baseball's first night games, *Scientific American*, 1 July

Schuman, H and Scott, J (1989) Generations and collective memories, *American Psychological Review*, **54**, pp 359–81

Stanley Hall, G (1906) *Adolescence: Its psychology and relations to physiology, anthropology, sociology, sex, crime, religion and education*, Appleton and Company, New York

Strauss, W and Howe, N (1991) *Generations: The history of America's future*, William Morrow and Co, New York

Thompson, D (2014) Millennials' political views don't make any sense, *The Atlantic*, 15 July

Zolfagharifard, E (2015) The wasted generation: even millennials think they are self-absorbed and lazy, claims study, *Daily Mail*, 3 September

The biology of stress and well-being

04

Introduction

Psychological concepts tend to be thought of as something that is 'in the mind' but that does not mean they are not also physical and biological. Stress is not just an abstract concept, it has real physical roots. Stress is hardwired into our brains, with organs that release stress hormones that have all sorts of physical consequences.

Many companies provide health coverage, and some even have benefits such as on-site doctors available to staff. Far fewer provide support for stress and mental health, despite the potentially huge cost savings that could be realized. Clever employers know that healthy workers are more productive workers. Yet estimates suggest that social costs of mental health problems in 2009–10 were £105 billion in England (CMH, n.d.), £3 billion in Northern Ireland, £7 billion in Wales and £9 billion in Scotland. Estimates suggest that about 17 per cent of the working-age population in Europe has a mild or severe depressive disorder (Gaspar and Müller, 2002). Yet already over-stretched government budgets make sufficient mental health-care provision another challenge to prioritize.

Findings from the European Agency for Safety and Health at Work (2000) suggest that 28 per cent of employees in Europe have had health problems as a result of workplace stress. ACAS, too, suggests that the economic costs of mental illness in the workplace are about £30 billion – between £8.4 billion in absence costs, £15.1 billion in reduced productivity and £2.4 billion replacing staff who leave work because of mental illness (ACAS, 2012).

This is not a social policy book, and while national support and services play an important role, employers can also make a difference, and many can do far more than they currently are. People spend one-third of their working life at work, so the topic of mental health at work is important. Consistent with previous findings, it is likely that these costs are now substantially higher (CMH, n.d.). A recent European study (Matrix, 2013) found work-related costs of depression to be €617 billion annually in Europe, including costs related to absenteeism and presenteeism of €272 billion and loss of productivity costs of €242 billion. To put that in context, total gross domestic product (GDP) of the European Union was €14.3 trillion (IMF, 2014). Reducing these costs by one-quarter would be equivalent to 1 per cent growth in European GDP. Some interesting research from Switzerland suggested that workplace stress cost the Swiss economy 1.2 per cent of GDP (Ramaciotti and Perriard, 2003).

Think of these costs as opportunities. Alongside the arguments about health, these costs indicate a huge opportunity for companies to save money. While 79 per cent of managers in Europe report concern about the levels of stress in their workplace, only 30 per cent of organizations in Europe have policies and procedures to deal with workplace stress, harassment and violence (EU-OSHA, 2014). Take, for example, a large national UK energy supplier who developed an employee support programme that offered psychological support for employees and trained over 1,000 managers in mental health literacy and improving well-being. They found that this programme saved £228,000 per year and increased job satisfaction from 38 per cent to 68 per cent (Mind, 2010).

The problem is similar all over the world. A recent study suggested that half of workers in the Greater Toronto area have had a mental health problem at some point in their working life. A related study suggested that mental health problems will cost that region alone $17 billion in lost productivity over the coming decade (CBC, 2016).

Mental health and well-being are not just something abstract that exists in the mind, they are connected with the chemistry and biology of our bodies. Understanding that while workplace environments, colleagues and job demands can impact stress and mental health issues, it is also important to understand the physical components. The majority of this chapter discusses practical implications, while some sections delve a little deeper into the biology of stress.

Again, as is an enduring theme in this book, *things can be improved*. Some of the findings in this chapter may seem disheartening. We would like to frame the costs and current problems as opportunities. Employers have substantial opportunities to improve and maintain mental health among their employees. This will not just make workplaces healthier, but will also improve productivity and profit. This chapter continues, discussing a case study of an employer that has a set of cohesive and comprehensive policies for improving well-being and reducing stress in the workplace. This example is used to discuss and demonstrate a concrete example of policies and practices that can improve well-being in the short and long term.

While this chapter primarily discusses the biology of stress in the workplace, this is connected to subsequent chapters in the book. Chapter 7 links intrinsic motivators with well-being. Chapter 8 moves the discussion forward to more positive outcomes, contrasting work engagement with the more negative factors of stress and burnout. Chapter 9 discusses the relationships between extrinsic motivators, stress and well-being in the workplace. Chapter 10 looks at how systematic factors like organizational culture can affect motivation and well-being in the workplace.

Stress at work

It is generally thought that workplaces are more stressful than ever before (Dugan, 2014). In a historical sense it would be difficult to say that today's poorly lit offices and overlit high-street shops are more stressful than a Victorian workhouse. In a more recent context it may be that the alleviation of threats to physical security may shift the focus towards psychological threats such as stress. Workplace fatalities halved from 1995–96 to 2014–15 in the UK (HSE, 2015a). Fatal injuries in the UK have fallen to one-sixth of their 1974 rate, since the Health and Safety at Work Act was introduced (HSE, 2015b). Research from the United States suggests that work-related injuries fell 90 per cent through the course of the 20th century, while the size of the workforce tripled (NSC, 1998). Conversely, rates of stress and related conditions have nearly doubled since the 1970s (HSE, 2015b).

There is a large 'stress industry' connected with stress too. Lawyers, psychologists, coaches, fitness instructors and pharmaceutical companies all make a great deal of money dealing with stress. No occupation is stress-free and some of the highest paid and most powerful positions seem to be the most stressful. Every occupation has its own source of stress, but no one is immune.

A worrying trend also appears to have emerged in competitive stressing. Stress is often related to personal struggle and hard work, and thus it is common to hear students, professionals and leaders competing over who is the most stressed. It is lauded as something valiant or ambitious, with the level of stress equated with level of personal effort. Students complain about exams, customer service workers complain about the customers.

Consultants emphasize how much stress their clients create, while clients are stressed by project managing their consultants.

There is an implication that if you are not stressed you are probably not trying hard enough, particularly in Britain, where modesty is an art form and the US positivity industry has not yet taken over. Complaining about stress is a type of negative boasting. Instead of talking about how happy, engaged and hardworking one is, one can still have a satisfying moan. Saying one is stressed, though, is often covert boasting about one's popularity, workload and level of ambition or similar.

If one takes a historical perspective of 100 as opposed to 20 years there is much evidence that work is becoming less dangerous. Offices are getting more comfortable. More people are moving away from physically demanding jobs. Employment legislation is getting more favourable for workers. Discrimination, bullying and harassment is not only illegal but is no longer covertly allowed to continue in most workplaces. Work is safer and working conditions have improved. Sick days, holidays, maternity and paternity leave are rights. But given major advances in employment legislation, legal protections for workers can only go so far.

A further issue is perhaps more interesting than the historical perspective and is a topic that is still controversial: background. Socioeconomic status, gender, age and other differences in people's background greatly affect experience in the workplace. More women are working. In 2013 in the UK 67 per cent of women aged 16–64 were in work (compared with 76 per cent of men (ONS, 2013)). But that is not the full story – we hear complaints from women about the challenges of juggling a personal and professional life, unspoken discrimination and a gender pay gap of 14 per cent. Gender differences, for example, vary widely between sector and job type. We discuss this in more detail in Chapter 10. As will be discussed further in Chapter 5, discrimination can be demotivating for those who are discriminated against. It can also diminish motivation for those with unfair advantages who may feel undeserving of a promotion or reward that has not been earned.

When people think of stressful jobs it is typically skilled professional jobs that come to mind. People with different backgrounds tend to go into different occupations and types of work. In a European Commission profile for 2013 it was reported that more than 42 per cent (42.3 per cent) of women work part time while only 11.5 per cent of men work part time. While women represent over three-quarters (76 per cent) of those working in teaching, training education and science occupations, only 19 per cent of those in engineering, manufacturing and construction occupations are women.

Supervisory boards are only 16 per cent women in the UK, and women fill only 34 per cent of managerial positions (EC, 2013). In the financial sector, women earn, on average, one-third more than the average pay for women. Yet within the financial sector men earn, on average, more than twice as much as women (Metcalf and Rolfe, 2009). Background, education and a host of other factors also complicate the matter. Not only does narrowing the gender pay gap to equitable levels improve motivation, it also increases labour-force participation, broadening the available talent pool (Dwyer, 2006).

But the reason for an increase in stress is more complex and it is difficult to pinpoint the sources. Generally, pay and conditions have been improving over the long term. And yet there seems to be convincing evidence that people say they are more stressed. Why? Where does this stress come from? Are some people just more prone to stress than others? Or are some jobs and industries more stressful than others? The answer, of course, is that both internal and external factors influence the experience of stress.

Internal factors

Some people are more prone to stress than others. Some people worry about their ability to do their job, whether their concerns are justified or not. Others worry about their colleagues and relationships in the workplace. Some people worry they are taking on too much at work while others become stressed when their career progression stalls. But as skills, abilities and experiences develop, stress and what people find stressful is bound to change.

Few doubt that there are dramatic, measurable individual differences in reactions to stress and that these have profound implications for work (MacRae and Furnham, 2014). What psychologists used to call neuroticism is now more often referred to as adjustment or emotional stability. Some people get stressed by almost everything whereas others are all but immune, and most people are somewhere in-between.

Levels of adjustment and sensitivity to stress are difficult to change, but irrespective of this there are healthy and unhealthy ways of coping with stress when it comes up. The healthy coping mechanisms include modest physical exercise, joining a support group, and time-management strategies are also useful. Less healthy coping strategies are often a fallback: beginning or increasing the intake of stimulants and depressants (pills, booze), lethargy in general and emotional outbursts are generally counter-productive. Fortunately coping strategies can be taught and, whilst personality and ability are fairly stable, coping can be changed.

External factors

The list of external stress factors is well known and everyone could come up with their own list. As we discuss in the subsequent section, almost anything can be a source of stress.

There are external sources of stress, but one must be cautious about using external factors to move all the blame externally. Acknowledging external sources of stress is useful if it leads to action, while blaming external factors and relinquishing control of one's own emotions is counter-productive.

We must also be cautious about seeing stress exclusively as a negative emotion, to be eliminated. Stress has an important function, and is hard-wired into our bodies. A little bit of stress, or manageable stress, may be useful. The problems emerge when stress is unnecessary or unmanageable.

The biology of stress

Stress is a natural part of life and is a response embedded in how our body works. It is a physiological response and part of what psychologists refer to as the general adaptation syndrome (Taylor and Sirois, 2009). Stress prepares the body to deal with challenges. A first, important distinction is the difference between stress and stressors:

- **Stressors** are events or situations that can be judged to be problematic, challenging, difficult or unwanted. These can be psychological stressors like performance reviews, e-mails or interpersonal conflict. Or, they can be physical stressors like hot or cold temperatures, health complaints, aches and pains. Stressors are not objectively stressful: that is, different people see different events as threatening. While some people become enormously stressed about looming deadlines, for example, others remain unperturbed.

- **Stress** is the body's response to stressors. It is the reaction that sends a flood of hormones throughout the body in preparation. This goes back to the animal part of our brain that creates a 'fight or flight' response. The animal brain suddenly sees a predator, and stress is the response to pull the body out of its resting state and spur a reaction.

That is why stress can have intense, physical manifestations. Startled people jump, stressed workers often have nervous tics or behaviours such as tapping pens, playing with their hair, obsessively checking their mobile phone, or impulsive shouting. In a threatening situation, stress is a normal and healthy response. It is the mind and body identifying a threat in preparation to react and, in the animalistic case, survive.

Stress creates physical effects as well as psychological ones. Stress hormones push the body into a state meant for short-term survival. The heart pumps faster and the spleen contracts, dumping red blood cells into the bloodstream, increasing the amount of oxygen the blood can carry to prepare for physical activity. The body starts sweating to remove the toxins the body produced from the increased metabolic rate. And the liver starts to convert glucose to fuel for the muscles to use. The digestive tract slows down and urine is retained, conserving water, which is an essential resource for the body. Stress puts the body on high alert.

It has significant effects across the body. The release of mineralcorticoids causes a retention of sodium, which causes more water to flow into the bloodstream with the consequences of increasing blood pressure. Gluccocorticoids cause proteins and fats to break down, to produce glucose to power the body, but this can lead to further blood pressure increases and reduce the inflammatory response that protects the body from illness. Stress is the body's compromise: use the body's full capacity immediately to survive the stressor. Once the stressor is gone, stress recedes.

Predatory animals are extremely rare in the contemporary workplace unless you are a zookeeper, or in a few rare other cases. But the body responds the same way to stressors whether it is a hungry lion or a presentation to a large group of people. The fight or flight response explains a great deal about reactions. Some people who are stressed by a deadline or presentation avoid and procrastinate (flight). Most good procrastinators know that putting it off does nothing to alleviate the stress, it just creates a looming sense of guilt, anxiety or concern that is constantly at the back of their mind. Others lash out, get angry or shout (fight). Both are instinctual reactions, but rarely do very much to remove the stressor.

The consequences of stress can vary from mild to severe:

1 **Minor health complications**: over the longer term, stress hormones – which increase blood pressure, deplete the body's reserves and suppress the inflammatory response that protects the body from illness – can lead to physical health problems. This explains why those who are constantly stressed are more likely to get sick.

2 **Cell and DNA damage**: prolonged exposure to severe stress can be damaging to the fundamental building blocks of a person, the cells and our DNA. Research has found (Epel *et al*, 2006; Epel *et al*, 2010) that prolonged exposure to intense levels of the stress hormone cortisol

actually frays the caps on our DNA (telomeres). This is potentially life-shortening (Aviv, 2004).

3 **Post-traumatic stress disorder (PTSD)**: PTSD, typically associated with extreme stress in the military, is another example of the potentially destructive effects of stress. This is not caused by general office stressors like running out of paper clips or getting a lower Christmas bonus than expected. PTSD is a psychological disorder that can result from life-threateningly stressful situations. These are events (most common in war-like situations, but possible anywhere) that create such intense stress from a life-threatening situation that the individual cannot recover once the stressor is removed.

4 **Death**: prolonged stress can be deadly. Again, this is not the daily irritation that is present in most workplaces, like colleagues chewing with their mouth open or not getting sufficient recognition from a supervisor. This is from prolonged stress that creates exhaustion by overworking the organs, dehydration and complete depletion of the body's resources. Being worked to death is not a feature of workplaces in most advanced economies that have developed labour standards; however, it still happens around the world (Oster, 2014; The Economist, 2007).

That said, it is not all bad. Prolonged exposure to stress can be problematic, but stress hormones like cortisol are not inherently 'bad'. Now, don't take the previous list and interpret it as 'stress is a toxic chemical', or telling people that their stressful job is ageing them (and definitely don't mention that you can *see* how their stress is ageing them). Think of stress in another way: as the body's alert system, it is also part of problem solving. When someone can identify the sources of stress (stressor), then the problem can (potentially) be solved.

Stress and optimal arousal

There is an optimal amount of stress, which does vary from person to person. Successful entrepreneurs often report feeling stress regularly and often. Some are constant worriers who are constantly stressing about their finances, their clients, their marketing plans, their short- and long-term prospects, their employees, their competitors and everything possible. They see many different things as threatening, and the stress focuses their attention on the stressors. Successful entrepreneurs are not just perpetual worriers though, they act on the sources of stress. They identify and then resolve the potential problem. Many entrepreneurs would describe themselves as worriers, but use their stress as a tool to identify, solve and overcome potential problems.

Thus, potential solutions are equally important. Potential stressors may not create stress if they are resolvable. As a rule of thumb consider the following two questions for managing employee (or your own) stress:

1 Is the stressor threatening?/Does it create stress?

2 Is it within one's capacity to solve?

The following three steps can be a helpful guide for mitigating stress and using it to improve performance after considering the previous two questions:

1 **Identify source of stress.** Be aware of signs of stress in your own body and behaviour. Tense muscles, negative thoughts or other signs of stress may be indicators of a stressor, even when one is not consciously aware of the specific source. Consider the reason for the stress, and if it is possible to address, go to step 2. An entrepreneur can justifiably be worried about an upcoming presentation to clients, but the source of this stress should not be ignored.

2 **Plan solution.** Consider potential solutions to the problem or ways of mitigating the source. Although some situations cannot be remedied, most can. The entrepreneur worried about the upcoming presentation may want to practise and spend additional preparation time to make sure they are ready and more confident.

3 **Implement.** This, as is a consistent theme in this book, is essential. Plans to reduce the stress must actually be implemented. If they are not, the previous two steps are just wasted time.

Stress as a negative emotion can be turned into a positive motivator when appropriate and constructive steps are taken to address the source. A feeling of worry can be transformed into pride in doing one's best to address the source of stress at work and improve performance.

The top two boxes in Table 4.1, clearly, are not the greatest concern. If the situation is not threatening it does not create stress. The lower two are the differences between potentially useful stress, and a stifling wet blanket of demotivating stress that reduces performance.

Consider a common example of stress without the capacity to deal with the problem. Many retail employees often have very specific job descriptions and limited authority; for example they cannot return products and refund

Table 4.1   Stress, capacity and threat levels

		Within Capacity	
		No	**Yes**
Threatening?	**No**	Not a concern, not stressful, 'someone else's problem/responsibility'.	Job demand that does not create stress. Typically the technical aspect of a job where the employee is an expert (eg an accountant filing taxes).
	Yes	A potentially threatening situation that the employee is not able to solve themselves. It may be beyond their experience, confidence or knowledge; or it might be beyond their authority or remit, but still fall to them (eg law student not qualified to give legal advice).	A situation is potentially threatening, could be challenging but is within the person's ability, and/ or they have sufficient authority to address the problem. These are development opportunities, and if well managed are an important part of learning. For example, giving a presentation with sufficient preparation time and knowledge of the subject.

money without supervisory approval. This may not always be threatening or stressful, but if a customer is angry, in a rush and being rude to the retail employee while the manager is unavailable, the situation is stressful because it is not solvable. But individual differences come into play as well, as some would find this situation stressful, others would not.

Bureaucratic organizations often report high levels of this type of stressful situation. Government organizations, for example, may put a low-paid worker in the position of processing forms. A series of requirements with accompanying stacks of forms need to tick every single box, otherwise it is rejected. Consider the employee(s) who have to send passport pictures back, rejected, because the subject is smiling. Overly bureaucratic organizations with Byzantine rules tend to create structures where the employee on the front line has no power or authority over the decision, but is 'customer facing' and has to deal with irate customers or clients. This can be incredibly stressful.

The other, optimal situation, is where a situation might be stressful at work, but the person has the capacity to deal with the stress.

A tip on stress, psychology and physiology

Stress is real, physical and physiological as well as being psychological. It cannot be wished away, but there is a lens that it goes through from being a stressor to becoming stress. Perception is an important part. That partially explains why most people are scared of public speaking, but not everyone gets stressed.

A little trick that can be helpful, when the stress is within one's capacity, is to reframe some of the stress symptoms. Excitement and stress have many of the same physiological effects. Racing heart, sweat, increase in blood pressure, which may be accompanied with physical changes like sitting up straight, becoming more alert. Is the reaction fear or excitement? In many cases it is the same thing, but one's own interpretation is important.

Long-term effects and the HPTI axis

Working with stress and managing it in the workplace takes a larger perspective than just taking away minor annoyances, making sure employees have the capacity to deal with their stress and day-to-day interventions. Changing workplaces takes a broader perspective, a strategic and long-term direction. Tactics like coping strategies workshops or motivational speeches can boost morale, but are ineffective without being part of a larger plan.

There has been one factor that has consistently been found to negatively impact a person's stress response – poverty (Taylor and Sirois, 2009; Evans and Kim, 2007). Child poverty is psychologically damaging for a number of reasons:

- **Psychosocial**: poverty is often associated with all sorts of challenges, including poor access to health care and education, and good housing. Children who grow up in poverty are less likely to learn (or have access to) healthy diets, learn about proper exercise and healthy behaviours. This may be unsurprising to most, but it is important, particularly because it is intertwined with biological effect.

- **Biological**: as discussed earlier, prolonged exposure to severe stress can be damaging. In children, it affects their development. Poverty and the consequent stressors affect young people's brains and biology. It can cause early disruptions of the hypothalamic-pituitary-adrenal (HPA) axis, the part of the brain responsible for regulating stress. In a variety of ways, the daily stressors associated with child poverty 'teaches' the developing mind and body to be more susceptible to stress.

For the sake of argument, let's ask why all this matters. Whose responsibility (see: fault) is poverty? Somewhere in government and the public sector, perhaps. The recruitment process does not start until people are working age, and all of those early developmental experiences are fully formed and it is too late to change someone's upbringing.

But that's short-term thinking, which is limiting and highlights why there is so much that can be fundamentally changed and improved in the workplace. What about employees' children?

Compensation structures and job security, among other perks and benefits, will have a profound impact on parents, and consequently their children's early environment. Profound lack of work–life balance for those who need it can pose difficulties for parents and children alike. But in every chance to minimize ill effects there is also another way to think about the problem, and create an opportunity.

Take the example of a large manufacturing company that constantly finds new ways to position itself as a 'family company' both to employees and customers. The company makes household products, and its values centre around being a family company. The entire benefits and compensation structure is designed to provide work–life balance, family holidays, time off, even down to providing fertility treatments for employees who are attempting to have children, and a company-owned holiday cottage available to all employees. These policies reduce stress that can be caused when work demands detract from family life, burnout caused by overwork as well as conflicting work and family priorities.

Everyone experiences stressful events in their personal and family life at one time or another, and an understanding manager and HR department can mitigate the stress at these times. Of course the organization cannot solve challenges in an individual's personal life, but it can reduce work demands as a stressor during these times.

The company in question also has many events and celebrations that explicitly involve families with children. But taking even greater steps they have 'take your kid to work day', and opportunities for children of employees to spend time in the company. They have summer internships/job placements and scholarship funds, to name a few. All seems nice, and it doesn't hurt to paint a positive image of the company. Kids get to learn what their parents do every day; parents have an opportunity to provide career guidance and introduce the world of work.

But in this type of environment, a 'family company', the children of employees are the upcoming talent pool. Most people talk about their families at work, particularly when their families are important to them. And of course, for many people, family and work–life balance is essential. Savvy interviewers know that asking about someone's children is a quick way to get many people to open up. These benefits within this type of environment will be appealing to many. Consequently, within the company, the well-involved HR practitioner or line manager knows that one of the employee's children just got excellent results on his exams and the other has excelled in university and is looking for a job in marketing.

Why not offer them a job placement, internship or company opportunity? Give them a scholarship for top results and offer a graduate placement. This may seem generous, and of course it is. But consider the opportunities involved, and potential long-term benefits for all involved. Chances are they already have a lifelong relationship with the company. One could not design a more immersive onboarding programme. Furthermore, it gives the company an opportunity to get a generation's recruitment a head start against the competition.

That is why really improving performance, building long-term success in an organization, combines so many elements. And when they are all aligned, sometimes they can have unintended consequences. Supporting employees with children and getting families involved in the workplace can be a nice perk of the job. And often policies that are well thought out, are intended to be constructive, fit with the company values and culture and are actually implemented have unintended positive consequences. They can reduce negative factors like stress as well as improving other factors like motivation and engagement (engagement is discussed further in Chapter 8). Who would have thought family benefits can create an exclusive talent management pipeline, straight into the company?

The more one considers the importance of early development, the more opportunities that can be developed and implemented to motivate employees, and develop the next generation of potential employees and promote success and performance.

A brief criticism

Just as successful accountants have to work long hours during tax season, and firefighters need to be physically fit, every different sector has its own opportunities, challenges and peculiarities. No company can cater to every attitude or interest, but the best companies make opportunities open to everyone who has the potential to succeed, and build on the company's strengths.

Just as some of these policies could not be reproduced in other companies or sectors, the big picture is most important. The policies have some important features:

1 **Positive intention.** The benefits stem from a genuine desire to make things better for employees. There may be beneficial consequences for the company as well as the employees, but they are designed to reduce stress and improve well-being.

2 **Cohesive.** A wide range of policies are complementary and fit nicely together. They are rooted in the same values, and contribute to the overall mission and vision of the company and those working in it.

3 **Implemented.** It is impossible to overstate the importance of implementation. It is so common for excellent, big ideas to never actually be implemented. Promises without follow-through is a rapid route to employee disillusionment.

4 **Inclusive.** Everyone in the company can be rewarded in meaningful and fair ways. Opportunities are open to everyone who is capable.

Critics might rightly argue that 'family' orientation would not appeal to everyone. Many of the benefits are geared towards people with children. Some people may not even want to talk about children at the office, let alone having regular company events where employees bring their family. This is an example of a cohesive set of policies, backed by a clear vision and strategy. Even the best company cannot be every thing to every person.

Conclusion and notes of caution

We should proceed with two notes of caution.

First, many people worry that organizational psychology, human resources and similar fields could descend into some sort of nightmarish attempt to squeeze the maximum amount of productivity out of people, using clever manipulation techniques. That could not be further from our aim in this book, nor is it the potential outcome from tools and recommendations in the book. Taking the example of creating and encouraging opportunities for employees' children to progress into the company is not some sort of multigenerational trap, brainwashing new generations to be eager employees of the benevolent company.

Cynical and manipulative interventions are destined to fail and are likely to disengage employees. Interventions have to be genuinely designed to improve things for employees, and it requires a knowledge of what the employees are really motivated by. The example from family-focused benefits works at the particular company discussed above because its size, and its culture, is so geared towards work–life balance. The policies integrate the company's target market, understanding of what employees are motivated by, and the resources to implement. This is a lesson that could be learned from, but would not fit every company culture.

That is the heart of a real (and successful) employment relationship. The individual works for the company, meeting specific objectives. The company motivates and supports that person to do their best, and learn to do even better. Help each other, and both do better; sabotage or manipulate each other and things will deteriorate quickly.

Taking lessons from psychology is not a destructive, manipulative way to improve productivity. The simple fact is that satisfied, engaged employees work more effectively. Mitigating stress reduces sick days and improves overall health. As will be discussed in greater detail in Chapter 8, well-being and engagement come with significant benefits. The most intelligent, motivated and engaged employees actually have the greatest capacity to leave the organization, and the most opportunities to search for and find another job. They are not forced to be there, and as some companies have found – if you get the motivation right, the job gets done even if employees are not even required to show up at the office (as will be discussed in Chapter 8).

Cynics and conspiracy theorists may see ill-intent in anything, but the real intention always gets revealed one way or another. The case study of corporate failure in Chapter 14 demonstrates this.

Second, in describing the opportunities for employee's children to join an organization we are not suggesting any sort of nepotism. Relying on family connections for jobs comes with other issues. We use this example to highlight the opportunities from a cohesive and well-designed HR policy, but this should be considered within a fair and equitable talent management framework. We discuss equity and its benefits in Chapter 5 and will add a best-practice example in Chapter 14.

Create the opportunities and the awareness, but the hiring/development process must be fair. Companies always suffer to some degree when unqualified people are favoured over the less able without the connections. Unfair procedures can also create problems for the employees – a job or promotion awarded based on privilege instead of merit will either be demotivating, or will fuel feelings of entitlement.

Strong, effective policy feeds into organizational strategy. As Henry Mintzberg suggests, an emergent strategic plan is one that considers emerging patterns: 'A relatively healthy organization will continue to pursue actions that are successful, and eventually actions emerge as pattern, things are done in a certain way, certain goals are pursued fairly consistently because they appear to be working' (Mintzberg, 1994: 25).

References

Advisory, Conciliation and Arbitration Service [ACAS] (2012) [accessed 10 October 2016] Mental Health in the Workplace is Costing UK Employers Billions [Online] http://www.acas.org.uk/index.aspx?articleid=3915

Aviv, A (2004) Telomeres and human aging: facts and fibs, *Science of Aging, Knowledge and the Environment*, **51**, p 43

Canadian Broadcasting Corporation [CBC] (2016) Mental health issues affect 1 in 2, Toronto, Hamiltron workers: CivicAction

Centre for Mental Health [CMH] (n.d.) [accessed 10 October 2016] Economic and Social Costs of Mental Health Problems [Online] http://www.acas.org.uk/index.aspx?articleid=3915

Dugan, E (2014) Going to work is more stressful than ever, poll reveals, *The Independent*, 2 November

Dwyer, M (2006) The economic rationales for narrowing the gender pay gap, report prepared for the National Advisory Council on the Employment of Women, New Zealand

Epel, ES, Lin, J, Wilhelm, FH, Wolkowitz, OM, Cawthon, R, Adler, NE, Dolbier, C, Mendes, WB and Blackburn, EH (2006) Cell aging in relation to stress and cardiovascular risk factors, *Psychoneuroendocrinology*, **31** (3), pp 277–87

Epel, ES, Lin, J, Dhabhar, FS, Wolkowitz, OM, Puterman, E, Karan, L and Blackburn, EH (2010) Dynamics of telomerase activity in response to acute psychological stress, *Brain, Behavior and Immunity*, **24** (4), pp 531–39

European Agency for Safety and Health at Work (2000) The state of occupational safety and health in the European Union – pilot study, Luxembourg: Office for Official Publications of the European Communities

European Agency for Safety and Health at Work [EU-OSHA] (2014) Calculating the costs of work-related stress and psychosocial risks – a literature review, Publications Office of the European Union, Luxembourg

European Commission [EC] (2013) The current situation of gender equality in the United Kingdom – country profile, European Commission

Evans, GW and Kim, P (2007) Childhood poverty and health: cumulative risk exposure and stress dysregulation, *Psychological Science*, **18** (11), pp 953–57

Gaspar, M and Müller, WE (eds) (2002) Depressionen: versorgungsstrukturen und behandlungsperspektiven, Springer

Health and Safety Executive [HSE] (2015a) Statistics on fatal injuries in the work-place in Great Britain 2015: full-year details and technical notes, Health and Safety Executive

Health and Safety Executive [HSE] (2015b) Historical picture: trends in work-related injuries and ill health in Great Britain since the introduction of the Health and Safety at Work Act 1974, Health and Safety Executive

International Monetary Fund [IMF] (2014) World economic outlook, International Monetary Fund

MacRae, IS and Furnham, A (2014) *High Potential: How to spot, manage and develop talented people at work*, Bloomsbury, London

Matrix (2013) Economic analysis of workplace mental health promotion and mental disorder prevention programmes and of their potential contribution to EU health, social and economic policy objectives, Executive Agency for Health and Consumers, Specific Request EAHC/2011/Health/19 for the Implementation of Framework Contract EAHC/2010/Health/01 Lot 2

Metcalf, H and Rolfe, H (2009) Employment and earnings in the financial sector: a gender analysis, Equality and Human Rights Commission, Manchester

Mind (2010) [accessed 10 October 2016] Taking Care of Business: Employers' Guide to Mentally Healthy Workplaces, *Mind* [Online] http://www.mind.org.uk/media/43719/EMPLOYERS_guide.pdf

Mintzberg, H (1994) *The Rise and Fall of Strategic Planning*, Pearson Education Limited, Ontario

National Safety Council [NSC] (1998) Accident facts, National Safety Council, Illinois

Office of National Statistics [ONS] (2013) Women in the labour market

Oster, S (2014) [accessed 10 October 2016] Is Work Killing You? In China, Workers Die at Their Desks, *Bloomberg* [Online] http://www.bloomberg.com/news/articles/2014-06-29/is-work-killing-you-in-china-workers-die-at-their-desks

Ramaciotti, D and Perriard, J (2003) Die kosten des stresses in der Schweiz, Staatssekretariat für Wirtschaft SECO, Bern

Taylor, SE and Sirois, FM (2009) *Health Psychology*, McGraw-Hill Ryerson, Ontario

The Economist (2007) Jobs for life: death by overwork in Japan, *The Economist*, 19 December

Measuring motivation

05

Introduction

One would assume workers get more committed, more motivated and feel more involved with a company as the duration of their tenure increases. Yet some surprising research from Gallup found a negative relationship between engagement and length of time at the company researched (Kular *et al*, 2008). Long-term employees should not be taken for granted, because they actually tend to get less committed and less motivated as their tenure increases. In explaining these results, Brim (2002) suggests that organizations do not effectively utilize many of their employees' strengths. Instead, many organizations constantly highlight skill deficiencies and employee shortcomings through training programmes that focus on addressing weaknesses instead of building strengths.

Thus, it should not be assumed that time heals wounds and length of tenure improves motivation or loyalty. And there is only one way to know what is really going on: measure it.

Motivation is one of the psychological factors that is relatively straight-forward to measure. People tend to be self-aware about their own motivation and honest about reporting it. It helps that there is no 'right' answer. However, just because it is straightforward does not mean it is easy to measure well. This chapter makes recommendations for measurement in general, and recommendations that apply to measuring motivation in the workplace.

Testing, assessment and valued characteristics

Collecting data about other people is often described as testing or assessment, and while the words tend to be used interchangeably there is an important distinction. Testing is a single, independent measure of a specific behaviour or attribute; assessment is a process of combining tests or other data sources to answer a specific question (Cohen and Swerdlik, 2010). Testing is a single method whereas assessment is a process that may combine any of the methods discussed in this chapter.

> **Testing.** A single independent measure of a specific behaviour or attribute.
>
> **Assessment.** A process of combining multiple sources of information to answer a specific question.

The chart in Table 5.1, adapted from Cohen and Swerdlik (2010) describes the important differences between testing and assessment.

This distinction is important, because it illustrates the difference between a specific tool and a more general question or problem. There is no one-size-fits-all test than can answer every question about motivation, performance

Table 5.1   Key differences between testing and assessment

	Testing	**Assessment**
Objective	Measure, with numbers, a particular attribute or behaviour.	Answer a question or solve a problem using various tests, data or measures.
Process	Standardized process with specific scoring and results.	Individualized or customized process that explores the *how* and *why* not just the results output.
Role of Evaluator	Evaluators are interchange-able, in that one individual or group is tested much in the same way as any other.	The evaluator is essential in this process, using knowl-edge and experience to customize the process.
Skill of Evaluator	Technical skills are required in relation to the particular test.	A broader base of knowl-edge and understanding of the context is required to customize the process.
Outcome	A standardized score or type of output is created based on predetermined rules.	A problem-solving approach is used to provide a more detailed analysis of the answer or solution.

SOURCE Adapted from Cohen and Swerdlik (2010)

and other factors within a company, just like there is no single tool that can be used to build a house or fix a car engine. The expert practitioner has a range of tools available that can be used and combined in order to come up with the best solution. This should highlight the importance of expertise in the assessment process: good tests are highly developed tools that have been created by experts. Creating psychometric tests is not a job for amateurs or hobbyists.

So, there are three essential considerations for any test:

1 **Reliability**: first, it is important that a good test yields consistent results for what it is intended to measure. A good thermometer always registers 25 degrees when the temperature is 25 degrees. If the thermometer is affected by other things, like tendencies to register higher temperatures earlier in the day or showing a different temperature after it has been shaken, it is not a very useful thermometer. The same is true of tests. That is not to say one person should always get the same results on a test, as factors like motivation can change. But, for a good test, changes in a person's score must reflect actual underlying changes.

2 **Validity**: tests must measure what they are intended to measure. A thermometer is not a very good measure of a person's intelligence. It may, indeed, be a valid measure of *something*, but not of intelligence. A valid measure of motivation must actually measure the person's motivation. That sounds straightforward, but the concept is far more complex than it seems on the surface. For example, try measuring motivation with a single question like 'Are you motivated by money or fame?' and you will get an answer, but that answer might not tell you anything valid about the person's true motivation. John and Soto (2007) provide an excellent in-depth discussion of validity.

3 **Utility**: the perfect test is useless if, in practice, it cannot be used. A thermometer would be useless for measuring room temperature if it were too large to fit in the room. A questionnaire that measures motivation but takes eight hours to complete is practically useless in an organizational setting. This issue of utility is not always given as much attention by researchers and psychometricians as it deserves, but the practicality and usefulness is an essential consideration in workplace testing.

There will always be trade-offs between validity and utility, and many academics balk at the notion of trading off any amount of validity to meet the practical needs in the workplace. Some practitioners will happily throw out any amount of validity in the interest of practicality. The reality is, without *both* validity and utility, a test is useless. A test with no validity is a waste of resources because it does not tell you anything. A test with no utility will never be used. That is where the role of expertise comes into assessment, achieving the optimal balance of each to achieve the best possible result.

Another consideration about testing and assessment is that it brings attention and focus to whatever is being measured. By its very nature, testing and assessment involves collecting specific information from other people. It is a basic fact about measurement that measuring anything forces it to conform to the way it is being measured. Testing in the workplace implies that whatever is being measured is important, desirable or useful. A valid test is a clear indication that whatever is being tested is of interest to the company and sends two clear messages (MacRae, 2013). First, *this attribute is important to us*. Second, it sends a message about the role, occupation or organization where testing occurs: *this position requires specific attributes that not just anyone will have.*

A brief (but useful) diversion

Most measurement systems can be complex, but have much of the complexity masked behind a final number. For example, IQ scores use 100 as a midpoint, the average score. Two-thirds of people score within the 'average' range (85 to 115) and anyone who knows that this is based on a normal distribution knows precisely how many people score within any particular range: 16 per cent of people score about 115, 2.5 per cent score above 130 and only 0.1 per cent of people score about 145. This is what statistics call 'normal' because nearly every psychological, and indeed physical, trait shows this pattern of distribution. Figure 5.1 shows the average height distribution of women in England and Wales. The average woman is 161.6 centimetres tall (ONS, 2010).

So what's in a number? If labelled with any other number would it mean the same thing? Different scales have different benefits and drawbacks. Using temperature as an example, Fahrenheit actually makes a lot of sense for day-to-day, informal, discussions about temperature. The 0 to 100 range of the scale covers a range of temperatures that most people live in. Celsius uses a different scale to measure the same thing. Celsius is the standard measure of temperature used in most countries, the 0 to 100 range aligned with freezing and boiling points of water.

The lesson is not to get too confused about the specific numbers or the particular scale being used. If you are not an experienced psychometrician, fear not! Even if you do not know exactly what the number means, it can

Figure 5.1   Distribution of height of women in England and Wales in 2010

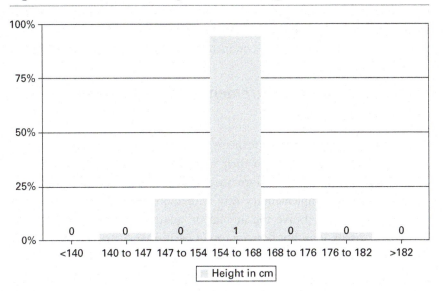

Height in cm

still be used as a guideline. In the same way one can say, 'It must be 40 (or 100) degrees outside!' to explain that it is a hot day – the score on a psychometric can be used as a guideline.

The HPMI test of motivation's scores is also aligned with a particular score. The scores have been aligned on a –100 to +100 scale in order to be more intuitive and easy to interpret. A score of 0 is average, meaning if you score a 0 that particular factor motivates you about as much as other people. If your score is +100 you value that factor at the highest possible level, more than everyone else with any score. Negative numbers, conversely, mean that you place less emphasis on the facet of motivation than the average person.

Similarly, some people get hung up on numbers in rating scales. It is, of course, important because different rating scales can give you different information of varying degrees of usefulness. If the performance review question is framed as 'Is the performance satisfactory?' with a yes/no answer, that pass/fail approach gives very limited information. If the question involves a rating scale, like 'Rate the performance from 0 to 2 (where 0 is poor, 1 is average, 2 is excellent)' that provides slightly more information but not very much. A rating scale of 0 to 6 (0 is extremely poor, 3 is average, 6 is excellent) provides even more information.

Of course this can descend into silly territory, moving to 25- or 100-point rating scales. Some would argue that a greater range offers even more information. Others, who analyse these things more rigorously and statistically, suggest the ideal range is between 4 and 7 points on the scale. Any less than 4 points and you start to lose information, anything above 7 provides negligible additional information (Lozano, García-Cueto and Muñiz, 2008).

Consider the following 10 recommendations for measuring performance.

10 points about measurement and performance appraisal systems

1   Yearly or semi-annual performance appraisal is a good start but can encourage people to be on their best behaviour for only a few days or weeks around the performance review. Day-to-day feedback can be used in a complementary way with more formally structured and delayed reviews. Leave the annual or quarterly reviews for the big-picture discussions, but keep on top of performance management issues that can and should be addressed immediately.

2   Conservative, cautious or weak managers will not give low marks. Performance appraisal should not end up being an exercise in giving everyone a 4/5 or 5/5. People need to be scored accurately, and sometimes conflict or hurt feelings might arise. Managers or evaluators must measure performance accurately and reliably, and cannot be afraid to provide criticism when it is earned. Make sure the full range of the scale is used in a way that accurately reflects everyone's performance.

3   Appraisal data may contradict other decisions about pay or development opportunities. If rewards, bonuses and recognition bear no relationship to the appraisal data it leads to some difficult questions. Appraisal data can, but does not necessarily have to, be linked to decisions about pay and promotions. The solution is to make it clear what performance appraisal data is used for, and on what criteria pay and promotion decisions are made.

4   Individual appraisals can be counter-productive when they encourage individual performance over group performance or team spirit and cooperation. Teamwork is often lauded, but often organizational cultures implicitly favour and reward individual performance. It is perfectly simple to appraise a team's performance instead of individual performance, or to do both depending on what is desired and appropriate (an example of this is provided at the end of this chapter).

5   Appraisals can be too inflexible to identify real differences between people or can be so trivial that no useful data is generated. The size and complexity of the organization can make comparisons difficult: the accounting department, legal team and sales team all need to be evaluated on different types of performance. There are two solutions to this. First, everyone beyond a certain level (say supervisor) can be evaluated based on leadership competencies and other general criteria. Then employees or teams can come up with their own criteria, defining what is desirable and optimal performance in their role.

6   If the performance management system is not used throughout the entire organization and certain groups are exempt, this can be unreasonable and unfair. It can be particularly unfair if employee rewards are tied to performance when management bonuses are not. This can happen, paradoxically, when the senior leadership – who should model ideal behaviour and exemplify performance – are the only exempt group from the company's typical performance management framework. Performance management systems can be flexible based on the role, but they must apply to everyone.

7   The skills and knowledge must be in place before any performance management system is implemented. Time, effort and money are needed in three phases: system design, implementation and maintenance.

8   Whatever ratings scale is used needs to have numbers and words that match, and can be applied to performance. Many rating scales used in performance appraisal are five-point scales with verbal descriptors, for example, 1 = under performance; 2 = marginal; 3 = satisfied; 4 = above average; 5 = excellent performance. It can be a recipe for disaster if it turns into a three- or two-point scale that effectively does not differentiate the good and the bad. Everyone gets between 2 and 4 and no one gets the top or bottom scores of 1 or 5. What is more, the description may leave 'satisfactory' performance in the eye of the evaluator. The scale must be clear and intuitive, on a sufficient range. Seven possible ratings is the best, with an anchor in the middle of the scale. Define what number represents minimum performance standards as well as average performance standards.

9   When conducting a cost-benefit analysis of designing, implementing and maintaining a performance management system it may seem like it simply is not worth the cost and effort. Additionally it has the potential to unearth performance issues that some within the company might prefer to keep hidden. Not all systems require months of super-consultant time and expense, but they also must not be amateurish or designed without proper expertise. The implementation is often as important as the design of a performance management system. Those within the organization

must be knowledgeable, supportive and trust in the efficacy of the system for it to be used well.

10 Employees are likely to feel alienated from the performance management system and view it as a standard or criteria they have to meet but have no control over. This is only the case if performance management systems are not properly piloted or introduced. In fact the precise opposite is most often the case: people complain about being over-consulted by HR over the contents of the appraisal form with which they are all too familiar.

Performance management, like measurement in general, is only useful and effective when it is done well. It is easy to point out examples of where vast sums of money and energy resulted only in bickering staff. This does not mean that measuring performance is necessarily demotivating. They simply did not do it right. It can work well and, as the blessed Lady Thatcher used to say: 'There is no alternative!'

Qualitative information

Numbers (quantitative data) are not the only way to evaluate people. Qualitative data can be useful as subjective information. One of the most common criticisms levelled at qualitative research is that it is not representative of a wider group or population. This is a misguided argument. Unlike a questionnaire or survey, and many of the quantitative methods, qualitative research is *not meant to be representative of a larger group* (Flowerdew and Martin, 2005). The purpose of qualitative research is not to replace numeric measurement; it is to provide more depth and detail and understanding to the meaning behind the numbers.

Academics have fierce and ranging debates about the merits of qualitative and quantitative research. The debate goes back for decades. Armstrong and Armstrong (1983) suggest a problem with qualitative data is that, 'explicit and, more often, implicit assumptions are built into the collection of these data ... which may serve to conceal or distort important aspects'. On the other hand, Miles (1979) says that, 'qualitative data tend to overload the research badly at almost every point: the sheer range of phenomena to be observed, the recorded volume of notes, the time required for write-up, coding, and analysis can all become overwhelming'. And that there are 'very few protections against self-delusion, let alone the presentation of "unreliable" or "invalid" conclusions to scientific or policy-making audiences'.

Being more practical about measurement in the workplace, we can put this debate aside and say both are correct and wrong at the same time. They are correct in all their criticisms, but a debate on one versus the other is not a debate worth having. Neither is better because they are like comparing apples and oranges, or arguing about whether Batman or Superman would win in a fight. They are different tools for different purposes. Of course when you use something for the wrong purpose it does not work.

A good example of this (discussed in detail in Chapter 9) is looking at people who are motivated by money. Imagine, on a scale from 1 (least important) to 10 (most important) a person's motivation to earn money is a 10. That's the quantitative piece. But why? Is it because they are on very low earnings and need that money to survive? Or is it because they have vast sums of money and want more? What about someone who scores a 1 on the same scale? They could be a Buddhist monk, a middle-class person satisfied with their income, or they could be a Rothschild. The quantitative 'how much' question is different than the 'why' question. Asking both provides more information, and sometimes the numbers identify the problem, whereas the qualitative information can give clues about the potential solution. If you know 90 per cent of the employees are disengaged, you have figured out there is a problem. More information is required to find the solution, and one should start asking why so many employees are disengaged.

Case studies

The only common feature of organizations, like individuals, is that they are all different. Company culture, organizational structure, policies, procedures and peculiarities always vary. Case studies are a type of qualitative data that can be very useful but must also be used with caution.

Business gurus and successful entrepreneurs naturally want to tell their own story, and explain how they became so successful. Often this fits into a nicely packaged narrative, with some sort of childhood spark, adolescent failure or life-changing experience. Some of these are well thought out with constructive advice, while many other autobiographies are self-satisfied, gloating about the author's own ability to overcome all challenges through sheer charm, ability and force of will (eg, see *Trump: The art of the deal*, 1987). Sign up to their workshop and learn the secrets of [their] success as it pours out from behind too many luminous white teeth.

Case studies, biographies and 'real-world examples' often become best-sellers when they combine the right amount of interesting narrative and entertaining stories, along with a few simple messages. Often these are uplifting and inspirational stories, which conclude that you, too, can be very successful if you do this one thing (three strategies, five disciplines, seven habits – like sins, self-help always comes with odd numbers).

Stories, allegories and fables from business should not be confused with other types of evidence. They tend to reveal more about that individual story than any substantial insight into general life, success and achievement. Arianna Huffington's *Thrive: The Third Metric to Redefining Success and Creating a Life of Well-Being, Wisdom, and Wonder* (2014) (remember, success always comes in odd numbers) describes a broken cheekbone sparking a realization and subsequent transformation. It would be unwise to recommend that specific course of action to others.

Case studies, just like all allegories, are open to interpretation, and will be interpreted through multiple lenses. First, the author adds their own slant, through which the reader can interpret the information. In any single story there are limitless interpretations. More notable characters and achievements tend to spawn ever-expanding numbers of biographies, all with different interpretations.

Stories are powerful. Stories (or case studies, case histories, as researchers like to call them) can illustrate a concept or specific point and add clarity. A case study can be an in-depth examination of an individual or organization to add more depth and clarity to the particular example of interest. Case studies can be useful to illustrate how and why things are as they are, how they got there and any circumstances or events that may have contributed. While it is relatively quick and easy to quantitatively test an employee's motivation, that test does not tell us anything about the reasons behind their motivation.

Case studies might also provide useful information about how an individual's attributes such as personality, motivation and experience helped or hindered that individual in a particular situation. Why does a trauma make some more resilient while making others more vulnerable? What individual circumstances are useful to know about? This is the question a case study can answer.

However, case studies must also come with an important caution. While a case study can show a real-world example, a case study should never be taken as proof of a wider concept. The very nature of case studies, their usefulness in understanding of that particular story, means they cannot be used with any certainty to explain another person's or company's story. We can learn lessons from history: empires tend to rise and fall for similar reasons and under similar circumstances (Turchin, 2003). But exploring, for example, stories of highly intelligent people who have failed catastrophically (see Chapter 14) cannot lead to the conclusion that highly intelligent people are doomed to fail.

We use stories, case studies, throughout this book to illustrate particular examples, to show how the concepts and theories are relevant within the workplace. They are also intended to be instructive in highlighting how important context is for motivation and performance within a particular team or organization. Do not expect to take one company's HR playbook and force it on another company. It must be adapted to fit within the business model, the organizational culture and those within it.

Returning to the initial three considerations for evaluating tests, included at the beginning of this chapter, let's apply these to case studies:

1 **Utility.** How useful and enjoyable is it to read? If the story is told well, the writing is good and the content engaging, a story can certainly be judged by its telling. But on this basis alone, the story may be no more or less useful than fiction. And indeed, one may be better off reading Mary Shelley, Dostoyevsky or Martin Amis to gain insight into human behaviour than another dull biography about Steve Jobs.

2 **Reliable.** Are the contents believable and accurate? Or is it a self-serving, ego-driven narrative to create an image of success? Or a tautological argument, defining success in order to make one's own approach appear successful? Unreliable accounts can certainly fit the first category, but are excluded from the third.

3 **Valid.** Do the conclusions fit with the scientific evidence? If it is a story, filled with personal accounts and opinions, it is never really possible to say whether or not those experiences, actions and attributes will have the same effect for anyone else. If the stories are used to illustrate concepts that have been well researched and validated, case studies may indeed be a valid way of telling the real story.

In the spirit of practicality, let's look at a few tips about workplace testing from a company that does just that, very successfully: Thomas International.

Tips from a successful assessment company

Thomas International is an internationally successful psychometrics company with offices in 60 countries and tests of characteristics such as personality, engagement and emotional intelligence in the workplace. As a rapidly growing psychometrics company, they are on the front lines of using psychometrics for practical applications in the workplace. To get some more information from the experts we spoke with Celeste McFarland, Content Executive at Thomas International, and CEO Martin Reid.

Motivation is important to their company, not just because it is a critical issue for their clients, but also within the business. Martin, CEO at Thomas, said one of his priorities is to keep the company motivated and maintain the 'start-up' mentality. That is, an entrepreneurial spirit inside the company, where everyone is motivated to improve the company, and where company growth will benefit everyone in the organization. This requires providing those within the company with the autonomy to improve. It also means keeping direct lines of communication open across the company (a similar example from an even larger company is discussed in Chapter 6). For example, Martin has scheduled days where anyone, from client to employee, can call him directly. This is clearly not a PR stunt or fad: just speaking with Martin shows he is not just affable and charismatic, he is genuinely passionate about growing the business and is always looking for new opportunities. This type of leadership, when genuine, can be incredibly motivating. More importantly, it models specific behaviours and sets the standard for the company culture (culture is discussed further in Chapters 8 and 10).

Thomas uses assessments for a range of different issues, and Celeste says the most common issues and challenges for their clients (many of which are discussed in this book) are:

- employee engagement (see Chapter 8);
- conflict management;
- teamwork;
- performance management (see Chapter 6);
- communication (see Chapter 6);
- succession planning (see Chapter 12);
- retention (see Chapter 10);
- change management (see Chapter 10).

Ultimately, motivation is an important component of each of these issues. For example, in their work with Siemens (the largest engineering company in Europe), they looked at recruitment processes, leadership development and 360 evaluations. The challenge involved developing Siemens's HR department and moving from a technical understanding to a broader view of talent and potential within the organization. The assessment process emphasized the need to give line managers more autonomy and focus on the value of employees and the broader contributions of employees to the organization beyond just technical expertise. Management training and development programmes created this change, along with the all-important implementation and follow-up. Siemens said:

> Ultimately the whole process changed the attitude, perception and behaviours of the senior management team. They have now bought into the understanding that people skills are just as important as technical skills.

Employment equity and equitable hiring

The most productive teams and the most successful teams, particularly if you're going into new areas, new markets, are diverse teams. You need a challenge. No CEO knows all the answers for a business.

Inga Beale, CEO, Lloyd's of London (Young, 2016)

Employment equity can raise the same concerns and suspicions as health and safety. The term employment equity has the power to strike fear into even the most confident HR manager. Some balk at the term, which can conjure images of gleeful employment lawyers, cringeworthy instructional videos about diversity and potential Twitter firestorms erupting from the wrathful depths of the most politically correct corners of the internet.

Fear not, it is going to be simpler and less controversial than you might think. We will also avoid any ideological arguments and stick to the facts. Employment equity means evaluating people based on criteria that predict performance. Employment equity has two key outcomes: 1) the moral argument; 2) the business case.

Employment equity means making decisions based on actual performance and fact-based evaluations of potential.

Employment equity can be intricately linked with motivation because organizations where discrimination limits opportunity for talented individuals, or provides unfair advantages for the unqualified or incompetent, can be incredibly demotivating. It is clear to see how organizations without equal opportunities based on talent and potential can affect motivation.

Intrinsic motivators can be stifled in many who are unfairly treated or evaluated, making it a difficult environment to be motivated by the value and satisfaction inherent to the work:

- **Autonomy** is diminished among those who have the capability but are not given the opportunity because of irrelevant factors.

- **Accomplishment** may not be possible for a segment of the workforce, stifling the desire among some to exceed expectations or improve performance for a company that is treating them unfairly.

- **Affiliation** can be incredibly different when standards are unfair and some groups are treated differently because of individual characteristics unrelated to work performance.

The three *extrinsic* facets are:

- **Security** can be affected when employees know a certain group is unfairly valued more than others. Those who are undervalued or overlooked will feel their place is less secure.

- **Compensation** will often be unfairly distributed when workplaces are not equitable and employee rewards are not based on talent, ability or performance.

- **Conditions** such as physical conditions may be less affected by equity, but unfair social or cultural conditions can negatively affect this factor.

It must be stressed that 'unfair' is not a matter of individual employee perspective; the entitled or oblivious individuals may complain about decisions or policies as 'unfair' simply because they dislike them. When we say unfair, we mean clear and measurable unfair situations such as the examples discussed shortly, where individuals are discriminated against for reasons like gender or ethnicity.

We're going to focus on the business case and leave the moral argument to others. Think of employment equity as bringing science and evidence to workplace policies and procedures. Hire people based on criteria that actually predict success. Compensate people in a fair way that reflects what they contribute to the company. Promote people based on who has the highest potential to do the job well. Use criteria that have been proven to predict potential. This is discussed in great detail in the book *High Potential* (MacRae and Furnham, 2014), including how it aligns with employment equity. It also means that those who are retained stay based on performance (not overlooking the corresponding implication: those who are *not* retained should be fired for the right reasons).

Bendl and colleagues (2015) outline four ways that employment equity can provide benefits for organizations:

- **Broadens the talent pool.** All sorts of discrimination can reduce the potential pool of talent available to hire. Homogeneous organizations that hire in their own image miss out on entire segments of potential employees (Wrench, 2007). For example, Grove (2010) estimates that while 70–90 per cent of people with mental illness say they want to work, only about 22 per cent are in work. This is often caused by the stigma about mental illness, instead of the individual's actual abilities. Many different studies of different demographic differences such as gender find that greater diversity and consequent access to talent provides benefits to business (Grosvold, Pavelin and Tonks, 2012).

- **Cost reduction.** There are costs associated with poorly managed diversity or equity policies from higher turnover, disputes and even possible lawsuits. Robinson and Dechant (1997) outline these potential costs and suggest that absenteeism also increases in workplaces that do not have effective employment equity policy and practice. Sanchez and Brock (1996) found that perceived discrimination lowered job satisfaction.

- **Representative of consumers.** If consumers are a diverse group, the company should be able to understand its customers. The knowledge of people with different backgrounds, experiences and knowledge can provide a greater range of insight within the organization (Bell, Connerley and Cocchiara, 2009). Subeliani and Tsogas (2005) indicated that a more diverse workforce is better positioned to understand new markets and customers.

- **Enhanced creativity and better decision making.** Some suggest that a more diverse workforce can generate more creativity, and improve the quality of decision making in groups (Tomlinson and Schwabenland, 2010). Research from McKinsey (Desvaux, Devillard and Baumgarten, 2007), for example, found that companies with greater gender diversity in top positions outperformed the sector averages in return on investment and stock-market growth.

Workplaces have improved greatly in past decades to become more diverse and use fairer practices. Some might ask, haven't we come far enough? Aren't workplaces now fair and open to everyone? The answer, is not yet. Unconscious bias is one of the serious barriers to equitable hiring. Briefly, here are three studies (of eight) identified by the Association of American

Medical Colleges (2009) that demonstrate the negative effects of unconscious bias:

- Steinpres, Anders and Rizke (1999) asked academic psychologists to rate curricula vitae (CVs) of real psychologists. The researchers randomized the gender of the name on the CV. They found both male and female raters were more likely to hire a male applicant, and more likely to rate male applicants as having adequate qualifications and experience. Heilman and Okimoto (2007) confirmed that a similar pattern was true of managers – men tended to be rated more favourably on various dimensions, even when the gender was randomized.

- King and colleagues (2006) asked participants to assess fictitious CVs, with the ethnicity associated with each CV randomized. They found African-Americans were rated least favourably, with Asian-Americans being viewed most favourably. They also found people made judgements about suitability for different types of work based on ethnicity, with Mexican-Americans being perceived as least suitable for high-status jobs.

- Goldin and Rouse (2000) examined the effects of 'blind auditions' in hiring musicians for orchestras. They found blind auditions, where the evaluators could not see the gender of the musician, increased the likelihood of hiring women by up to 55 per cent.

There is a great deal of evidence to indicate workplaces could be more diverse, and there are opportunities to improve. Only 15 per cent of FTSE board members in the UK are women, 12.6 per cent in the United States, 16.6 per cent in France and 12.9 per cent in Germany. The highest proportion of women on boards is in Norway, with 36.3 per cent (Gladman and Lamb, 2012).

Interesting findings from the Shaw Trust (2006) show there is a gap between employer perceptions and facts. Their findings indicated that 45 per cent of employers thought none of their current employees would experience mental illness and 89 per cent thought no one in their organization had a mental illness. Yet about half of people will be diagnosed with a mental illness in their lifetime and every year about 25 per cent of people are diagnosed with a mental illness (Mental Health Foundation, n.d.). Lack of awareness means many employers and businesses are not planning for problems that will be a certainty to arise for any organization.

> It is not that individuals in the designated groups are inherently unable to achieve equity on their own, it is that the obstacles in their way are so formidable and self-perpetuating that they can not be overcome without intervention. It is both intolerable and insensitive if we simply wait and hope that the barriers will disappear with time. Equality in employment will not happen unless we make it happen.
>
> Judge Rosalie Silberman Abella
> Royal Commission on Equality in Employment, 1985

Employment equity as good science

Irrespective of the moral arguments and the business case, we also argue that equitable employment practices are just good science. Good science involves making informed decisions based on good evidence. Employment equity does not mean treating everyone in the same way, it means treating people fairly. It can involve treating people equally despite their differences. For example, company theft must be met with the same consequences irrespective of differences. Or it can mean treating people as equals by accommodating their differences (HRSDC, 2011). For example, installing ramps and lifts so that people with physical impairments have access to the workplace.

A common fear is that employment policies will lead to a 'reverse discrimination', quota systems or reduced opportunities for other groups not identified in the employment equity policy. This is not what we are advocating; every group should have equal opportunity to compete for a position in a free labour market, with positions going to the most capable candidates. The purpose is not to give any group an artificial advantage but to ensure everyone who is capable has a fair opportunity.

Another common fear is that employment equity means hiring unqualified people. This too is a misconception. No one should get a job simply because they are part of a group or because of their demographic background. Selection, hiring, promotion, development and retention should focus on qualified and qualifiable individuals. No one, irrespective of group membership, should be hired or promoted if they are unqualified or incompetent.

Employment equity programmes should focus on ensuring policy does not create unnecessary barriers to employment that exclude potential talent.

The 'barriers to employment' can seem complex and sometimes unclear because many different things can be a barrier. Whether a barrier is unnecessary also depends on the type of work. For example, requiring a driver's licence is a fair requirement for someone who drives a taxi or is a delivery driver. In Canada, it is common for employers to ask if job candidates have a driver's licence. A review of a local newspaper's classified jobs advertisements showed that about 10 per cent of nearly 1,000 job postings required a driver's licence. Less than 70 per cent of those that required a licence were for a job that involved driving a vehicle: jobs including cleaners, restaurant servers, labourers, elder care attendants and pharmacy assistants, to name a few. A driver's licence is not actually needed for most jobs, and this is a barrier that tends to be biased against less affluent candidates (and these requirements would actually be illegal under Canada's Employment Equity Act). These types of barriers are surprisingly common. One of the authors recently saw a handwritten sign in a shop window in north London that said, 'FEMALE CLEANER NEEDED': clearly the advertiser saw nothing wrong with the advertisement, which was displayed prominently.

If there is nothing in the job requirements or 'qualifications' that indicates a factor like gender or possession of a driving licence is required for the work, it should not be a consideration in the selection process. It is unlikely that the previous examples were done maliciously or with the intention of excluding particular groups. However, it should be apparent that work cleaning a restaurant does not require a driver's licence or that the employee be a specific gender. The reason driving licences are commonly advertised as a job requirement in Canada is that public transport is limited and often unreliable. Many employers believe that employees should be able to drive to work in order to be reliable. In this case the real issue of punctuality and reliability can be addressed fairly and equitably. If one of the job requirements is 'must be extremely punctual', then, any issues with punctuality can be addressed as a performance issue without precluding those without a car.

Another example of a potential barrier in a hiring process is in the way a job is advertised. If the job is advertised by word of mouth only, that is potentially a large barrier. If jobs are only made available to those within the direct social circle of company employees this may favour certain groups and exclude others. Again, this may not be deliberate exclusion but the effect is much the same. There are many simple and low-cost mediums to advertise jobs, including on social media and free job-listing services. If the purpose of hiring is to get the best person for the job, a broader reach of potential talent can only improve the process.

Some would argue that employment equity should be left up to labour market forces. They would argue that the most talented will rise to the top using their intelligence and ability no matter their background. This may be true in some instances, but often there are systematic barriers that make this impossible. For example, parents often struggle to balance work schedules and childcare, and this challenge unduly affects women in a variety of ways (Poduval and Poduval, 2009).

Essentially the concept of employment equity is simple: hire, develop and retain people based on characteristics that predict performance or potential, and remove any unnecessary barriers to being hired, promoted or retained. This should not be demotivating to any group, because it is not about bringing anyone else down, but about providing the same opportunities for everyone to succeed. This is motivating to groups that may previously have had fewer opportunities. It also should be more motivating to those who previously had unfair advantages – in an equitable organization they can take pride in succeeding within a system that rewards real performance.

For additional reading on the topic of employment equity, Standing and Baume (2001) provide a very comprehensive analysis. A guide to employment equity produced by the University of Western Ontario (2014) provides more practical advice and recommendations.

Conclusion

Motivation can be measured, and doing so provides many opportunities to improve individual and company performance – from employment equity broadening the talent pool, to understanding motivation within organizational culture and policy to bring about change for the better. The key message of this chapter should be that motivation needs to be measured to be understood. There are a variety of ways to measure motivation at work that fit with different objectives, situations and companies.

There are still incredible opportunities to improve productivity, performance and well-being in the workplace and measurement is a strong step to short- and long-term improvement. However, it is not a solution in itself. Measurement provides information, but implementation and real change are essential for improvement. The example of Ryan LLC, which is discussed in Chapter 8, demonstrates how measurement led to an identification of problems and substantial improvements in both profitability and employee well-being within an organization.

Further reading

A more detailed guide to measurement and research is far beyond the scope of this book. The earlier sections in this chapter are intended to provide a brief introduction, some guidelines and tips for measurement in the workplace. To explore these areas in greater detail, the following six books are recommended, ordered from the most accessible to the more technical:

The Free Management Library (2016) provides a free, online, guide to research methods from a business perspective. It is a fairly brief overview to the key concepts with a few facts and figures that are clearly designed for readers from a business perspective. They focus on describing the most common data collection methods.

Baumberger, Rugh and Mabry's book *RealWorld Evaluation* (2006) provides a very good, practical and accessible guide to research and evaluation projects. The book's subtitle 'Working under budget, time and political constraints' highlights the practical emphasis of this book.

Wheelan's (2014) book *Naked Statistics: Stripping the dread from the data* presents an entertaining and amusing discussion of statistics. It is a light read that provides a bit of insight, but should not be used as a reference guide or to provide deep or comprehensive understanding of statistics. It is a nice, easy read for anyone who wants to learn some statistics basics, but who cannot get through a dry statistics textbook.

Anderson's (2013) book *Research Methods in Human Resource Management* is a useful guide to research for the HR practitioner. It is clearly structured in textbook format with learning outcomes and practical recommendations through each chapter, with discussion questions to highlight each point.

Landers and Nelson (2013) present an introduction to statistics from a business perspective. It covers the most common types of statistical analysis and gives practitioners all the basic tools needed to understand scientific research and publications. Chapters are structured around examples from business.

Cohen and Swerdlik (2010) provide a more technical but still very accessible book primarily aimed at psychology students. They discuss in great detail statistics, testing, test development and considerations such as validity, reliability and utility. Even their discussions of statistics are fairly accessible and easy to read for anyone who is interested but does not have a background in these areas.

References

Anderson, V (2013) *Research Methods in Human Resource Management*, CIPD, London

Armstrong, P and Armstrong, H (1983) Beyond numbers: problems with quantitative data, *A Critical Review*, 6, pp 1–40

Association of American Medical Colleges (2009) Unconscious bias in faculty and leadership recruitment: a literature review, *Analysis in Brief*, 9 (2)

Baumberger, M, Rugh, J and Mabry, L (2006) *RealWorld Evaluation: Working under budget, time, data and political constraints*, Sage, London

Bell, M, Connerley, M, and Cocchiara, F (2009) The case for mandatory diversity education, *Academy of Management Learning & Education*, 8 (4), pp 597–609

Bendl, R, Bleinjenbergh, I, Henttonen, E and Mills, AJ (2015) *The Oxford Handbook of Diversity in Organizations*, Oxford: Oxford University Press

Brim, B (2002) The longer workers stay in their jobs, the more disheartened they become, *Gallup Management Journal*, March

Cohen, RJ and Swerdlik, ME (2010) *Psychological Testing and Assessment*, McGraw Hill, New York

Desvaux, G, Devillard, S and Baumgarten, P (2007) *Women Matter: Gender diversity, a corporate performance driver*, McKinsey and Company, New York

Flowerdew, R and Martin, D (2005) Philosophies underlying human geography research, in *Methods in Human Geography: A guide for students doing a research project*, Pearson Education Limited, Harlow

Gladman, K and Lamb, M (2012) Women on Boards Survey, Harvard Law School Forum on Corporate Governance and Financial Regulation

Goldin, C and Rouse, C (2000) Orchestrating impartiality: the impact of 'blind' auditions on female musicians, *American Economic Review*, 90 (4), pp 715–41

Grosvold, J, Pavelin, S and Tonks, I (2012) *Gender Diversity on Company Boards*, Voxeu

Grove, B (2010) Stigma and discrimination – overcoming the barriers to employment, in A Baumann and M Muijen (eds), *Mental Health and Well-Being at the Workplace: Protection and inclusion in challenging times*, World Health Organization

Heilman, ME and Okimoto, TG (2007) Why are women penalized for success at male tasks?: The implied communal deficit, *Journal of Applied Psychology*, 91 (1), pp 81–92

Human Resources and Skills Development Canada [HRSDC] (2011) *Employment Equity: Myths and realities*, Government of Canada

John, OP and Soto, CJ (2007) The importance of being valid: reliability and the process of construction validation, in RW Robins, RC Fraley and RF Kreuger (eds) *Handbook of Research Methods in Personality Psychology*, Guilford Press, New York

King, EB, Saaid, AM, Madera, JM, Hebl, MR and Knight, JL (2006) What's in a name? Multiracial investigation of the role of occupational stereotypes in selection decisions, *Journal of Applied Social Psychology*, 36 (5), pp 1145–59

Kular, S, Gatenby, M, Rees, C, Sone, E and Truss, K (2008) Employee engagement: a literature review, Kingston Business School, Working Paper Series No 19

Landers, RN and Nelson, PJ (2013) *A Step-by-Step Introduction to Statistics for Business*, Sage, London

Lozano, LM, García-Cueto, E and Muñiz, J (2008) Effect of the number of response categories on the reliability and validity of rating scales, *Methodology*, 4 (2), pp 73–79

MacRae, IS (2013) Practical consequences of occupational testing and assessment, *Assessment and Development Matters*, 5 (3)

MacRae, IS and Furnham, A (2014) *High Potential: How to spot, manage and develop talented people at work*, Bloomsbury, London

Mental Health Foundation (n.d.) [accessed 10 October 2016] Managing Mental Health in the Workplace, *Mental Health Foundation* [Online] https://www.mentalhealth.org.uk/publications/managing-mental-health-workplace

Miles, MB (1979) Qualitative data as an attractive nuisance: the problem of analysis, *Qualitative Methodology*, 24 (4), pp 590–601

Office for National Statistics [ONS] (2010) 'Average' Briton highlighted on UN World Statistics Day, Office for National Statistics

Poduval, J and Poduval, M (2009) Working mothers: how much working, how much mothers, and where is the womanhood? *Mens Sana Monographs*, 7 (1), pp 63–79

Robinson, G and Dechant, K (1997) Building a case for diversity, *Academy of Management Perspective*, 11 (3), pp 21–31

Sanchez, JI and Brock, P (1996) Outcomes of perceived discrimination among Hispanic employees: is diversity management a luxury or a necessity?, *Academy of Management Journal*, 39 (3), pp 704–19

Shaw Trust (2006) Mental health – the last workplace taboo, Shaw Trust, Wiltshire

Standing, H and Baume, E (2001) Equity, equal opportunities, gender and organization performance, Workshop on Global Health Workforce Strategy, Geneva, Switzerland: World Health Organization, Department of Health Services Delivery

Steinpres, R, Anders, KA and Rizke, D (1999) The impact of gender on the review of the curricula vitae of job applicants and tenure candidates: a national empirical study, *Sex Roles*, 41, p 509

Subeliani, D and Tsogas, G (2005) Managing diversity in the Netherlands: a case study of Rabobank, *International Journal of Human Resource Management*, 16, pp 831–51

The Free Management Library (2016) *Basic Research Methods*, The Free Management Library, Minneapolis, MN

Tomlinson, F and Schwabenland, C (2010) Reconciling competing discourses of diversity? The UK non-profit sector between social justice and the business case, *Organization*, **17** (1), pp 101–21

Turchin, P (2003) *Historical Dynamics: Why states rise and fall (Vol. 41)*, Princeton University Press, Princeton, NJ

University of Western Ontario (2014) *The Employment Equity Guide*, University of Western Ontario, Ontario

Wheelan, C (2014) *Naked Statistics: Stripping the dread from the data*, W W Norton and Company, London

Wrench, J (2007) *Diversity Management and Discrimination: Immigrants and ethnic minorities in the EU*, Ashgate, Aldershot

Young, K (Presenter) (2016) 'Inga Beale' (radio series episode), in Drysdale, C (producer), *Desert Island Discs*, BBC Radio 4

The power of communication and conversations $\qquad$ 06

Introduction

Communication is intricately connected with thought (Vygotsky and Kozulin, 2012) and consequently motivation. In this chapter we discuss different forms of communication, from body language to electronic forms of communication where the nuance that can be conveyed through body language is absent. The focus of this chapter is very practical, with focus on more recent and electronic forms of communication.

Work runs on conversations. Teams, clients, line managers and leaders, stakeholders and direct reports all communicate. Successful teams thrive on communication; dysfunctional groups put up barriers to block communication. When information is secreted away and protected, even the most motivated employee can be thwarted.

There are increasing numbers of communication mediums, amplified by technology, which have the potential to improve communication. It is now possible to communicate instantly with almost anyone, almost anywhere in the world, at no cost.

Performance management systems, compensation structures and benefits packages all affect extrinsic motivation. These policies exist in the background to mitigate potential dissatisfiers. But the day-to-day motivation at work runs on conversations. Any work involving a group requires good communication to be effective. Poor communication can be irritating in the short term, and destructive in the long term. The importance of conversations can be overlooked because they are frequent and informal. Yet conversations shape the communication networks and culture of the organization, and the way people speak with each other can have profound effects on motivation.

If most people had mastered communication it would not need to be discussed – but this is far from the reality. All forms of communication, from body language to e-mail etiquette and use of emoticons is fraught with peril. The peril is only increased when it is at one's fingertips at all hours of the day and night.

Body language at work

The best place to start is with the more familiar (for most), in-person forms of communication. Body language influences communication whenever the interacting parties can see each other. Nearly all HR or business-type courses have a component dealing with non-verbal communication. About 70 per cent of information communication comes across through body language. This means that non-verbal cues are more than twice as important as the words being spoken. In negotiation skills course trainers emphasize how to 'read' one's opponent; in selection skills course instructors emphasize how one may detect dissimulation in applicants; in appraisal workshops consultants point out how video feedback indicates how pleased or disappointed appraisees are with particular feedback. And, of course, no sales course is without advice on how and what to watch for in customers in order to maximize sales.

Curiously, research in the United States (Lynn and Mynier, 1993; Drago, 2008) has shown that the size of a waiter's all-important tip is affected by non-verbal behaviour. Three behaviours were shown to increase or diminish the size of a waiter's tip. First, whether the server touched the diner. Apparently, diners in the United States enjoy physical contact with the person bringing their food. Second, whether the server initially squatted in their interaction with the diner, as opposed to stood. Diners in the United States apparently prefer the squatting waiter. Third, the size and 'authenticity' of the waiter's initial smile increased the tip. These same behaviours in Britain might lead to withdrawal of the tip, and perhaps a rapid retreat by the dining party. These findings highlight another important point about non-verbal communication: different behaviours are desirable in different cultures and circumstances.

There are different dialects of body language. Just as American English has a tendency to turn nouns into verbs, body language has its own peculiarities. Of course, as communication between cultures increases, these peculiarities spread more quickly within and between cultures. Business communication, too, has its own eccentricities. Turning nouns into verbs is a good example of this. 'Actioning', 'tasking', 'unfriending', 'incentivizing' or 'Googling' are all commonplace. But body language has its own equivalents. What about the intimate handshake, popularized by Bill Clinton, which involves grasping both hands and intense eye contact – might the 'Clinton handshake' seem a bit threatening for an introductory-level greeting?

Debrett's (arbiter of British culture) notes on handshakes: 'Handshakes are brief, and should preferably be accompanied with direct eye contact. Do not complicate the greeting with other forms of touching – hands on the back, double-handed handshakes etc. Britain is still a comparatively non-tactile society' (www.debretts.com).

Like Mexican wine, American football or Greek financial systems, some winks, gestures and postures do not travel well. Japanese inscrutability is partly a function of very different rules associated with body language. Americans, conversely, may be very skilled at hiding their true feelings with excessive emotionality.

Body language may be coded in verbal language. Consider the following examples taken from the different areas of non-verbal communication:

- **Emotional-spatial distance**: emotional distance is often reflected in physical distance. People often approach those they feel emotionally close to, and physically distance themselves from people they are trying to keep at an emotional distance. Proximity typically implies intimacy.

- **Eye contact**: making and maintaining eye contact indicates focus on the other person, and openness. Excessive or unwarranted eye contact may be seen as threatening.

- **Posture**: a slouched posture can indicate relaxation or carelessness. A more upright posture can indicate either poise or prudishness.

Those who focus on body language are quick to read signs and signals in every gesture. Playing with hair, fiddling with jewellery, side glances and half smiles can all be interpreted and overinterpreted. But different behaviours and tics mean different things to different people, and vary widely between cultures. Averting one's eyes can be an indicator of lying or a mark of respect. Maintaining eye contact can indicate interest or irritation. Any good poker player knows that body language behaviours can easily be faked or repressed.

Similarly, body language is often imitated in groups. Even when it is not done deliberately, most people automatically act to fit in with the group. People tend to reach for their glass and take a drink in synchronization. A person sits up a bit straighter in the presence of others with good posture.

A person taking a glance at their phone can trigger a wave of phone checking across the group.

There are no hard and fast rules about what gestures necessarily mean what. But there are a few extremely important points to consider with respect to body language. It does follow certain rules, particularly in lying:

- Delayed responses: the time between the question and the answer can indicate false responses. Generating lies takes longer than responding with the truth. However, some questions do merit a certain amount of consideration, particularly when the consequences are serious.

- Distancing pronouns: there is less use of 'I' or direct pronouns. The story becomes more abstract and less personal when the truth becomes more distant.

- Slow and uneven speech: inventing the story interrupts the flow of speech. Coming up with lies on the spot can make speech more uneven. Pre-prepared lies can also come out stutteringly, if not sufficiently rehearsed.

- Too much detail: liars often keep talking when it is unnecessary. They fill silences with inconsequential details to make the story sound more convincing. More detail creates more of a problem when it can be confirmed or contradicted later. Good investigators learn this trick and hold silences longer, wait for details, and check for consistency.

- Rising pitch: statements get more shrill towards the end of a sentence. The pitch rises and sounds like a question 'You believe me?' There are some linguistic exceptions to this, such as Australians, New Zealanders and some Californians.

- Excessive movement: people who are emotionally uncomfortable often have trouble getting physically comfortable and move around too much, squirm and twitch.

- Excessive eye contact: liars often overcompensate, almost as if challenging the person to question the veracity of their statements – and excessive eye contact can be a bluff.

- Inadvertent truths: speech errors often increase with nervousness and sometimes reveal a person's true thoughts. Generally, an increase in speech errors and clumsy phrases accompanies anxiety.

- Flattening voice: in an attempt to avoid any expression or tone that would give the person away, they remove any expressiveness from their voice.

These signs can be indicators for certain lies, or certain people who tell untruths. But remember these are not always accurate. These signs are indicators of stress, but it is not just the liars who become uncomfortable in social situations. When people are shy or the stakes are high, nervousness often follows. Public speakers, those practising a second language, interviewees and attendees at an important lunch with the CEO may all be nervous. Nervous habits closely resemble the signs of those telling untruths.

Pathological liars believe their own fantasies and can fabricate with more truth than the genuinely truthful. And the best poker players often learn that the most effective way to mislead is to tell the truth in a way that no one else believes it.

Body language is a primarily learnt behaviour. With few exceptions, much of body language such as gesture and posture is learnt as part of growing up. Family, friends and teachers all influence body language in different ways.

Even without words, body language can send direct messages. Gesture, posture, touch and dress send clearly interpretable messages. A sly glance or a wink can be enticing or mocking. A smile can be encouraging, accommodating or diminishing. Body language can be used to restate and hence reinforce messages. Or it can negate an entire statement and indicate sarcasm. But often it functions to regulate and coordinate all communication. Body language helps to let people know when it is their time to talk, when yes means no (and vice versa), when things are getting rather embarrassing, and so on.

Yet we cannot automatically assume the primacy of body language. Communication without body language is now possible using many different mediums. Some methods of electronic communication have even added their own substitutes for body language, which will be discussed later.

Take two examples. Imagine dividing a large group of people randomly into three smaller groups. One reads a message from the CEO; another hears a broadcast of exactly the same message; a third group watches a video presentation, again with the same message. They all have exactly the same amount of time in which to receive exactly the same message but through different media: print; audio-only; audiovisual. Afterwards you test their memory. Who remembers most? The print group remembers most, the audiovisual group least. Why? First, reading requires more mental effort and processing of the material, which results in better memory. Second, readers go at their own pace, not that of a possibly idiosyncratic CEO. Third, the picture of the CEO – that terrible outfit, the awful glasses, the bad haircut – can interfere with concentration on the storyline. In this sense, the two things – picture and sound – are not synchronized. Forget the power of television if you want to remember facts.

The second example is that, rather surprisingly, it seems that it is easier to detect people lying through verbal cues only (that is, on the telephone) than in face-to-face communication. Verbal cues include response latency (taking longer to reply to questions because of having to think through the answer); verbal distancing (saying 'one cannot be said to' rather than 'I'); slow but uneven speech; an overeagerness to fill silences (because liars overcompensate for silences); and too many pitch rises instead of pitch drops at the end of a sentence (which sounds like 'Do you believe me now?').

The message is not that in-personal, audiovisual or older methods are superior to newer forms of communication. It just means that the cues are different and, more importantly, the traditions and etiquette involved in electronic communication has its own culture and peculiarities.

Formal communication and types of conversations

Formal communication tends to be structured, ordered and unidimensional. Marketing letters, a message from the CEO and written policies are formal communications written and directed at one particular group. No response is required, or any response has a specified format with guidelines. Conversations, on the other hand, are informal and mutual. A conversation can be between two or more people, through any medium, but has fewer conventions. Most jobs involve dozens or even hundreds of conversations every day.

Conversations are not just face-to-face chats. As with so many things, conversations are moving. And managing that communication effectively can have a substantial impact on motivation. Good communication is motivating; poor communication can be demotivating.

There are now so many ways to have a conversation, one almost needs an etiquette guide for using different modes. It may seem complicated, but balancing different communication mediums is fraught with challenges and opportunities.

A challenge to communication – especially managing conversations and e-mail and text messages and other mediums – is there are rarely specific guidelines. Before delving into more specifics, there are three points to use as guiding principles. This is not just about politeness, but managing communication is actually crucial to well-being and productivity. A deluge of unmanaged and disorganized messages can drown the recipient. A few general guidelines:

- **Organize communication**: different communication channels provide an opportunity to organize and prioritize information. Managing communication, particularly digital communications, is one of the greatest soft skills that is rarely taught.

- **Prioritize communication**: there is a simple fact about e-mail – the more e-mails you send, the more you are going to receive. Most people know the nagging guilt that can accompany an inbox full of unanswered mail; and the satisfaction (or relief) accompanied by an empty inbox. But, not everything is urgent. Delayed responses can improve productivity and reduce stress. Answering 50 e-mails in the morning almost guarantees the inbox will be refilled by noon. Consider which are necessary.

- **Remove ambiguity**: one of the real generational differences (although the lines are nowhere near clear-cut) is in experiences and practices using communication channels. Conflict, frustration and stress emerge from misunderstandings, so a clear policy about communication can be a huge advantage. Which mediums are acceptable for work communication? What are expected response times? What is the preferred communication medium?

Communication is, of course, a fundamental part of keeping people motivated, but it can also be incredibly demotivating if used inappropriately.

In this chapter we are going to spend a substantial amount of time discussing electronic communications. This is for two reasons. First, because it is pervasive. Over 100 billion work e-mails are sent every day, and that number is rising. E-mail is constantly reported as a source of stress at work: 37 per cent of smartphone users feel overburdened with e-mail; 12 per cent of those without a smartphone felt overburdened by e-mail (Huessner, 2010); 96 per cent said they could not handle more than 50 e-mails per day – the average business user received 88 e-mails per day, projected to rise to 97 e-mails per day in 2018. But e-mails are no longer the only method of electronic communication.

The average office worker spends 13 hours a week – 650 hours a year – on e-mail. At this rate, the average office worker could expect to spend three years of a 45-year career on e-mail. This fact should not be alarming in itself: without communication you have no business. But the reason it is so important to discuss, instead of shrugging it off as an annoying reality, is that improvements can be made. There are increasing varieties of electronic messaging platforms and their use is only growing. According to Goode (2016) over 60 billion messages are sent every day using WhatsApp and Facebook messenger, three times the number of text messages. Up to 200,000 iMessages are sent every second (Leswing, 2016). About 9,000 Snapchat picture messages are sent every second (Mulshine, 2015). These figures were accurate at the time of writing, will likely be higher at the time of publication, and likely will continue to grow rapidly until they are surpassed by another medium. Samuel Goldwyn said, 'Never prophesy, particularly about the future.' But if current growth rates persist, messaging services will soon surpass e-mail. Electronic communication is part of everyday life, but like any innovation we need guidelines to use it most effectively.

E-mail compulsivity

E-mail created an immediacy and directness that surpassed geographic boundaries and the speed of all previous methods of communication. Delays in e-mail are measured in milliseconds or seconds, which is inconsequential in the context of written communication. It is easily available, cheap and open to anyone. So is a conversation with your friendly, local pub drunk – yet e-mail has the advantage of specifying any recipient, anywhere in the world.

But e-mail has led to problems. Most people get frustrated with spam and marketing e-mails, or with the moderately unstable uncle with extreme political beliefs who insists on sending group e-mails to everyone in the address book. Indiscriminate cc'ing means being included on so much inconsequential conversation at best, and an accidental 'reply all' can be a terrible electronic faux pas. Not only that, there is the sheer demand of the e-mail inbox. On the plus side, everyone else is accessible. The downside is that you too are always accessible.

Yet when e-mail is down, panic quickly ensues. The constantly open communication can become compulsive, and when it is inaccessible some people develop anxiety that can be near to panic attacks. Being deliberately unavailable is the fantasy, but being out of the loop is terrifying. You might be missing crucially important communication. Lost opportunities, lost income, lost gossip. Hence the love–hate relationship with e-mail. The problems of e-mail can be neatly divided into two categories: volume and interpretation.

The volume problem is obvious to all. Despite spam detectors and other filtering devices, most users complain about the sheer volume of messages they receive. An obvious problem is that it is initially very difficult to differentiate the important from the unimportant. There are basic filters in most e-mail programs to misdirect the offers from foreign princes and invitations to solve erectile dysfunction. But there is no easy or automatic way to prioritize the important e-mails from real friends, colleagues and contacts.

The second problem, of interpretation, is slightly more challenging. That is everything lost in translation, without the normal body-language cues that exist in everyday conversation. As data gets cheaper and faster to send, more complex types of information become easier to send. But new additions to the language are always as controversial as they are useful. The reason for this is remarkably simple. Those who have developed a mutual or cultural understanding enjoy the new additions to language. Those who are out of the loop are anxious, curious or angry.

Some draconian rules

Some organizations have decided to bite the bullet. Faced, paradoxically, by reduced efficiency because staff spend all day sending and receiving, they have tried to devise new rules. Some rules can seem offensive or defensive. But rules should be aimed at doing a bit of filtering and helping with prioritizing. Consider the following:

- E-mails should not be sent to people in the same room, on the same floor or in the same building.
- Subject lines of chevrons indicating urgency should be used cautiously. Limit per day the number of e-mails that can be marked urgent.
- No one is allowed to send more than 10 e-mails per day.
- CC-ing is allowed only once per day and never to more than seven people.
- No e-mail may be less than 20 words or more than 150 words, and whilst bullet points are encouraged, seven is the maximum.
- If an e-mail is not responded to within 48 hours it should be deleted.
- On-holiday or out-of-office auto responses should be set so that senders are aware of your absence.

While some of the rules listed above may be reasonable (holiday autoresponding, avoiding e-mails with those in the same room), these draconian rules ignore many of the realities of business. Stricter rules on e-mail may be reasonable when moderating communication between people who work in the same office.

One of the limitations of e-mail is tone and body language. Without face-to-face voice tone it is often easy to misinterpret e-mails. The most primitive hieroglyph of that colon, dash and bracket emotional encoding – ie :-) – helps very little. Hieroglyphs in text communication is becoming more sophisticated with emoticons and other images, but emoticon literacy is still varied and extremely deficient at the office. Capitals are seen as shouting; spelling or typing errors as carelessness or ignorance.

It is often those with low emotional intelligence or poor social skills who choose to communicate via e-mail when in-person communication is more efficient. They think it is easier. It isn't. It is harder to read the hidden agenda in e-mails. Some of the advice given to people when receiving traditional letters may apply:

- Never reply immediately if the e-mail causes strong (negative) emotions. You don't have to sleep on it but give it a few hours.

- Beware forwarding e-mails that contain jokes, asides or personal comments that can be very contextual.

- Re-read your responses, particularly to emotionally charged e-mails, at least once.

- Realize that not all e-mails get delivered.

E-mail etiquette and advice seems to be needed in the contemporary office. Improper use of e-mail can be demotivating for the sender as well as the receiver, and e-mail addiction can be both compulsive and counter-productive. First, let's consider the challenge, then look at some salves and frameworks for managing e-mail in a productive way.

E-mail is one of those daily headaches for most working people that is difficult to avoid. The e-mail inbox is a constantly expanding and often unrelenting to-do list of requests, advice, information and discussion. The authors of this book send and receive tens of thousands of e-mails every year. We write and receive more in e-mail every year than the total contents of this book. A lot more. We can commiserate that e-mail can be a source of stress for many people.

But, how many companies have a formal (or even informal) e-mail policy? Very few. How many have policies covering other forms of electronic communication? Fewer still. Surely sending images of certain body parts to fellow employees over Snapchat would be covered by a company harassment policy. But more is needed. The prevalence of electronic messaging means it should be explicitly discussed. Even companies that do have an e-mail policy often focus on negative behaviours such as using a work e-mail to send chain letters, distributing copyrighted material without permission or for personal uses. These policies miss the bigger picture.

When are employees expected to be on e-mail? How is e-mail to be treated out of hours?

But e-mail has been around for decades, and at least a few conventions have been established for its use. The potential problems and opportunities have moved far beyond e-mail – because most people now have a device in their pockets that receives e-mails, and it is not just e-mail. The immediacy and urgency of e-mail has been surpassed with messaging apps.

And it has gone even further, because there are different applications, all on the same handheld device that can be used to communicate audiovisually, with e-mail, through direct messaging, or by sending captioned snapshots, or even discussion while playing online games. Alternative ways of communication capture the attention of savvy marketers, concerned commentators and the security services, who are extremely interested in what is discussed over new communication mediums. Decision makers within the workplace should also take notice.

However, sometimes the old rules remain relevant, particularly when they are elegantly phrased, such as Lewis Carroll's *Eight or Nine Wise Words About Letter-Writing*, which are all still relevant to e-mail and a highly recommended read (Carroll, 1890).

Texting/messaging

Mobile phones are nearly ubiquitous, and along with various messaging services most people also have a combination of e-mail accounts along with other messaging services in their phone. Texting or similar messaging services are being used by more people to have work conversations. There is little real difference between an e-mail and a text message in a practical sense except that text messages are always sent directly to a phone and come with a greater sense of immediacy and urgency.

Beware of instant messaging for work conversations: it's a trap! Keep this for personal use and for non-work conversations. Unless absolutely necessary, or by prior agreement, keep the messaging apps for personal communication. Or, have a separate messaging app to be used for work.

The appeal of instant messaging services is revealed in the name: instant. However, there are very real risks of moving work communications into a medium that tends to be used for personal conversations.

There has been much recent research on the topic of mobile phones. We are not going to argue they are bad, but the evidence is clear: mobile phones are distracting. Whether you are driving a car, or just having lunch with a colleague, the closer you are to your phone, the more distracting it is. Of course, using a phone is incredibly distracting and incredibly dangerous when in control of a vehicle (APA, 2006). That distraction is not going to be fatal in the workplace, but it will be disruptive.

The surprising findings by Thornton and colleagues (2014) shows that you do not have to be using a phone for it to be distracting. When your phone is on the table in front of you, it can be a major distraction. Even if you are not using the phone, and do not intend to use it, the presence detracts from attention that can be focused on tasks. Distractions reduce productivity. They make it harder to get started, and interrupt thought processes. Research shows that having a mobile phone, face up, on a desk will reduce intelligence test scores. These findings should not be taken too far: mobile phones do not make people less intelligent. But, the continual presence of a distraction reduces ability to concentrate, reduces effectiveness and capability.

It actually takes a surprising amount of mental effort to ignore something. Advertisers who create billboards know this: flashing lights and loud noises are almost impossible to ignore. It takes more mental energy to deliberately ignore a distraction than to let it command your attention. The same is true of mobile phones. They are effective tools when used appropriately, and managed effectively. But like any resource, they are only valuable when used effectively.

So, there are three concerns with texting and messaging applications:

- **Distraction.** Messaging, e-mail and phone notifications in general can be distracting. The research suggests 'out of sight, out of mind' really is true in the case of mobile phones. Leaving a phone face-up on your desk will be distracting. If it remains there for the entire workday it will reduce productivity, interrupt flow of thoughts, and detract from overall motivation. A phone is a useful tool, but needs to be used appropriately and put in the proper place. For most occupations, its place is hidden away, for occasional and purposeful use.

- **Boundaries.** In most situations there should not be any reason why a text message is an improvement on an e-mail. There is no need for your boss or colleague or direct report to be able to contact you in eight different ways, particularly when every single message ends up in the same place: your phone's notifications dashboard. Keep different communication mediums separate. This makes it easier to switch between work and personal notifications and 'turn off' different types of messages when appropriate or necessary.

- **Notifications.** Imagine a situation where a colleague walked into your office and asked you a question, sent you a message, or gave you a picture of a kitten every eight seconds. How much work would you be able to get done? Phone, e-mail and other notifications are remarkably similar. Each time a notification pops up, even if you choose to ignore it, it is a distraction. Other than certain occupations such as physicians, police officers and firefighters, most occupations do not require a response time that is measured in seconds. All devices have filters that can prioritize information from certain applications, people, or during certain times. Use these.

On emojis, gifs and hieroglyphs

We would be remiss to discuss body language, but leave out the hieroglyphs that are being used as electronic substitutes for body language. Language purists and puritans always bemoan the changing nature of language. As long as people have been writing about language there have been writers complaining about how new developments, and often younger people, are ruining the 'proper' language. Every time the *Oxford English Dictionary* adds a new tranche of words such as 'twerking' or 'bank of mom and dad', there is grumbling and tutting across the country for a few minutes. But language is constantly evolving to meet the new conditions and environment. Somehow, new methods of electronic communication and cheap data have introduced hieroglyphics into the English language.

Those not familiar with the trend should be introduced to two concepts. First, emoticons are illustrations of faces, people or objects that can be incorporated into text-messaging systems. They are like more sophisticated versions of the text smiley face ':)' or 'J' that has been in use for a long time in e-mail. A now popular, copyrighted, type of emoticon was originally created in Japan. When Apple introduced this type of emoticon and similar images into their phones in 2012 their use took off around the world. In 2015, the *Oxford English Dictionary*'s Word of the Year was 'Face of Tears with Joy'. Although it sounds like the title of a particularly bad early

20th-century painting or piece of conceptual art, Face of Tears with Joy is actually used more in electronic conversation than some letters of the alphabet (OED, 2015).

Emoticons add much of the context that text messaging systems lose from the lack of intonation and body language. Whether or not emojis themselves have any longevity, similar systems for communication of facial expressions and body language are in their ascendancy.

Second, animated gifs are like soundless video clips that are only a few seconds long and typically convey an extreme emotion, reaction or point. Often the clip will have subtitles, showing what was said in the brief clip. These are less prevalent than emojis, but they are often used to communicate a clear message quickly, often with emotional reactions. They are often clips that involve recent pop-culture references, so the most typical examples cannot be shown for copyright reasons.

Love or loathe the increasing popularity of including images in written text, it adds depth and complexity to textual information in the same way that body language adds depth to face-to-face conversations. As they increase in popularity it is equally unsurprising and amusing to see 'emoji workshops' training for less savvy managers in the same way that social media is now taught. Their popularity does not justify their use in a professional setting, but they will be, and already are, used in work communication. The ability to convey powerful emotions like excitement, disgust, frustration or disappointment in a single image in a message or e-mail can be extraordinarily useful when both the sender and the receiver understand the meaning.

But herein lies the challenges. Just as body language is culturally learned and developed, the use of imagery like emoticons and gifs is based on shared understanding of their meaning. Out of context, or with the wrong person, they can seem wildly inappropriate, unprofessional or disrespectful. Conversely, mutual understanding, particularly shared humour, can go a long way in building relationships and keeping people motivated. There are two key recommendations, one for employee users and one for those managing others.

For emoji users

As with most new media and communications, keep it formal, and avoid using anything your intended audience might not understand. Never use an emoticon or related addition to a message in an initial contact at work. Sending off a CV to a prospective employer and 'Thanks for considering my application – smiley face' is an error. As with any type of communication, err on the side of caution and formality.

For employers and managers

Anyone who has not grown up with using cartoonish hieroglyphs as a part of communication may have difficulty understanding how embedded they can become in language. In the same way, any generation has slang words that may sound unprofessional or frivolous when they are first used, but quickly become passé. Once something enters into common use it can become an unconscious part of language.

Equally, being overly keen to use emoticons or similar with younger, new employees is not to be advised. In the same way, using slang from the wrong generation can be embarrassing, and erring on the side of caution and formality is advisable.

The following eight points are general guidelines that can be used to inform or guide a digital communications policy. These guidelines can also be applied at an individual level, to make communication more efficient and prevent digital communication from interfering with motivation:

- **Compartmentalize accounts.** When possible, use specific accounts for specific purposes. Different e-mail accounts can be used to sort multiple roles or responsibilities, and many systems exist to manage multiple e-mail accounts in one space. Keep specific types of messaging applications for personal use only. This way you can 'turn off' the work accounts, and when the phone purrs or lights up it does not instantly remind one of work.

- **Initiate communication respectfully.** Often introductions happen electronically where it is difficult or impossible to learn about the person on the other end. If you do not know their preferred form of address, how formally they use language or their expectations of digital communication, keep it polite and respectful. Use the most respectful form of address in the first e-mail and then see how they sign off an e-mail in order to determine their preferred form of address. Just like any communication or relationship, the communication style can change once more familiarity is established (but, it may not).

- **Clarify expectations.** If you prefer that a particular messaging service only be used for personal communications, make that clear. Not everyone has the same expectations of what forms of communication are appropriate, so it is always best to clarify. If you choose to be on e-mail evenings or weekends, make it clear you do not expect a response outside of work hours, particularly if you are in a position of authority.

- **Keep it short.** Unless there is a good reason, keep e-mails short and to the point. This is particularly important when sending unsolicited e-mails, making introductions or with requests. It may be tempting to give flourishing details and comprehensive information about one's background when making an e-mail introduction. If there is a chance you may not receive a response it may also be tempting to include every question one could possibly need to ask immediately. This is most often an error, and it places an unfair burden on the receiving party. Keep your introduction as short as possible, while still making it clear who you are. If you feel more explanation is needed, attach a CV or link to more detailed information about you. Never ask more than two questions in the initial e-mail. If more questions could be forthcoming, the third question should be either 'Do you mind answering a few more questions?' or 'Is there anyone in your organization who could answer a few more questions?'

- **Remember, if it's written down, it's 'on record'.** Assume that everything that is written down and sent or stored electronically will be stored permanently. This is true for a few reasons. First, messages often get forwarded on to others than the initially intended recipient. Or, an extra recipient might accidentally get added to the list. Second, electronic messages are always stored somewhere, and that location may not be under your control. No matter how secure a server is or who is protecting the data there is a potential for anything to find its way into unintended hands. Data 'leaks' every day, and can end up publicly available. This is not to say one must be constantly paranoid about every word, but always be cautious about making disparaging remarks or disclosing confidential information.

- **Avoid negativity.** Avoid the long e-mail rant, written in anger and/or under the influence of alcohol *at all costs*. E-mails sent in frustration and anger can get the sender into a lot of trouble in many different ways. Often passionately written e-mails can be regretted the next day. And as per the previous point, that message could easily be shared around the office. Most communication can, to varying degrees, safely move to digital forms of communication. But, the more extreme the sentiment, the more digital ways of expressing that emotion should be avoided in the workplace. Conflict can be much more effectively resolved in conversation, or in person. Even the most kindly worded, thoroughly revised message of criticism, no matter how constructive, is entirely one-sided. This can quickly escalate if the other person feels the need to defend themselves. Once an angry e-mail war breaks out it can become extraordinarily hard to defuse without multilateral disarmament and a skilled negotiator.

- **Think what you would do in person.** This is not a perfect rule, but is generally a good rule of thumb for what is acceptable through electronic communication. Sending someone multiple e-mails when they have not responded to the first one is the equivalent of knocking on someone's door unrelentingly. Sending text messages asking whether someone has seen your e-mail yet is like trying to kick down the door to check if someone is at home. It is not appropriate in the workplace. If you are not sure what the proper etiquette is, consider the closest equivalent to a face-to-face interaction.

- **Include wisely.** There are situations where an entire group or team needs to be included in an e-mail, or adding colleagues to the list of recipients makes them feel included. There are times, but this is not most of the time. Of course keeping those who need (or want) to be included in electronic conversations can be constructive. Often excessively cc-ing is counter-productive. The more people are bombarded with superfluous information, the more likely they are to miss or ignore the important information. This is, of course, also a matter of personal taste. Some colleagues do want to feel 'involved' in everything, need or want to be well informed. Others want to be included as a recipient only when absolutely essential.

Interviews and a good lunch

A personal, face-to-face conversation can be incredibly powerful. Never underestimate the power of a good lunch. This is often used as an interview technique by savvy interviewers. An office environment creates all sorts of expectations and anxieties. Why not try a good lunch? Much more can be learned over lunch than at a stuffy panel interview with predetermined questions.

Of course, some would argue this is by no means scientific, and not a replacement for a sound interview process. And they are correct. A good lunch is an alternative method for an alternative purpose. Can the other person do small talk? Do they have more of a tendency to being interested or being interesting? Can they have a casual conversation about the topic beyond a pre-prepared interview script? The better the lunch the more that can be learned.

It also gets at the *motivation* in the way that a more formal discussion process may not be able to. The time given for a long conversation over lunch allows the conversation to go beyond *performance* to *motivation*. A performance review process often looks at the behaviours, but rarely investigates why. Lunch can be less judgemental when it is not a formal performance review. There may be performance issues, but there is no discipline over lunch, we're concerned with *why*. What else is going on, what is the motivation at the moment, what factors are influencing the performance? There is often time to delve deeper into motivations with amusing anecdotes and pleasant discussion. What was the worst job you ever had? The anecdote may be interesting, but the reasons why it was the worst job, the description and details included or omitted are all telling. How's your partner? Your parents? Your children? Your dog? What else is going on that might be affecting your work performance?

Relationship building

This should not sound like a cynical attempt to catch unsuspecting employees or colleagues off guard, or being manipulative to get information that can be used later. A good lunch requires give and take for it to be any good. One needs to model the type of openness that is expected, and be prepared to answer any questions that one asks. A cynical attempt to gain information makes for a dull lunch, and will probably be demotivating as soon as the other person discovers that intent.

However, for most people, building relationships is motivating. Learning more about the people around them, their vision and their motivation makes it easier to identify and feel a sense of belonging. This is particularly true when a senior figure makes the time to have a *conversation* instead of a bulletin, a speech at the annual Christmas party or a webcast.

If used constructively, it is also an extremely valuable tool to find out what is really going on. If people have the chance to discuss their work honestly with someone they know is listening, it can be surprising how much they will disclose. Annual surveys and questionnaires are fine, but only the blissed out and pissed off will give much detail about what they really think.

Give a retail cashier an opportunity to describe all the problems in their workplace and they will tell you every problem in the store and, for each problem, have five examples of how things have gone wrong (and probably will suggest solutions). We will elaborate on the opportunities here in Chapter 6, but people from different parts of the company or at different levels of seniority may have information that never makes its way to a senior leader's direct reports or through the 'open door' that every HR department seems to advertise.

Motivating

Psychologists call it the talking cure, but often just having someone to listen can help to alleviate stress and counteract the demotivating forces that can spring up in every workplace. But a good lunch with a charming boss can turn the day around, and sometimes a single spark of motivation creates an upward spiral.

The misguided inspection

When a conversation is not really a conversation it can be informal, over-structured, impersonal and incredibly demotivating. Some sort of inspections or 'site visits' are commonplace in most workplaces, particularly larger organizations. Some leader from head office receives the red carpet treatment, the franchisee comes in to inspect the branch or the politician makes sure they are well-photographed at the coal face.

This is a huge opportunity that is often missed. A prime example of this is from an international coffee retailer. The company structure means there are many levels of management, each of which schedules site visits. The stated purpose, of course, is to maintain quality standards, physically ensure the operation is running smoothly and maybe the presence of successful leaders will inspire the employees to work harder.

The reality, unbeknown to the benevolent inspectors, is quite different. Food is overstocked to give an impression of abundance, and then thrown away at the end of the day. Bathrooms are scrubbed and counters are polished to add a shine that is not normally visible. Staff are on their best behaviour, smiles polished and plastered on liberally. Extra staff are called in to ensure customers are served quickly.

It is slightly reminiscent of Politburo-style inspections where factories would show off their thousands of newly produced tractors. The polished facade conceals the fact that the tractors will never actually have engines. When this happens it is not just a missed opportunity, it can be incredibly destructive. Employees become disillusioned and demotivated. Real problems never reach the attention of senior management, and the company wastes resources and may even divert them from areas of actual need. It damages motivation and profits.

First, it is a missed opportunity because there are so many opportunities for good during a visit. This should not be a regal visit where the staff are lined up to shake hands, and will be asked 'have you come far?' while a Potemkin Village is erected to conceal the real desolation of your empire. It is a chance to see how things really operate on the front line, how people are working and what they are thinking. Just one quick and honest conversation would reveal that apparatchik inspections are costing money and reducing profitability.

The second missed opportunity is the chance for a leader to know exactly how the company is running. The value of this should not be underestimated, as concealed problems have a tendency to grow. Of course this is not as easy as it sounds. To get honest answers the questions and the approach must come from genuine concern. If the questions are asked and solvable problems are raised, they must be addressed. Organizational values are meaningless if they are not lived. If the actions don't match values, that does little to improve motivation.

At the coffee retailer, this was often compounded by an inspection being announced, prepared, scheduled and then forgotten. About half the planned site visits never occurred. Staff were instructed to prepare for the site visit, but the inspector never arrived. It is not difficult to see how this would compound the demotivating factors. Not only do a dozen employees work their hardest to create an image that their owners want to see, the owners do not even participate in the charade.

But this is a huge opportunity to get information and these conversations have the power to be motivating if they are done right. A visit takes some planning, but it can be designed to have minimal inconvenience. If your staff end up working extra hours to keep things pristine for your visit it is unlikely they will be huge supporters of your leadership. But being able to have a conversation with someone in a position to make changes in the company is motivating. Problems at work are only demotivating if they go unaddressed and unresolved. The process of actually solving problems is motivating. Being part of a solution is motivating. Knowing that your expertise is valued is motivating.

Performance reviews and regular 'check-ups'

Performance management is rarely done well. The common 'annual review' is a yearly event that is often too late to identify any problems, too infrequent to accurately capture the performance over the intended period and too dull for words.

Of course, increasing the regularity of performance reviews can be a burden if it involves excessive paperwork and far too much bureaucratic box-checking. But, if done well it should not be a burden. Again, conversations to the rescue. We would recommend some sort of review monthly, but it can even be done weekly in small organizations and with the right approach.

Documentation is an important part of the performance review, in maintaining records and tracking over time. But this does not mean that a long form has to be filled out for each performance review. More formal performance reviews within a performance management structure may occur at longer intervals. A conversation can be a brief performance review.

One of the authors once worked in an office of about 20 people. Every morning the manager would make the rounds, and speak to three or four people. No forms, no scores, no ratings, and it was all done in such an informal and friendly way it just seemed like a friendly chat. Of course the innocent questions 'How are you doing', 'What are you working on', can sound like small talk – but they are essentially performance management questions.

The weekly check-up can be unfeasible in some organizations, but the heart of the process is making sure everything is going well. No problems, no red flags, and it doesn't need to go any further. Any problems or issues are identified on the spot and can be addressed quickly. Of course talking to people can be time-consuming but keeping on top of things and dealing with problems immediately can save a great deal of time, stress and expensive turnover in the long term.

References

American Psychological Association [APA] (2006) [accessed 10 October 2016] Driven to Distraction: Driving and Cell Phones Don't Mix [Online] http://www.apa.org/research/action/drive.aspx

Carroll, L (1890) *Eight or Nine Wise Words about Letter-Writing*, Emberlain & Son, Oxford

Debrett's (2015) [Online] www.debretts.com

Drago, C (2008) Nonverbal communication and restaurant personnel, MSc dissertation, Oregon State University

Goode, L (2016) Messenger and WhatsApp process 60 billion messages a day, three times more than SMS, *The Verge*, 12 April

Huessner, KM (2010) Tech stress: how many e-mails can you handle a day? *ABC News*, 20 July

Leswing, K (2016) Apple says people send as many as 200,000 iMessages per second, *Business Insider UK*, 12 February

Lynn, M and Mynier, K (1993) Effect of server posture on restaurant tipping [electronic version], retrieved from Cornell University, School of Hospitality Administration

Mulshine, M (2015) This mind-blowing graphic shows how many Snapchat photos are sent per second, *Business Insider UK*, 28 May

Oxford English Dictionary [OED] (2015) [accessed 10 October 2016] Oxford Dictionaries Word Of The Year 2015 Is... *OED Blog*, [Online] http://blog.oxforddictionaries.com/2015/11/word-of-the-year-2015-emoji/

Thornton, B, Faires, A, Robbins, M and Rollings, E (2014) The mere presence of a cell phone may be distracting: implications for attention and task performance, *Social Psychology*, 45 (6), pp 479–88

Vygotsky, L and Kozulin, A (2012) *Thought and Language*, MIT Press, London

Intrinsic motivation

07

Introduction

In what job are people most happy? Doctors, bankers, pilots or engineers? Clergy, artists, potters or writers? Farmers, IT specialists, nurses or architects?

Every so often the results of big international studies are published on this topic. The results are nearly always a surprise: jobs that come top are not always well paid, but are often challenging, complex or personally rewarding. Often people emphasize the satisfaction with seeing the products of their work, or creating something. For example, *The Guardian* (Ferguson, 2015) reported that construction workers, clergy, engineers, teachers and gardeners reported the highest satisfaction.

Forbes (Adams, 2015) reported the happiest and unhappiest jobs in 2015 (see Table 7.1, overleaf).

The happiest jobs consistently involve a level of independence, social contribution or creating new things. The lowest satisfaction ratings consistently involve jobs with very little flexibility or independence, along with minimal personal contribution or creativity in the job.

Many well-paid jobs seem to come way down on the list. A study in the journal *Psychological Medicine* (Roberts, Jaremin and Lloyd, 2013) reported that medical doctors, dentists, veterinarians, estate agents, lawyers and those in the financial services report the highest rates of depression and suicide. But why?

It seems that money has not a lot to do with it. Individual differences in motivation are far more important. Interestingly, the answer is that the most satisfying jobs are those that do not appear to the job holder as a (conventional) job. They are paid to do what they love most. They are employed at an activity that enchants and captivates them. One where all their abilities and passions coincide. The technical term for this is intrinsic motivation.

Table 7.1 *Forbes*, happiest and unhappiest jobs in 2015

Ranking	Happiest	Unhappiest
1	Principal	Security Guard
2	Executive Chef	Merchandiser
3	Loan Officer	Salesperson
4	Automation Engineer	Dispatcher
5	Research Assistant	Clerk
6	Oracle Database Engineer	Research Analyst
7	Website Developer	Legal Assistant
8	Business Development Executive	Technical Support Agent
9	Senior Software Engineer	Truck Driver
10	Systems Developer	Customer Service Specialist

The job is satisfying for its own sake: it is not the money and the perks that are motivating or important. The job speaks to one's interests and passion.

What good work does for you

Not everyone loves their job, but work can be a source of satisfaction and can improve health and well-being. Psychologists such as Marie Jahoda (1980) are fascinated in understanding the plight of people without work. What does work provide that is so psychologically healthy? Why is work good for you? She listed various psychological benefits of a good job, such as strong relationships, realistic self-esteem, self-direction and productivity, which help us to understand intrinsic motivation.

One should start thinking about motivation at work from the very beginning, when starting (and even before starting) the job. The following section discusses five reasons why being positively motivated at work is good for individual well-being. Then we consider the importance of these elements to an onboarding process.

An effective onboarding process is not just about training new employees and getting them ready for their new job with the company. An onboarding process should be a well-planned and managed introduction to the company and its culture. But it should also engage new hires from the very beginning of the process. A well-designed onboarding process will get new employees motivated to start work. It can also be a powerful motivational process and tool, if it incorporates the five elements:

1 **Work structures time.** We are creatures of habit. Some of us are morning people and some evening people. Having a regular routine is what most people seek, with of course, the option to change it if they so wish. Work structures the day, the week and even longer periods. The loss of a time structure can be very disorientating. A predictable pattern of work, with well-planned 'rhythms', is what most people seek (see Table 7.2a). To have flexitime and to be able to work at times when it most suits your personal circumstances and rhythms is terribly important.

The sample schedule in Table 7.2b reflects a more traditional sector such as manufacturing, financial services or professional services. Other sectors like technology or sales may focus more on fun activities, team cohesion or communicating the particular culture of the organization through the activities.

2 **Work provides regularly shared experiences.** Most people's friendship network comes from the world of work. Many of us spend more time with people at work, than outside work.

Table 7.2a Structured time

Factor	Effect	Example
Structured Time	The timing and occurrence of onboarding activities should be planned out ahead of time, clearly communicated and predictable.	Informal and formal activities can be scheduled.
	This reduces uncertainty, particularly at a time where new employees might be nervous. A well-structured onboarding process can demonstrate the value of structure, organization and communication within the organization.	Formal training involves learning about policies, procedures, regulation, roles and responsibilities, etc.
	Of course, if the process is unclear or disorganized, this is also an instructive introduction to the organization.	Informal onboarding provides less structured opportunities to learn about colleagues in a social setting. This could be lunches, drinks or group activities. *See the sample schedule in Table 7.2b*

Table 7.2b Sample onboarding schedule

Day	From	To	What	Who	Objective
MON dd/mm/yy	9:00am	10:00am	Welcome Breakfast	Hiring Manager	Introduce new hires, with time for informal conversations and introductions over breakfast
	10:00am	11:00am	HR Orientation	HR Manager	Basic introduction to policies and procedures, key contacts in HR
	11:00am	12:30pm	General Introductions	Hiring Manager	Walk around the office, outline of different roles and responsibilities of each department, introductions to key contacts in each
	12:30pm	1:30pm	Lunch	–	Unstructured lunch hour
	1:30pm	2:30pm	IT Overview	IT Trainer	Simple introduction to IT systems, e-mail access, computer logins, and introduction to IT help contact(s)
	2:30pm	3:30pm	Activity/Challenge		Task to practise knowledge gained from initial activities; for example, independent or group assignment to gather information based on IT tools and key contacts introduced previously
	3:30pm	5:00pm	Unstructured time + individual introductions to personal mentor	Personal Mentor	Unstructured time to try out computer systems, access, e-mail; personal 15-minute introductions to personal mentor
	5:15pm	onwards	Company Drinks	Hiring Manager, key contacts	Informal, optional after-work drinks

Regular contact with non-nuclear family members provides an important source of social interaction. Social isolation can be related to stress, loneliness and mental-health problems. Social support from friends, family and colleagues mitigates many causes of stress and increases coping ability. Those with strong and diverse social support networks tend to be more resilient to stress and have greater resources to solve problems and deal with challenges. This consequently can improve mental and physical health. One of the most frequently cited sources of job satisfaction is contact with other people. We are, in short, social animals.

3 **Work is a source of activity.** All work involves some expenditure of physical or mental effort. Whereas too much activity may induce fatigue and stress, too little activity results in boredom and restlessness, particularly among extraverts. People seek to maximize the amount of activity that suits them by choosing particular jobs or tasks that fulfil their needs.

4 **Work provides experience of creativity, mastery and a sense of purpose.** Both the organization and the product of work imply the interdependence of human beings. Take away some sense of relying on others, and

Table 7.3 Shared experience

Factor	Effect	Example
Shared Experience	Shared experience in the onboarding process should provide opportunities for all new employees to work together, along with less formal social time.	Start new hires together as a cohort instead of staggering entry. Minimize training costs by combining groups and provide more opportunities for team cohesion and shared experience.
	Ideally, it should also include time with employees who are experienced, knowledgeable and potential sources of information or mentors for the new hires.	Provide early opportunities to meet people from across the organization, including potential social supports from HR, management or mentors.
	Establishing a sense of belonging early on can be a powerful motivator.	Connections with people from other departments provides a greater breadth of knowledge across the company. These contacts may also offer more unbiased support than immediate team members.

Table 7.4 Work is a source of activity

Factor	Effect	Example
Activity	Activities, training and events should be challenging but also be realistic and achievable for the new hires.	Formal, structured training must be part of any onboarding process. But challenges, and opportunity to practise the new skills, is also important.
	The level of activity or challenge should be appropriate to the job the new hires are being prepared for, and prepare employees for the level of activity that is to be expected during the work.	Combine training time with opportunities to practise the new skills.
	The type and focus of activity should also align, for example if the job is always conducted in an office environment, a week of outdoor or entirely off-site onboarding activities are probably not appropriate or relevant.	

Table 7.5 Work gives a sense of mastery

Factor	Effect	Example
Mastery	New hires may be nervous about their capability to get the job done, uncertain about their role, or concerned about developing relationships and fitting in.	Provide training, resources and information combined with tasks of incrementally increasing difficulty.
	An onboarding process and any associated training should provide new hires with confidence in their ability to get started, and the knowledge and connections to learn and adapt quickly to their new role.	As onboarding and training progresses, new hires should get more flexibility and independence to complete their tasks.
		Support should be available if needed, and the new hires given a balance of challenging, yet realistic tasks.
		Increase autonomy whenever appropriate to accommodate different rates of learning.

them on you, and the unemployed are left with a sense of uselessness. Work, even not particularly satisfying work, gives some sense of mastery or achievement.

5 **Work is a source of personal status and identity.** A person's job is an important indicator of personal status in society – hence the often amusing debates over job titles, such as 'sanitary engineer' for street cleaner. Furthermore, it is not only to employed people that jobs give a certain status, but also to their families. The employed person therefore is a link between two important social systems – family and home. Unemployed people have lost their employment status and hence identity. Not unnaturally, there is a marked drop in self-esteem during unemployment.

Creative activities stimulate people and provide a sense of satisfaction. A person's contribution to producing goods or providing services forges a link between the individual and the society of which he or she is a part. Work roles are not the only roles that offer the individual the opportunity of being useful and contributing to the community. Jobs help us to feel useful and have a sense of purpose.

Never underestimate the importance of job titles. You are what you do. You take on the reputation of the organization you work for. And your job title speaks to your success at your job.

Table 7.6 Work is a source of personal status and identity

Factor	Effect	Example
Identity	The onboarding process should clearly establish what the new hire's role should be, how they fit into the organization, and the importance of their work.	Some companies provide new employees with a personal mentor from day one.
	Introduce the new hires to people who will rely on their work, or who can emphasize the value they can be adding.	This is a less formal relationship than a line manager or trainer, and is someone who can provide informal advice, introductions to others in the company and impartial support.
	Provide examples of who has done well in the job in the past. Explain what value that has to the company, its customers, stakeholder or others.	

Drive at work

In 2010 Daniel Pink wrote a book entitled *Drive: The surprising truth about what motivates us*. It turned out to be a best-seller. He acknowledges as a science journalist that most of the ideas are not his but mainly derived from self-determination theory developed by Deci and Ryan. The message of the book is clear. Carrot-and-stick motivation does not work any more.

Pink proposes that businesses should adopt a revised approach to motivation that fits more closely with modern jobs and businesses, one based on self-determination theory. Human beings have an innate drive to be autonomous, self-determined and connected to one another, and when that drive is liberated, people achieve more and live richer lives. Organizations should focus on these drives when managing their human capital by creating settings that focus on our innate need to direct our own lives, to learn and create new things, and to do better by ourselves and our world.

There are three components of intrinsic motivation, three factors that are measured in the HPMI motivation assessment that was introduced in Chapter 2: autonomy, recognition and affiliation. Each component is related to specific outcomes and related steps that can be taken to improve performance in the workplace:

1 **Autonomy**: provide employees with autonomy over some (or all) of the four main aspects of work:

   - *Time (when they do it)*. For many types of work, the output or deliverables are more important than the time spent at a particular location. Consider switching to a ROWE (results-only work environment) that focuses more on the output (result) rather than the time/schedule, allowing employees to have flexibility over when they complete tasks (see Chapter 14 for a successful example of this).

   - *Technique (how they do it)*. When you know employees are capable and competent they can be given flexibility in how they get the job done. When people are capable of getting their job done with limited supervision, don't dictate how they should complete their tasks. Provide initial guidance and then allow them to tackle the project in the way they see fit rather than having to follow a strict procedure.

   - *Team (whom they do it with)*. Although this can be the hardest form of autonomy to embrace, allow employees some choice over who they work with. This can take a number of forms. Involve employees in the selection process, interviewing prospective hires and evaluating peers' performance. If it would be inappropriate to involve them in the recruitment/selection process, instead allow employees to work on open-source projects where they have the ability to assemble their own teams.

- *Task (what they do).* There are many different ways to allow employees the freedom to choose their own paths. Provide paid time for volunteer work, particularly when volunteering allows them to use their skills – and emphasize the value of those skills. Some accountancy firms support their staff in providing tax or financial planning advice to those on low incomes. Allow employees to have regular 'creative' days where they can work on any project/problem they wish – there is empirical evidence to show that many new initiatives are often generated during this 'creative free time'.

2 **Recognition**: people like to be recognized for their skills and abilities, for adding value in their work and doing something well. Allow employees to become better at something that matters to them:

- *Provide 'Goldilocks tasks'.* Pink uses the term 'Goldilocks tasks' to describe those tasks that are neither overly difficult nor overly simple – these tasks allow employees to extend themselves and develop their skills further. The risk of providing tasks that fall short of an employee's capabilities is boredom, and the risk of providing tasks that exceed their capabilities is anxiety.

- *Create an environment where mastery is possible.* To foster an environment of learning and development, four essentials are required – autonomy, clear goals, immediate feedback and Goldilocks tasks.

3 **Affiliation**: feeling involved, part of the workplace and contributing to a greater cause can be an important motivator. Take steps to fulfil employees' natural desire to communicate the organization's overall vision and the team's specific objectives. Making a valuable contribution to a greater goal can be incredibly motivating:

- *Communicate the purpose.* Make sure employees know and understand the organization's purpose goals, not just its profit goals. Employees who understand the purpose and vision of their organization, and how their individual roles contribute to this purpose, are more likely to be satisfied in their work.

- *Place equal emphasis on purpose maximization as you do on profit maximization.* Research shows that the attainment of profit goals has no impact on a person's well-being and actually contributes to their ill-being. Organizational and individual goals should focus on purpose as well as profit. Many successful companies are now using profit as the catalyst to pursuing purpose, rather than the objective.

– *Use purpose-oriented words.* Talk about the organization as a united team by using words such as 'us' and 'we'; this will inspire employees to talk about the organization in the same way and feel a part of the greater cause.

Energy at work

There are many ways of describing someone who is energetic at work: ambitious, excited, engaged, aspiring, driven, enterprising, enthusiastic, and more. There are some less positive ways of describing energy, including pushy, impatient, desperate, bold and brash. But typically energy is a very desirable characteristic, particularly when it is directed towards productivity and efficacy. Energy is often associated with youth, health and happiness.

Having personal energy and directing it appropriately is the essential component of intrinsic motivation. Energy is a rather amorphous and unscientific term, but it is a useful one when described using three dimensions.

The first is physical energy. Older people often have less energy than younger people. Sick people have less energy than healthy people. Sleep-deprived people are less energetic than the well-rested. Physiology can be incredibly limiting when a person does not have the capacity to direct their energy and use it in their work. Being malnourished, sleep deprived or out of shape can limit the capacity of otherwise capable individuals.

Physical energy and well-being is not just a matter of physical health. Colds, flu, illness, aches, pains, insomnia and physical fitness can all affect this. Yet mental health and well-being is equally important. It is also one of the greatest potential areas for improvement, and has the potential to reduce absenteeism and improve productivity. This was discussed in detail in Chapter 4.

The second dimension is psychological energy. This has been conceived of in different ways. The Freudians define a psychic energy: a force that drives us to want and do things we barely understand. Thus we can be driven to a-rational, irrational, bizarre behaviours because of these unconscious libidinous springs. The pseudoscientifics use energy as a more spiritual term to describe a melange of perfectly useful psychological constructs, from intelligence to personality to motivation, values and emotional intelligence.

Personality traits are related to psychological energy. Extraverts are outwardly focused, social animals who appear more (socially) energetic but can burn up easily with their impulsivity and impatience. Introverts find social situations tiring, and feel recharged when they have a chance to recuperate on their own. But introverts can have a much slower burning fuse and are often able to focus their attention and energy even in situations that their more extroverted colleagues would find boring. Neurotics waste their energy burning it up on the irrelevant and the imaginary. They can easily become anxious, then depressed, by small things. They fritter away their additional nervous energy rather than conserve it for the long haul or the really important. Paradoxically then, they appear to have more energy than their stable opposites but waste it on worry.

But the most important trait, consistently associated with greater performance, is conscientiousness. The conscientious employee could be described as self-motivated, achievement-oriented and the broad, omnipresent CV requirement 'able to work well independently or as part of a team'. It is the capacity to get started, motivate oneself and direct one's physical energy and intellectual capability towards the tasks that actually matter.

Third there is intellectual energy. The bright have more intellectual energy: more curiosity, more openness to new experience. They use their energy more efficiently. Indeed one definition of intelligence is about energy-efficient brain processing.

In other words, there are three broadly important concepts that contribute to motivation, performance and potential:

- health;
- conscientiousness;
- intelligence.

These three components affect a person's potential levels of achievement; motivation is about whether or not the individual has the drive and direction to work towards that potential (MacRae and Furnham, 2014).

Flow at work

The concepts of energy and work engagement are not new. In 1990, Csíkszentmihályi wrote a book called *Flow*. His objective was to talk to people who were creative and successful, in an attempt to learn the secrets of their success. He was not concerned with the occupation or task. It could be in a profession or trade, but equally could be as a concert pianist or climbing up large rocks.

His research questions were not particularly unique: 'What makes people successful?' has been asked countless times over. His findings, too, may not seem particularly surprising: people are at their best when they love what they are doing.

His methods, though, were novel and demonstrated these findings in an interesting way. He called his method 'experience sampling'. All participants carried a beeper (remember, this research was conducted in the 1980s), and an alarm sounded eight times per day. Whenever the alarm sounded, participants were required immediately to write down exactly what they were doing and how they were feeling.

People felt best, he found, when engrossed in some challenging activity. During flow they lost track of time, felt more capable, more sensitive and more self-confident, even though the activities may be work-based challenges. The activity was its own reward: intrinsically motivating. Flow banishes depression, distraction and creeping dispiritedness. So what are the preconditions of flow?

Csíkszentmihályi identified the following factors as accompanying an experience of flow:

1   Clear goals (expectations and rules are discernible and goals are attainable and align appropriately with one's skill set and abilities). The challenge level and skill level should both be high.

2   Concentrating – a high degree of concentration on a limited field of attention (a person engaged in the activity will have the opportunity to focus and to delve deeply into it).

3   A loss of the feeling of self-consciousness, the merging of action and awareness.

4   Distorted sense of time, one's subjective experience of time is altered.

5   Direct and immediate feedback (successes and failures in the course of the activity are apparent, so that behaviour can be adjusted as needed).

6   Balance between ability level and challenge (the activity is neither too easy nor too difficult).

7   A sense of personal control over the situation or activity.

8   The activity is intrinsically rewarding, so there is an effortlessness of action.

9 A lack of awareness of bodily needs (to the extent that one can reach a point of great hunger or fatigue without realizing it).

10 Absorption into the activity, narrowing of the focus of awareness down to the activity itself, action awareness merging.

Vallerand (2012) believed flow was the consequence of (harmonious) passion. Thus for flow to be experienced at work a person needs a clear goal in mind, reasonable expectations of completing satisfactorily the goal in mind and the ability to concentrate; also being given regular and specific feedback on their performance, and having the appropriate skills to complete the task.

One can observe flow in those jobs where people experience greatest work satisfaction. They include mainly artisans – potters and painters, writers and weavers, thatchers and designers. They exercise their talents, work at their own pace and can see the results of their production. Engrossing professional jobs report the same type of flow. Physicians, teachers and software developers also report a high level of flow when they are occupied and engrossed in their work. When they are successful, they can see the products of their success. They are what they produce. Their identity and abilities are caught up in the work they are doing.

How to foster passion, energy, flow and drive

There seems abundant evidence that the intrinsically motivated, harmoniously passionate person at work experiences vigour, flow and well-being. The question is how to pick the right people and adopt the optimal management style and corporate culture to maximize it. The literature on intrinsic motivation, passion and flow all suggest similar ideas. These include:

- **Challenge**: goals need to be set by both worker and supervisor that involve an optimal amount of difficulty/challenge in attaining them. People do best when working on meaningful goals where tasks are of intermediate difficulty. They should be stretching goals and seen as part of a development plan. Thus let people set personally meaningful goals and targets that are related to their self-esteem. Give them feedback so that they can see how they are doing.

- **Curiosity**: activities that stimulate an employee's attention and interest are best. This means introducing novelty and stimulating questioning that takes them beyond their present skills and knowledge. Changes and challenges stimulate curiosity. The idea is to foster a sense of wonder. It is about job enrichment.

- **Control**: allowing employees to have a choice in what happens. This sense of – and actual – autonomy is most important. Leadership roles, even temporary ones, create a higher sense of engagement and recognition. People at work need to understand cause-and-effect relationships. They need to know and believe that their effort and outcomes have real and powerful effects. But most importantly they must be able to freely choose what and how they learn.

- **Contribution**: most of us like to believe that we are doing something useful and meaningful at work and making a contribution to the welfare of others. People like to have pride in their work in that it shows what they are capable of but also that the products of their labour are recognized as useful.

- **Fun and Fantasy**: using imagination and games to promote learning in the workplace. The idea is to turn work into play.

- **Competition**: comparing the performance from one employee to another more as a source of feedback than in the spirit of trying to win a competition. This can, however, have negative consequences if it reduces cooperation.

- **Cooperation**: encouraging employees to help each other to achieve goals. This means working in self-organized teams. People enjoy helping as much as being helped. Cooperation improves interpersonal skills.

- **Recognition**: celebrating employees' accomplishments and successes. This means recognizing employees for a job well done and praise for doing a great job. Where possible, praise should be public; gather your team together for a moment and celebrate an accomplishment. Spend your day looking for and recognizing great performance.

Money, intrinsic and extrinsic motivation

There is one point that nearly everyone remembers from Herzberg and that is clearly correct. Extrinsic motivators have more power to make people dissatisfied than satisfied. Money, in particular, has more power to demotivate than motivate. It is a disenchanter not an enchanter.

The essential point for the two-factor theory is that the factors that lead to motivation are different from those that lead to dissatisfaction. Those that block or interfere with motivation are not the same as those that facilitate engagement. Moreover it is surprising how quickly a person can be swayed by one or another.

One topic that never goes away is money, and more importantly its ability to motivate the average worker. Economists argue that money is the only serious motivator. It is certainly true that people will do anything for money! But this is the essence of extrinsic motivation.

The simple fact is that money is but one motivator. Job security, a pleasant environment and a considerate boss are all motivators as well. Consider the following: would you prefer £1,000 (tax free) or a week's extra holiday? £10,000 or a new job title? £50,000 or a job guarantee for life? £100,000 or meaningful and intrinsically satisfying work? Put like that, as a choice between money alone or other motivators, the power of money may decline.

If, indeed, money is a powerful motivator or satisfier at work, why has research consistently shown that there is no relationship between wealth and happiness? In fact there are four good reasons why this is so:

- **Adaptation:** although everyone feels 'happier' after a pay rise, windfall or lottery win, one soon adapts to this and the effect very rapidly disappears.

- **Comparison:** people define themselves as rich/wealthy by comparing themselves to others. However, with increased wealth, people usually move in more 'upmarket' circles where there is always someone wealthier than themselves.

- **Alternatives:** as economists say, the declining marginal utility of money means that as one has more of the stuff, other things such as freedom and true friendship seem much more valuable.

- **Worry:** an increased income is associated with a shifting of concern from money issues to the more uncontrollable elements of life (eg self-development), perhaps because money is associated with a sense of control over one's fate.

Money does not always bring happiness. People with £10 million are no happier than people with only £9 million. Yes, everyone wants more money. Economists are right: money does act as a work motivator, but to a large extent in the short term, for some workers more than others, and at a cost often to the morale of the organization. Psychologists are also correct – money is only one of many motivators of behaviour.

In fact, there is surprising research from athletics that shows the greatest reward does not always lead to the most happiness. Think of Olympic athletes who win medals. This could be seen as the pinnacle of athletic achievement – competing with the world's best at a particular sport and winning a medal demonstrates an ultimate level of achievement. So with three medals, symbolizing a hierarchy of success, who do you think reports the highest levels of happiness?

1 Gold

2 Silver

3 Bronze

If a gold medal is the highest level of achievement within the three, and bronze is the lowest of the three, surely happiness should follow in the same order. But satisfaction and psychology rarely align with token economics. The order of most satisfied actually looks more like:

1 Most Satisfied: Bronze

2 Satisfied: Gold

3 Least Satisfied: Silver

So why is the bronze medallist the most satisfied within the group? It is not a matter of highest rank equalling greatest satisfaction, but the bronze medallist is happy considering the other alternatives. Not only has the bronze medallist won against that fourth-place competitor (winning a spot on that podium) they have beaten all the other competitors who ran slower, or did not perform as well as they did. Often it is only a fraction of a second or a few centimetres in which they earned their position in that honoured triumvirate. Bronze medallists consistently rate the greatest satisfaction. The bronze medal is a huge accomplishment, and there is always that silver and gold medal to continue striving for.

The silver medallists have, technically, outperformed the bronze medallists yet they report being less satisfied than their other two colleagues. In comparison, the silver medallists might be even happier than the bronze medallists – but not more satisfied as they are not thinking of winning against the other competitors. They often report disappointment with not getting the coveted gold. The silver medallist may have 'lost' the gold medal by only a fraction of a second, and that sense of loss and social comparison with the gold medallist reduces satisfaction.

The gold medallist is, of course, incredibly satisfied. Yet most competitors in the very top position will note a sense of dread that quickly creeps in when holding the highest position. There is no higher award than that gold medal, and it comes with an inevitable burden: there is never any higher award and someone else will eventually overtake you.

The same lesson applies to economics and compensation at work. The main value of money is that one lives in a world in which its importance is overestimated. The research on compensation shows money does not really increase happiness, and only decreases happiness when its absence is a source of stress. This can happen for two reasons.

First, when a person or a family cannot afford basic necessities like food, clothing, housing, utilities and the basic costs of living. Income level beyond basic needs has little long-term effect on happiness (Veenhoven, 1991; Veenhoven and Vergunst, 2014). Second, when people overextend themselves financially. Making £1 million every year is less satisfying when one is spending twice that amount. And the happiness or satisfaction associated with greater spending is short-lived. A larger house, a more expensive car and a more costly label on clothing can provide a momentary boost of excitement. It does not contribute to any sort of long-term happiness. Money only affects happiness in a relative sense. Spending/earning less money leads to dissatisfaction while spending/earning more money only provides a temporary high. Like any addictive substance, people get used to income levels very quickly and that becomes the new normal. Only changes in that level create emotional reactions.

It is true that money doesn't buy friends. The accumulation of money does not end people's troubles; it merely changes them. There is a common psychological illusion called the environmental fallacy: 'I'm unhappy here; if only I could get away from this town/job/neighbourhood/apartment I would be so much happier.' Anyone who has ever gone for a long holiday with their partner in an attempt to salvage a failing relationship knows that having the same argument in a more exotic location does not solve the underlying problems.

The power of money as a motivator is short-lived. Furthermore, it has less effect the more comfortable people are. Camus (1963) was right when he said it is a kind of spiritual snobbery to believe people can be happy without money. When given or earning a modest average amount, the value of other work benefits become greater. Kohn (1993) offers six reasons why this seemingly backward conclusion is, in fact, the case:

- **Pay is not a motivator:** whilst the reduction of a salary is a demotivator, there is little evidence that increasing salary has anything but a transitory impact on motivation. This was pointed out more than half a century ago by Herzberg, Mausner and Snyderman (1959). Just because too little money can irritate and demotivate does not mean that more money will bring about increased satisfaction – much less, increased motivation.

- **Rewards punish:** rewards can have a punitive effect because they, like outright punishment, are manipulative. Any reward itself may be highly desired; but by making that bonus contingent on certain behaviours, managers manipulate their subordinates. This experience of being controlled is likely to assume a punitive quality over time. Thus the withholding of an expected reward feels very much like punishment.

- **Rewards rupture relationships:** incentive programmes tend to pit one person against another, which can lead to all kinds of negative repercussions as people undermine each other. This threatens good teamwork.

- **Rewards ignore reasons:** managers sometimes use incentive systems as a substitute for giving workers what they need in order to do a good job, such as useful feedback, social support and autonomy. Offering a bonus to employees and waiting for the results requires much less input and effort.

- **Rewards discourage risk taking:** people working for a reward generally try to minimize challenge and tend to lower their sights when they are encouraged to think about what they are going to get for their efforts.

- **Rewards undermine interest:** extrinsic motivators are a poor substitute for genuine interest in one's job. The more a manager stresses what an employee can earn for good work, the less interested that employee will be in the work itself. If people feel they need to be 'bribed' to do something, it is not something they would ordinarily want to do. Alas, it is more common to see disenchantment.

Conclusion

Intrinsic and extrinsic motivation are not opposite ends of a scale, they are two different scales. Most people are part intrinsically and part extrinsically motivated at work. All jobs have a mixture of the two factors. For some people a job choice is a trade-off between choosing a job that they love versus choosing a less desirable job with very good rewards such as salary, pension, perks or holidays.

It is not uncommon to read in the newspaper about very well-paid professionals who suddenly give up their highly paid jobs to do something very different. In this situation, money is not a motivator, but a tool that can be used to pursue a passion and intrinsic motivation. When people have the freedom to trade extrinsic motivators for intrinsic passion, most will jump at the opportunity. They will often talk about 'it not being worth it'; 'life is too short' and other comments to show that, perhaps because they have made a lot of money, they would much prefer to do something they really enjoy and that they think is really meaningful. In many cases they do the same job, but are so much more motivated because they are 'doing it for themselves'. That is, in short, intrinsically motivating.

References

Adams, S (2015) The happiest and unhappiest jobs in 2015, *Forbes*, 26 February

Camus, A (1963) *Notebooks*, Alfred Knopf, New York

Csíkszentmihályi, M (2002 [1990]) *Flow: The psychology of happiness – the classic work on how to achieve happiness*, Rider, London

Ferguson, D (2015) The world's happiest jobs, *The Guardian*, 8 April

Herzberg, F, Mausner, B and Snyderman, BB (1959) *The Motivation to Work*, John Wiley & Sons, New Jersey

Jahoda, M (1980) Work, employment and unemployment: an overview of ideas and research results in the social science literature, SPRU Occasional Paper Series, University of Sussex

Kohn, A (1993) Why incentive plans cannot work, *Harvard Business Review*, **71**, pp 54–63

MacRae, I and Furnham, A (2014) *High Potential: How to spot, manage and develop talented people at work*, Bloomsbury, London

Roberts, SE, Jaremin, B and Lloyd, K (2013) High risk occupations for suicide, *Psychological Medicine*, **43** (6), pp 1231–40

Vallerand, RJ (2012) The role of passion in sustainable psychological well-being, *Psychology of Well-Being: Theory, Research and Practice*, **2** (1), pp 1–21

Veenhoven, R (1991) Is happiness relative, *Social Indicators Research*, **24**, pp 1–34

Veenhoven, R and Vergunst, F (2014) The Easterlin illusion: economic growth does not go with greater happiness, *International Journal of Happiness and Development*, **1** (4), pp 311–43

Work engagement, organizational health and culture

08

Introduction

Extrinsic motivation is important, but motivation is not always enough. Implementing effective policies and building a strong company culture is essential to moving from good intentions to real results. Get it right with motivation, values and rewarding employees and job satisfaction increases, employees are more engaged.

It used to be called morale, but the positive psychologists have taken over the territory and prefer the term 'work engagement'. Engagement has become overused and has been turned into one of those ghastly management-speak essentials. It has been mercilessly transformed from a noun into a verb, a common affliction of language in the world of business jargon. We will distinguish work engagement as a distinct concept from uses of 'engage' such as 'engage staff in conversation' (see: meeting); 'engage in dialogue' (see: speak to); 'engage customers in our newest product offerings' (see: spam). And we'll leave morale behind because it too has been overused beyond the point of usefulness, often used interchangeably with many other terms. Peterson, Park and Sweeney (2008) for example, found 14 different usages of the term morale across the research.

Work engagement is an interesting and more useful concept because it is both a scientifically valid concept and is strongly connected with constructive (and profitable) workplace outcomes. It is a measure of individual well-being, distinct but related to concepts like organizational health, which we get to later in this chapter. Therefore an individual can have high well-being at work, even in a dysfunctional team, or an individual may have low engagement within an otherwise effective, functional and healthy team (Hallberg and Schaufeli, 2006).

Hallberg and Schaufeli (2006) initially developed the concept of work engagement as a contrast to *burnout*. Burnout at work covers most of the negative ground, intended to describe a smothering, wet-blanket concept that extinguishes motivation, leads to emotional exhaustion and cynicism (Schaufeli, Leiter and Maslach, 2009). The concept of burnout emerged in the 1970s and Schaufeli and colleagues (2009) worked to develop a positive psychology measure to be the opposite of burnout.

Schaufeli and colleagues, as positive psychologists, wanted to move an overwhelming amount of burnout research (they identified over 6,000 books, articles, dissertations and journal articles) into a more positive dimension. Thus, they propose work engagement as the opposite of burnout. They suggest work engagement is a state of optimal functioning at work, characterized by vigour, dedication and absorption. Individuals who are highly engaged in their work have a continual energy and sense of satisfaction in their work.

The concept of work engagement sounds incredibly attractive, it is what everyone would like in their work. And, importantly, low work engagement is related to many workplace outcomes. Those who are less engaged have higher turnover rates, greater cynicism, more negative perceptions of the organization, emotional exhaustion, depressive symptoms, other physical and psychological health complaints, and decreased commitment to the organization. Higher levels of work engagement have been proved to be linked to measures of individual physical and psychological health (Hallberg and Schaufeli, 2006) as well as performance and productivity.

Yet, findings from around the world show there is much room for improvement in work engagement. A large workplace study from the UK found that a minority of employees could be described as 'engaged' (Buckingham, 2001). International research by ISR (2004) with 160,000 workers across 10 advanced economies found engagement highest in the United States and Brazil (75 per cent of workers engaged) and lowest in France (only 59 per cent of workers). In 2014, Roberts reported that in the UK only 37 per cent of workers believed innovation was encouraged, one-third of employees reporting a poor relationship, and fewer than half (49 per cent) felt valued at work. This is a big problem, or what coaches refer to as a 'development opportunity'.

Improving work engagement is a huge opportunity to improve employee well-being as well as company profitability. Ott (2007) found that higher workplace engagement was related to higher earnings per share among publicly traded businesses. High engagement was related to improved outcomes, including 12 per cent higher customer advocacy, 18 per cent higher productivity, and higher profitability. Low engagement was associated with negative outcomes: the least 25 per cent engaged companies had 31–51 per cent higher turnover, 51 per cent more inventory shrinkage (an accounting term for when products go missing) and 62 per cent more workplace accidents.

The performance delusion: a path to disengagement

Some employers don't think too much about their employees, their personal lives, or individual and professional accomplishments – other than when individual achievement involves company performances. Good companies understand the values of support from an employer in difficult times as well as when business is thriving.

Support is often thought of in terms of something people need in difficult times, and this is absolutely true. We know from the research on social support networks (Agneessens, Waege and Lievens, 2006) that those who can be supported, know who to turn to, and have a shoulder to cry on are better able to weather the difficult times. Most people know this implicitly, and know who to turn to in a crisis. In turn, most people acknowledge that in a time of personal crisis, emergency or extreme difficulty they are prepared to support their close friends in any manner, at any time of day or night. Even if not called on, that can be a comforting thought to people facing difficult times. It may not have reached the level of difficulty that requires emergency emotional, professional or financial support.

But what about in times of success? Of course it is widely assumed that people need support in times of failure but periods of success show employee independence, ability and competence. Professional success especially does not need to be supported in the same way as failure… right?

There is much talk about the Peter Principle: people tend to get promoted to their own level of incompetences. The Peter Principle (Peter and Hull, 1969) is when employers choose characteristics based on current performance instead of future potential and capacity in the new role. This often leads to derailment and failure. It is common in almost every sector that a high-performing employee is promoted from a job of specialist knowledge into the fundamentally different role of managing people. It is easy to forget the challenges inherent in this. Most assume that career trajectories are a ladder where climbing means managing the people you used to work with. This is one of the most fundamental fallacies in the workplace, the performance delusion (MacRae and Furnham, 2014). Those who have trained extensively to learn a specialized skill, and spend years of time and energy mastering that skill, are not always willing, able or capable of transferring those technical skills to the very different type of work that is leadership. The best nurse will not necessarily make the best manager; the best teacher will not necessarily be the best head teacher. Leadership career trajectories are fundamentally a different type of job than mastering a particular role (MacRae and Furnham, 2014). The commonplace belief is that if you are the highest-performing specialist in the team or department, you should get promoted to a managerial or leadership position. Without proper training, preparation and development that can be a quick path to demotivation and disengagement.

This happens all the time. And it is an unfortunate problem that stems from poor career planning and poor development pathways. For many specialist roles, mastering one's abilities and maintaining current knowledge is a full-time job and a lifetime career development. Take, for example, findings from MacRae (2010) from a group of physicians working in a hospital reporting very high work engagement. It is a very challenging job, with constant demands on time, ability, knowledge and expertise. Working in a hospital is a difficult environment, yet these physicians report high engagement. They report that their work fills them with energy, their work is full of meaning and purpose, and they become immersed in their work.

This is common in specialized jobs, where the person is competent (and motivated). Doing a challenging, interesting and rewarding task provides the sense of work engagement that is often referred to as flow (Csíkszentmihályi, 2008). It is a sense that we get when the work is pleasurable and satisfying. The work is challenging enough to be interesting and that enjoyment results in people losing track of time, feeling more capable and more confident. The activity or task is its own reward, that is, intrinsically motivating. During flow people lose track of time because the work is enjoyable, and they feel more capable, more sensitive and more self-confident even though the activities may be challenging.

Promoting someone from a position where they were engaged, productive and effective into a managerial position can be a huge mistake. It can be a collective delusion, where the promoter creates the impression of managing the team as a better or more important job while the employee imagines a step 'up' as a step in a better direction.

This fallacy can be maintained and stoked for a very long period of time. How long can someone work their way up the management ladder, only to realize 20 years later that they really were happiest when they were doing the job themselves instead of watching and supervising others doing that job.

Improving engagement requires not just promoting the most engaged top performers, but moving (or retaining) people in the job where they can perform best and be most engaged in the work. For some, this will be leadership, others are most engaged honing their craft.

For some, working from home is the solution to many problems, for others it creates more problems than it solves. Many people fantasize that being their own boss, owning their own company, consulting or working from home is their path to freedom and engagement in their work. However, motivation and engagement is not always that simple.

An initial caution on working from home

Work is an action, not a place. Most work tasks can be done anywhere. Where you work, the people you work with, and your surroundings affect health, happiness and productivity. A different city, neighbourhood or office location can hugely affect all sorts of other decisions in your life. What route you take to work, how long you spend in the community, where you stop by on the way to work or back home. No one knows this better than those who work from home.

Not everyone goes to the office any more, and not everyone needs to. Between the wide variety of communication methods available, it is feasible to be part of an office without ever going into the office. And the number of people working from home is growing. Estimates from the Office of National Statistics (ONS, 2014) suggested the amount of people working from home grew to 4.2 million (13.9 per cent of workers), from 2.9 million (11.1 per cent) in 1998 when records of this began (ONS, 2014) in the UK.

Optimistic proponents of working at home would say that it:

- reduces the time and stress of commuting;
- provides greater autonomy and flexibility in the work;
- improves work–life balance, and is useful for parents, people with disabilities, carers;
- increases the size of the talent pool;
- can provide an environment free of office distractions.

Cynics embraced working from home for the financial benefits. Those who work from home reduce costs because they take up less office space. But people who work from home often have to make themselves available outside of regular office hours and contexts. International assignments or even vacations may not offer respite because airports and hotels offer 24-hour connectivity, and even airlines are providing WiFi access on their flights, which allow (or perhaps inflict) the user with uninterrupted access to the workplace. Even above 39,000 feet, no one is safe from e-mail and, as we discussed in Chapter 6, e-mail can be a burden as well as a boon. Disengagement and demotivation can result from e-mail compulsivity and excessive work demands.

It works for some people, for different reasons, but it is not flawless. Consider the following 12 problems with working at home. Some are more easily solvable than others, but working from home is not always a paradise of teleconferences in the bathtub, sleeping in and working however and whenever you want:

1　**Expenses and costs.** In an office, the organization pays all the bills but who pays for all the expenses in a home office? There is no IT department, maintenance department or even any obliging colleagues to make the tea. There is no HR department to help with problems, or finance department to simplify the billing and pay-cheque for the self-employed remote worker. To save money from expenses the home worker may have to hire an accountant to keep track of expenses, tax deductions and credits alongside expenses.

2　**Workplace health and safety.** Workers may not be working in a space designed for their work, chairs may not be ergonomic and the only facilities available may be what a person has in the household. What about insurance implications if an employee falls down or injures themselves while working?

3　**Corporate culture.** What is the corporate culture of your spare bedroom? It can be more difficult to bring corporate culture out of the workplace and into a person's home. Should all workers be required to spend some time in the office, or with their colleagues? Or can that flexibility be part of the company culture?

4　**Monitoring performance.** In some occupations performance is easier to measure than in others. Electronic messages and communication make monitoring easier, but this can still be challenging in some types of work. There are two ways to address this. First, performance management should be focused on results. Targets should be clear, reasonable and measurable.

5　**Learning opportunities.** People learn from each other's success and mistakes and through personal communication in the office. If one does not come into the office, it is easier to lose touch with colleagues and the company, and you may miss out on opportunities that others receive by being in the right room at the right time.

6   Communication. Flexible working hours may lead to different working schedules. That is great when it improves work–life balance, but difficult when the manager or head office cannot get in touch. A series of missed calls and a game of voicemail tag ensues and frustrates those on both sides. There needs to be at least some formal guidelines, scheduled availability and other policies to ensure communication is effective. Electronic communication has different subtleties and information that can be conveyed in different ways than face-to-face communication. Misunderstandings and conflict can be worse over electronic communication because subtleties, humour or much of the context can be lost.

7   Exclusion. Physical distance can be a significant factor in excluding colleagues either deliberately or unthinkingly. Often the employees whose achievements are most visible are selected for pay rises and promotions. If the performance of the home worker goes unknown, they are unlikely to be recognized and rewarded for it.

8   Family/friend interruptions. Parents working from home might be distracted by their children; family members might intrude on much-needed working hours; and friends, neighbours or others might see being at home as being available. They might know you are 'working from home' but do not see why you cannot have a quick break and a chat.

9   Burdening/family friends. It is often nice to have someone to talk with about your work, and the home worker does not have the break-room or water-cooler opportunities to talk with interested colleagues. Even the most sympathetic spouse does not want to become the home worker's on-site counsellor.

10   Mobile working. The ability to work anywhere can be a huge asset, but can also be a huge irritant in public spaces. Working on-the-go can lead to dangerous egocentrism, commandeering public spaces as one's own personal workplace. The loud and boorish work discussion on a train carriage can be extremely disruptive for others. Mobile workers introduce greater security risks too. For example, a laptop, mobile phone or portable hard drive with sensitive company data left in an airport, train carriage or coffee shop.

11 **Diminishing work–life balance.** While working from home can be a boon to work–life balance, it can also be a threat. If you work from home, you are always at work. There may be greater temptation to check e-mail, do a bit of work, or do other work excessively. Colleagues, clients and supervisors, too, might not respect that home workers need 'out of office' hours even if they live in their office.

12 **Motivation.** Some people are motivated by the autonomy that working at home provides, and are most productive when they are working from home. Others find being at home provides innumerable distractions and opportunities to procrastinate when they are not in the structured office environment. It's not for everyone, some people just cannot seem to get work done without going into the office.

There is no holiday party to celebrate a festive season or employee's birthday, no colleague in the lunch room to chat about the morning's events. Many people really miss going for dinner or drinks after work with colleagues. Some people procrastinate, doing a bit of housework, tidying up, realizing the day before a looming work deadline that they absolutely *must* clean out their entire closet and donate some of the unworn clothes to a charity to free up some space – and then realize at the end of the day that they spent the rest of the afternoon researching the best charity. It works better for some than others, and if workers are allowed to work from home, the appropriate supports and structures are still required in order to improve engagement and productivity.

Those who work from home, too, can do many things to improve their working environment. Some join clubs or networks of people in similar positions for advice, social support and learning. Others arrange to meet up regularly with colleagues, while some are perfectly happy working in their own splendid isolation. It is not just about increasing flexibility and reducing overheads, it's a different style of life and self-management. It's great for some, but not for everyone.

Complete flexibility: a case study from Ryan LLC

So how to make working from home... work? It's possible, and some have done it. The following example provides a model of how it can be done, and done well to improve productivity.

CASE STUDY   Ryan LLC

Ryan is a multinational tax services firm. Their work includes tax advisory and consulting services, tax recovery, credits and incentives, tax process improvement and automation, tax appeals, tax compliance and more. They do tax.

Ryan have developed one of the most flexible workplaces: employees can work from anywhere, teams manage and set their own schedules, have no required office hours, no time tracking. The performance of over 2,000 employees is measured entirely based on outcomes, and employees are given the flexibility to manage their time however they choose.

The principle is that employees are expected to uphold the 'three Cs':

- Communication
- Collaboration
- Consideration

Working on flexible schedules or out of the office is not to come at the expense of relationships with peers, clients or leadership. Communication is essential to ensure all employees have clarity about projects, performance, timelines and availability. Their system myRyan helps this by focusing on six core principles:

- Employees focus on results, not hours.
- Employees have flexible work schedules and locations.
- Employees eliminate activities that waste time and money.
- Employees collaborate and support each other.
- Employees thrive in a guilt-free work environment.
- Employees have the freedom to achieve work–life success.

These values sound good, but what about implementation? There are two key areas that suggest they are living the values, and their exceptional policies are translated into an excellent culture.

First, they are a best-practice model for performance management systems. They track all the information centrally, in their customer relationship management (CRM) system (myRyan) and have industry-leading tools and policies at all stages of the employee relationship, from onboarding through to exit interviews. This will be discussed further as a best-practice example in Chapter 14.

Second, they are regularly lauded for their company policies and culture. Great Places to Work regularly rates Ryan as one of the best places to work around the world including in Canada, the United States and the Netherlands. Fortune (2016) rates them as one of the best companies for flexibility. Their flexible system has had excellent uptake with 90 per cent telecommuting and 100 per cent of employees make use of the flexible work schedules.

Third, employees vote with their feet. Employee turnover is 10 per cent at Ryan, which compares with an average annual employee turnover of 27.8 per cent in professional services. Using estimated turnover costs from MacLean (2013), even a very rough estimate suggests a company like Ryan with 2,000 employees would lose about 350 fewer employees every year, compared with the industry turnover average, saving about US $3.5 million per year.

The example of Ryan is discussed further in Chapter 14.

Cautions from context

This model, of course, is not universally applicable. This is a highly skilled, very demanding type of work and workplace. And even within this company, the way employees use their flexitime varies widely. Some still like to be around colleagues, to come into the office. They like being around others, contributing in person to a team (affiliation motivation). Some are motivated by the structure of an office environment, and find themselves less productive at home.

Others are motivated by the flexibility and independence offered outside the office (autonomy motivation), others like the comfort and ease of working from home (conditions motivation). The flexible workplaces also provides excellent flexibility for those with family or other responsibilities outside of the workplace, and this contributed to Great Places to Work rating Ryan as one of the top five 'Best Workplaces in Canada for Women'.

There is no right or wrong motivation, but those who are qualified, capable and act like grown ups should be treated as such. Everyone benefits.

Organizational culture

While work engagement is an individual measure of well-being, organizational (or corporate) culture can be described as the overall (non-physical) environment that exists across the company. Teams and departments, too, often develop their own culture and environment, although these are often firmly rooted in the overall organizational culture. Organizational culture is important because it affects individual motivation. Hartmann (2006) suggested that cultural practices like honest and direct approaches to communication are more motivated to innovate, and that fragmented organizational cultures made management actions less effective. Guiso, Sapienza and Zingales (2015) found that in companies where employees view their organizational culture as trustworthy and ethical, firm performance is higher.

Some examples should help to make the meaning of organizational culture clear. Hospitals often have a crisis-driven organizational culture. Everyone is rushing from crisis to crisis, many work long hours under difficult circumstances, and no matter how hard everyone works, genuine life-threatening emergencies pop up as quickly as they can be solved. Technology companies such as Google eagerly promote an image of organizational culture that is relaxed, friendly and fun by having things like play areas and whimsically themed conference venues (Stewart, 2013). Even organizations that, by design, have a laissez-faire approach – letting each employee shape their environment, or giving every manager free rein to shape their team's culture – will influence the overall company culture. A free-for-all environment where employees are pitted against each other can create a competitive, aggressive or cut-throat culture.

Ravasi and Schultz (2006) neatly define organizational culture as shared assumptions about acceptable behaviour. Thus:

Organizational policies: are written and codified standards of behaviour.

Organizational culture: the unwritten, but known, acceptable standards of behaviour.

There can be some overlap between culture and policy because policies are one tool that can be used to influence organizational culture. If, for example, a company has an unwritten, but generally known environment where sexual harassment goes unreported and unpunished – that is part of the culture. To combat this culture, a zero-tolerance policy might be developed, where the consequences (along with a set of policies, procedures, supports, etc) of sexual harassment in the workplace are clearly codified.

Understanding the culture is essential for getting the policy right. To continue the example, a company culture may exist where sexual harassment is tolerated or ignored even when there are formal policies against sexual harassment. But if a culture exists where complaints are ignored and complainants are blamed for reporting inappropriate behaviour, culture is unlikely to change. In this example, understanding the culture could mean adding additional measures to combat the behaviour, and make it clear that the behaviour will not be tolerated. For example, an anonymous, independent third-party hotline to report abuse, with an independent counsellor or mediator, and with independent advice and support would make it clear that the culture is changing. Often culture is difficult to change, but without serious action it is impossible. As will be discussed further in Chapter 13, inaction or inattention is often the source and sustenance of toxic culture.

Industries, as well as companies, develop and reinforce their own cultures. In a discussion with a former financial services CEO (see MacRae, 2014), he suggested that the 2008 banking crisis and subprime mortgage meltdown was fuelled and propagated by a culture of greed and negligence in the financial sector. Not every company in the sector was caught up in it, nor was every individual, but the culture in the industry greatly affected the culture of most companies within the sector.

Organizational culture is difficult to shape, and ultimately comes from the top. As described in MacRae (2014), and reinforced (O'Reilly *et al*, 2014), culture comes from the top. As discussed in detail in MacRae and Furnham (2014), the ultimate accountability is the leadership. Constructive, healthy culture needs to come from the top. And negligent leaders can create negligent culture. But the values and actions need to be adopted up, down and across the organization. It needs to move from the leader to the leadership team, to every department and location. A leader with inspiring vision and admirable values cannot create or change culture without implementation.

To try to assess/measure the concept of organizational culture, in an easy way that anyone can do, ask a number of employees to list the behaviours that are assumed to be acceptable in the workplace, but not formally written or codified in policy. This can be done qualitatively or quantitatively. Consider the following checklist: which of the following behaviours are not covered by company policy, but are encouraged in the company culture?

- philanthropism;
- profit seeking;
- helping colleagues;
- drinking alcohol;
- gossip;

- long hours;
- sharing information;
- keeping information to oneself.

Go further, go online and complete the brief questionnaire – at www.highpotentialpsych.co.uk/motivperformance – to see a snapshot of your organizational culture. It only takes five minutes, and there is no cost. Share on social media and see how your organizational culture compares with others, or see how your colleagues see the organizational culture.

Organizational health

If organizational culture is a rather open-ended description that could be anything, it is useful as a descriptive but not an evaluative term. Therefore, we define organizational health as a constructive, effective organizational culture. There is no one 'right' culture – it is based on the experience of those within the organization.

There are two clear-cut dimensions along which organizational health can be measured (see Table 8.1):

- **Productivity.** A productive company successfully accomplishes its mission or purpose. This can, but does not necessarily, have to include profit.

- **Physical and psychological health.** Those working within the company are given every appropriate opportunity to be physically and psychologically healthy at work.

The low/low combination in Table 8.1 is a toxic organization whereas the high/high organization could be described as a healthy organization.

Recommendations for a healthy organization

The World Health Organization (Kuhn, 2010) suggests four key components for improving the health of an organization:

- **Integration**: connect workplace health with relevant policies and ensure implementation.
- **Participation**: involve employees in planning and policymaking processes, as well as implementing and evaluating the actions taken.

Table 8.1   Levels of organizational health and productivity, with examples

		Productivity	
		Low	**High**
Health	**Low**	Employees are not healthy, or their health is under threat and the organization is unsuccessful.	Employees are not healthy, or their health is threatened, but the organization is successful.
		In the commercial world these companies shut quickly; in the public sector they are sometimes maintained for ideological or political reasons.	In the commercial world, these companies often compensate with extrinsic motivators like reward and punishment.
		Example: the majority of coal mines are unprofitable (Ker, 2015) and the organization tends to have a pessimistic and fatalistic culture that discourages seeking help for mental health issues, despite the prevalence of problems (Law, 2012).	Example: London's investment banking sector is infamous for being highly profitable, with an unhealthy culture. An article in the *Financial Times* described it as 'an unhealthy treadmill' with an 'entrenched culture of overwork' (Gapper, 2014).
	High	Employees are treated well and are happy and healthy at work, but the organization is failing.	Employees are healthy and well treated in an effective/ productive company.
		These can be toxic organizations where the individuals or leaders prioritize self-interest and maintaining the status quo over the objective of the organization.	These are the most effective organizations, and the type of company everyone wants to work for.
		Example: Powa, a tech company described as 'a textbook example of how not to run a business' (Cellan-Jones, 2016) was probably an exciting and engaging place to work before it was run into the ground.	Examples: Ryan in this chapter, Thomas International in Chapter 5.

- **Balance**: improve the working conditions and quality of the work at an individual, employee level.

- **Based on need**: ensure action is taken based on an analysis of the health requirements, and ensure a process of continual evaluation and improvement.

We will revisit these principles in the final chapter, illustrating with a case study a company that has excellent policies and culture that supports these four points.

Berkels and colleagues (2004) conducted a review of good practice in mental health promotion across Europe, and in the report with a predictably catchy title the European Union is so loved for – '*Project F 1607 – mental health promotion and prevention strategies for coping with anxiety, depression and stress-related disorders in Europe. Final report 2001–2003*' – it concluded that interventions can be classified into three categories at different levels of intervention:

- **Individual level**: individual interventions and improvements such as improving coping skills, mitigating stress and improving interpersonal relationships.

- **Social environment**: supportive environments (including organizational culture) that prevent against things such as discrimination, harassment and bullying.

- **Working conditions**: improving workplaces as well as supports for work–life balance, and things like balancing work and childcare for parents.

The Canadian Mental Health Association (2010) provides a great deal of useful information about mental health in the workplace, and they propose eight strategies to promote mental health:

1 **Participation in decision making.** Encourage employees to be involved in decision making. Griffin, Rafferty and Mason (2004) found that initiatives where group members had direct involvement and ownership resulted in higher levels of group well-being.

2 **Clearly define employee duties and responsibilities.** We discuss this at length in Chapter 6 about communication.

3 **Promoting work–life balance.** The example of Ryan's flexible working policies earlier in this chapter is a prime example of this.

4 **Encourage respectful behaviours.** Perceived support from administration is an important contributor to employee well-being (Jones, Flynn and Kelloway, 1995; Parker *et al*, 2003).

5 **Managing workloads.** Overworked people are less productive as well as less healthy, as is demonstrated at the beginning of this chapter.

6 **Allow continuous learning.** Development is important, more so to some than others. In Chapter 4 we discussed an example of lifetime development opportunities.

7 **Conflict resolution practices in place.** Fair resolution is essential if problems will be addressed. Avoiding problems makes them worse, while resolving problems quickly minimizes potential problems.

8 **Recognize employee contributions effectively.** Understand how employees want to be recognized and motivated, and do it. How to do this is the focus of the next three chapters.

A quirky option: walking meetings

A set of policy templates and HR guidelines can only go so far. It can lay the framework for a healthy organization, but the best organizations have their own unique culture and behaviours that reflect and reinforce what makes them different. It is what makes people feel a sense of belonging in a unique workplace; and when it is done well, it will also align with the corporate image. Google works hard to create and sustain their 'fun' culture, which would hardly be appropriate in a legal firm or unemployment benefits office.

Big-picture policies can shape the culture, but sometimes the little, quirky policies can have their own impact. Consider the following idea. Meetings can be dreary, torpid affairs. The purpose, content and participants in a meeting vary, so sometimes stuffy boardrooms are necessary. But often, meetings are just conversations between a few people.

If you are in a job that involves many meetings, why not move some of them outside? Weather, geography and other parties permitting, a brisk walk can be refreshing and exercise has many benefits to physical and psychological health. It does not need to be a frivolous excuse to leave the office. Make a plan. Perhaps three agenda items, a 30-minute walk on a three-kilometre route, with one agenda item to be concluded every kilometre.

It may not always be professional, or palatable to the other party, so this option is not always appropriate. But it can brighten up a day, inspire new creativity, and even if it ends up being another useless meeting rehashing the same old problems, it has done a little to improve health.

A similar method can be used for workers who spend hours on e-mail. On a nice, sunny day, why not take the mobile phone and tackle that Sisyphean inbox over a leisurely walk in the park?

Conclusion

Work engagement is a positive state with many benefits for employers and employees alike. There are many opportunities and many new and emerging approaches that can boost engagement, motivation and profitability at work. There is no one-size-fits-all approach that can be applied to every organization, but examples such as that of Ryan show it is possible – it takes a bit of imagination and the potential increases in productivity and profitability are enormous. Engaged workers improve company performance as well as individual well-being.

While we discussed the potentially damaging effects of stress in Chapter 4, an effective organization can go further than mitigating harm. In fact, boosting engagement is not the same as mitigating harm. Mitigating harm involves improving the lowest standards or the most damaging policy, while increasing engagement requires building on current strengths. Both are complementary and have positive effects, which will be amplified and reinforced if both can be addressed.

References

Agneessens, F, Waege, H and Lievens, J (2006) Diversity in social support by role relations: a typology, *Social Networks*, **28**, pp 427–41

Berkels, H, Henderson, J, Henke, N, Lavikainen, J, Lehtinen, V, Ozamiz, A, Van den Deede, P and Zenzinger, K (2004) *Mental Health Promotion and Prevention Strategies for Coping with Anxiety, Depression and Stress Related Disorders in Europe (2001–2003) – Project F 1607*, Federal Institute for Occupational Health and Safety, Dortmund

Buckingham, M (2001) What a waste, *People Management*, 11 October, pp 36–39

Canadian Mental Health Association [CMHA] (2010) [accessed 10 October 2016] Workplace Mental Health Promotion: A How-To Guide [Online] http://wmhp.cmhaontario.ca/wordpress/wp-content/uploads/2010/03/WMHP-Guide-Final1.pdf

Cellan-Jones, R (2016) [accessed 10 October 2016] Powa Failure: Where Did the Money Go? *BBC News* [Online] http://www.bbc.co.uk/news/technology-36070904

Csíkszentmihályi, M (2008) *Flow: The psychology of optimal experience*, Harper Perennial Modern Classics, New York

Fortune (2016) [accessed 10 October 2016] 50 Best Workplaces for Flexibility [Online] http://fortune.com/tag/50-best-workplaces-for-flexibility/

Gapper, J (2014) Bankers and lawyers are on an unhealthy treadmill, *Financial Times*

Griffin, MA, Rafferty, AE and Mason, CM (2004) Who started this? Investigating different sources of organizational change, *Journal of Business and Psychology*, **18** (4), pp 555–70

Guiso, L, Sapienza, P and Zingales, Z (2015) The value of corporate culture, *Journal of Financial Economics*, **117** (1), pp 60–76

Hallberg, UE and Schaufeli, WB (2006) 'Same same' but different? Can work engagement be discriminated from job involvement and organizational commitment? *European Psychologist*, **11** (2), pp 119–27

Hartmann, A (2006) The role of organizational culture in motivating innovative behaviour in construction firms, *Construction Innovation*, **6** (3), pp 159–72

ISR (2004) [accessed 10 October 2016] International Survey Research [Online] www.isrsurveys.com

Jones, B, Flynn, D and Kelloway, K (1995) Perception of support from the organization in relation to work stress, satisfaction, and commitment, in Sauter, S and Murphy, L (eds) *Organizational Risk Factors for Job Stress*, pp 41–52, APA, Washington, DC

Ker, P (2015) Two thirds of world's coal output is loss-making Wood Mackenzie estimates, *The Sydney Morning Herald*, 10 December

Kuhn, K (2010) Challenge of modern working life to mental well-being and social inclusion: workplace-related mental health problems – risk and prevention, in Baumann, A Muijen, M and Gaebel, W (eds) *Mental Health and Well-Being at the Workplace: Protection and inclusion in challenging times*, World Health Organization

Law, BM (2012) Coal miners' dilemma, *Monitor on Psychology*, **43** (4), p 20, American Psychological Association

MacLean, EL (2013) Reducing employee turnover in the Big Four public accounting firms, CMC Senior Theses

MacRae, I (2010) [accessed 10 October 2016] Organizational Well-Being and Communication in a Medical Setting [Online] https://open.library.ubc.ca/cIRcle/collections/undergraduateresearch/42496/items/1.0086055

MacRae, I (2014) Assessing and developing value(s) in the financial sector: a case study, *Assessment and Development Matters*, **6** (1), pp 15–17

MacRae, I and Furnham, A (2014) *High Potential: How to spot, manage and develop talented people at work*, Bloomsbury, London

Office of National Statistics [ONS] (2014) Record proportion of people in employment are home workers

O'Reilly, CA, Caldwell, DF, Chatman, JA and Doerr, B (2014) The promise and problems of organizational culture: CEO personality, culture and firm performance, *Group Organization Management*, **39** (6), pp 595–625

Ott, B (2007) Investors take note: engagement boosts earnings, *The Gallup Management Journal*, 14 June

Parker, CP, Baltes, BB, Young, SA, Huff, JW, Altmann, RA, LaCost, HA and Roberts, JE (2003) Relationships between psychological climate perceptions and work outcomes: a meta-analytic review, *Journal of Organizational Behaviour*, **24** (4), pp 289–416

Peter, LJ and Hull, R (1969) *The Peter Principle: Why things always go wrong*, William Morrow and Company, New York

Peterson, C, Park, N and Sweeney, PJ (2008) Group well-being: morale from a positive psychology perspective, *Applied Psychology*, **57** (1), pp 19–36

Ravasi, D and Schultz, M (2006) Responding to organizational identity threats: exploring the role of organizational culture, *Academy of Management Journal*, **49** (3), pp 433–58

Roberts, H (2014, March) [accessed 10 October 2016] UK Near Bottom of Employee Engagement Ranking, *HR Magazine* [Online] http://www.hrmagazine. co.uk/article-details/uk-near-bottom-of-employee-engagement-ranking

Schaufeli, WB, Leiter, MP and Maslach, C (2009) Burnout: 35 years of research and practice, *Career Development International*, **14** (3), pp 204–29

Stewart, JB (2013) Looking for a lesson in Google's perks, *The New York Times*, 15 March

Extrinsic motivation and rewards

09

Do you know the only thing that gives me pleasure? It's to see my dividends coming in.

ATTRIBUTED TO JOHN D ROCKERFELLER (LEWIS, 1908)

Introduction

Rewards motivate. When people cannot or will not motivate themselves, external (extrinsic) rewards can have a profound effect on behaviour. Money is, of course, one of the most universal and transferable extrinsic motivators, but all sorts of perks and benefits can be used to motivate or coerce people into behaving in the desired way.

Rewards, even money, are not unique to humans. In the mid-20th century BF Skinner suggested and subsequently demonstrated that many animals can be influenced to behave in certain ways (Ferster and Skinner, 1957). This was not a new idea, but he perfected the techniques. The idea is relatively straightforward. All actions have consequences, and the consequence of any behaviour will determine how likely the individual is to repeat that action. Rewards encourage behaviour, punishment deters behaviour.

Skinner and colleague Charles Ferster (Ferster and Skinner, 1957) showed that it was relatively straightforward to train rats with simple rewards in a process he called *Operant Conditioning*. In this case, the rats were rewarded with food. Many parents use a similar tactic to encourage behaviour in children. This type of training with desirable rewards can be used to encourage almost any behaviour. Rats can be encouraged to press levers and run mazes. Dogs are trained to sit, roll over, run obstacles courses and do any number of tricks. Skinner even trained some of his pigeons to play ping-pong. With great confidence in his method he even proposed a missile guidance system using pigeons, although the system never took off (Darling, 2011).

Even complex tasks such as playing ping-pong or guiding the trajectory of a missile can be encouraged and taught by breaking down the task into simple, component steps. Research has yet to demonstrate that pigeons have any instinctual knowledge of ping-pong or ballistics. But they have the capacity to learn, and to understand cause and effect. A pigeon can quickly learn that when it turns its head to the left, it receives food. The pigeon learns the pattern, and repeats the turn. When the rewards stop, the pigeon will try similar actions: a turn in the other direction, a bob of the head, a larger or faster turn in the first direction. Rewarding larger and larger turns can quickly escalate into a pigeon spinning in circles at an astounding velocity.

From concrete to abstract rewards

Rewards can go far beyond food, and of course humans are far more complex and need more sophisticated rewards than food to encourage behaviour. Sometimes. Want to get a group of university students to participate in a focus group? Try pizza. Bring a plate of freshly baked pastries into an office or boardroom and see what happens. Savvy facilitators who want to end the session at a particular time arrange for an appetizing array of food to arrive 5 or 10 minutes before the desired completion time. Motivation to argue, discuss, debate and rehash may be diminished when it stands in the way of a good lunch.

Another clear finding from psychology is that rewards can be interchangeable. One type of reward can be substituted for another, when the relationship between the two types of rewards have been learned. Often animal research uses items of food because it is straightforward, and one of the two rewards that animals seek with most determination (we will get to the second shortly). Yet animals, like humans, can develop a system where symbolic tokens have meaningful values. Research from Chen, Lakshminarayanan and Santos (2006) showed that monkeys, too, could make use of and be motivated by money. They studied a group of capuchins: small and highly intelligent monkeys that have complex social structures and hierarchies (although they have not yet developed unions).

Chen and colleagues introduced a currency system to a group of capuchins, by first introducing small tokens. The macaques had little interest in the tokens until researchers demonstrated how the tokens could be redeemed for a tasty treat, like a grape. As intelligent little monkeys, they quickly learned that the tokens had value, backed up by a real commodity they wanted, in this case perhaps the 'Grape Standard'. Once they realized the value of the tokens, the macaques would trade, use and redeem the valuable tokens.

The little monkeys did not just redeem the tokens for food, they quickly traded the currency and developed an economy within the group. Unsurprisingly, one of the first observed financial transactions between the monkeys (Dubner and Levitt, 2005) involved a macaque giving a token to another in exchange for sex (that is the second reward animals pursue; difficult to justify to the ethics board). The obliging macaque collected payment from the client and immediately redeemed it for a grape.

The research in monkey economics continues, and further studies (such as Lakshminarayanan, Chen and Santos, 2011) have shown that monkeys behave in similar ways to people when currencies or commodities change in value. If the value of a token increases from one to two grapes, the entire group react predictably and rationally to the change in value, and in the same pattern as humans. When the value falls, people (and macaques) tend to buy more. And the financial behaviour of monkeys follows the exact same patterns as that of human gambling or investing in the stock market.

Rewards can influence behaviour, but rewards can be replaceable or interchangeable. Money is the standard unit of compensation for units of work because it is widely interchangeable for other desired rewards. And, indeed, money can be a powerful motivation tool. It would be foolish to suggest that money has no importance in most workplaces. The most important questions are *when* and *how* money can be a motivator at work.

The research consistently shows that beyond a minimal level, there is no link between wealth and happiness. Not having enough money to survive at a very basic level can lead to chronic stress and adversely impacts well-being. But being moderately wealthy, extremely wealthy or extravagantly wealthy makes little meaningful difference on happiness. The effects of financial rewards depend on four (Argyle and Furnham, 1998), important factors:

- **Adaptation.** Most will report they are 'happier' after a bonus, pay rise, inheritance or other influx of money. However, the effects of the money disappear very quickly. People learn to think of increasing income levels as their new normal. Continued exposure to affluence requires greater financial rewards to produce the same effect.

- **Comparison.** People compare their income and earnings to the people around them. Those within a very well-paid team tend to compare their compensation with their team members, instead of the average level of compensation in the company or the country. No matter how large the bonus, most people will be unsatisfied if their bonus was smaller than their colleagues.

- **Alternatives.** No matter how much money one has, there are always other difficulties, and there are always problems that money cannot solve. Economists refer to this as the marginal utility of money, but it really means that the more one accumulates, the less valuable it seems. Other things that may be scarcer, like true friendships or free time, may seem far more valuable.

- **Worry.** Higher incomes often lead to shifting priorities. If money is not a worry, it leaves the mind open to wander to other things to worry about. Relationships, family, friends, self-development, philanthropic work and any number of other concerns can seem more important than money. And it is often true that the more one accumulates, the more stuff there is to worry about.

An incredibly useful finding by Ferster and Skinner (1957) also shows that *how* and *when* rewards are provided affects their impact on behaviour. Rewards can be compared on two dimensions:

- **Timing**: rewards are provided either based on the amount of time elapsed or a fixed time frame. In a *fixed interval* rewards are provided based on a predetermined amount of time, for example, every five minutes. In a *variable interval* schedule the timing of rewards is random and unpredictable.

- **Condition**: the number of responses, frequency of the behaviour or similar factor determines the number of rewards. In a *fixed-ratio* schedule, there are a set number of responses required to obtain the reward. For example, every time the dog sits, it receives a treat. As training progresses this could be every fifth, tenth or fiftieth time. In a *variable-ratio* schedule the number of responses required to provide the reward is random and/or unpredictable to the person trying to obtain the reward. Casinos have learned that this is the most effective way to encourage a behaviour.

All these schedules encourage behaviour, but not all are equally effective. The list below (and shown in Figure 9.1) shows how effectively (from most to least) each of the reward schedules encourage behaviour:

- **Variable-ratio** reward schedules are the fastest and most effective at encouraging behaviour. This is the type of reward that draws in gamblers. The reward is unpredictable, but it could just be the next spin. Just

Figure 9.1 Types of reward schedules

Fixed Interval	Variable Interval
Rewards at predictable timing at consistent intervals	Rewards at unpredictable or random intervals of time
Example: annual salary	*Example: supervisor brings in pastries some mornings*
Fixed Ratio	**Variable Ratio**
Rewards based on predictable and consistent criteria	Rewards at unpredictable intervals, based on a specific condition or performance
Example: performance bonuses, specific amount for every 10 widgets sold	*Example: company lottery for salespeople, every sale is rewarded with another chance to win*

one more time, one more bet could result in the big win. Variable ratio rewards are often used with sales teams. Let's say every completed sale is rewarded with a draw in the team lottery: every additional sale is another chance to win (but not a guarantee).

- **Fixed-ratio** rewards are also very effective at encouraging behaviour, but tend to act more slowly than variable-ratio rewards. Say the sales staff receive a bonus for every tenth sale they make, or those in a factory are rewarded for the number of products they make. This often encourages people to work harder and/or longer but can often lead to burnout and compromising quality for quantity (how to mitigate this in a performance management system is discussed shortly; how intrinsic versus extrinsic motivators affect quality versus quantity of performance is discussed later in this chapter).

- **Variable-interval** rewards also encourage behaviour, but in a more moderate way than the two described above. Consider checking the company e-mail, if an e-mail can be described as a 'reward'. E-mails come in at unpredictable times, and so checking one's e-mail is rewarded at seemingly unpredictable intervals. It is, of course, also influenced by behaviour to a certain extent: sending e-mails typically leads to responses. But imagine if the number of e-mails received depended on the number of times you checked your e-mail (fixed ratio). If reloading the e-mail page made an important e-mail response come through more quickly, imagine how much more compulsively some would check their e-mails.

- **Fixed-interval** rewards are the weakest way to encourage a particular type of behaviour. However, they do encourage the behaviour in that the reward requires a minimal level of performance, such as showing up for work. A pay cheque every two weeks is conditional only on a basic level of performance. A salaried employee receives a rate of compensation at a fixed level, irrespective of other factors.

The problem with any single reward schedule is that encouraging one type of behaviour often has consequences for other factors. Pay a writer based on the number of words, and they will fill newspaper column inches but not necessarily with the best content. Paying factory workers based on their output can lead to compromising quality. An estate agent is paid for their sales volume, not their ethical conduct. Increased hourly compensation for 'overtime' work encourages longer hours, but does nothing to encourage productivity within those hours.

Thus, compensation frameworks must consider the most important outcomes, and find ways of balancing the rewards and encouraging the desired outcomes without compromising others (see Table 9.1). Consider an example from a logistic company, which pays warehouse employees performance bonuses dependent on the number of items they pack and ship. Employees have a minimum hourly rate, but receive a multiplier on the base

Table 9.1 Examples of compensation schedules with advantages and limitations

Type	Schedule Type	Notes	Behaviour rewarded	Limitations/ Drawbacks
Hourly Rate	Fixed-ratio/ interval	Bi-monthly payment, also dependent on number of hours worked	Being at work, number of hours worked	Limited effect on performance
Volume Performance Bonus	Fixed-ratio	Minimum number of items required to be shipped; higher performance adds wage multiplier	Number of items shipped	Prioritizing speed over accuracy and safety
Error Rate	Fixed-ratio	Target error rate is a condition of receiving the volume	Accuracy	Inhibits or limits speed/ volume performance

NOTE Monetary rewards can be effective when properly understood and used effectively, but they are not the only motivator and must be considered alongside other motivators such as power, fame, recognition and autonomy.

rate, which can be increased by shipping more items. So, an employee may have a minimum number of items they are required to ship within each pay period. If the minimum target is 100 items, and the employee ships out 150 items, their pay for that week is multiplied by 1.5. Also important is that this is based on the number of 'correct' items shipped. Shipping 25 flowers to the client instead of 25 bags of flour should not be rewarded. For this reason, error rates are built into the reward system. A maximum error rate is set, which if exceeded, negates the volume performance multiplier. This means volume is rewarded only when it does not compromise the quality (accuracy) of the work.

Need for power

Would you rather have power or fame? Would you rather have power and influence that no one knew about, or be a powerless, well-renowned figurehead? How much money would you spend to obtain a powerful position? If a political office were for sale, how much would it be worth? Some people would spend any amount of money for power and control, others have no interest.

Unashamedly pursuing power and influence at work may raise concern around the office, but many people are motivated by power, influence or control. They want to have an impact. They probably have a vision for their group, their company or society at large and they achieve their ends by attempting to convince, influence and persuade others. Some try giving unsolicited help and advice; others attempt controlling or regulating others. They directly command others, or use influence behind the scenes to achieve their goals. Need for power is expressed by attempting to gain influence and control. The tactics can vary greatly.

It can sound sinister, seeking power and control in order to achieve your own objectives. However, it is essential to distinguish between constructive and destructive needs for power. Researchers (McClelland, 1970; Magee and Langer, 2008) would call this the drive for socialized versus personalized power. Alternatively we can make the distinction between those who want power for themselves, and those who seek power as a tool to improve the lot of others. Those who want personal power make decisions for personal benefit irrespective of the effects on others. Conversely, those who seek the power to help others are much more likely to make decisions that reduce harm to others and benefit the greatest number of people, even when it requires personal sacrifice.

A study from David Writer (2005) showed that those who were motivated by achievements were successful in business but failed in politics. Conversely, the desire for power is much more predictive of success in politics. The career politician must present a consistent and controlled image to consolidate power. They need to manage and control those around them, balance support and use creative tactics to maintain their control. Idealistic politicians often say that principles are more important than power. Others would say principles are useless without the power to change things.

Business and politics are different. Whereas politicians have to face and answer endless questioning and criticism from many people, this is much less true of business. Politicians get criticized for changing their opinions irrespective of sense or logic. Business people who can quickly change course are lauded for their agility and adaptability. In business there are a few very clear indicators of success and failure, usually to do with money.

The need for power can be a powerful motivator. So too can the lack of power. Demotivated, disillusioned employees with no control often find less than constructive ways to extract a personal power or control over their own work. And when employees become pissed off, they quickly realize that destructive behaviours afford them a different type of power, influence or control. The key lesson here is that the power to be autonomous is a very strong motivator (see Chapter 7). Employees can be very motivated by the power to do their job in their own way, and feelings of power over one's own work (referred to by psychologists as *locus of control*) has many benefits, from reduced stress (Karimi and Alipour, 2011) to job satisfaction and adjustment at work (Spector *et al*, 2002).

The desire for fame, and narcissism

Money is not the only reward on offer and not everyone wants to take control. Everyone wants to have their good work recognized and appreciated to some degree. Most people want to belong to a group, be respected by others and maybe even receive the occasional compliment. Some people seek fame while others flee from the spotlight. Some people become famous for their achievements, while others seek fame as an achievement in itself.

Another way to describe an obsessive desire for fame is narcissism. Narcissists are boastful, pretentious and self-aggrandizing, who overestimate their own abilities and accomplishments while simultaneously deflating others. Their inflated version of their own importance appears to be secure, but is often punctuated by the need for everyone around them to know how truly special and important they are. Narcissists have fragile self-esteem, needing to be bolstered up by constant attention and admiration from others. They expect their demands to be met by special favourable treatment, and develop relationships with the intention of getting some personal benefit from them. In doing so they often exploit others because they see others as tools to make themselves look or feel better. They are well known for their arrogance and their disdainful, patronizing attitude. As managers their difficult-to-fulfil needs can lead them to have difficult social relationships and to making poor decisions.

Narcissists often find that these attributes can be extremely valuable in business. Self-confidence is typically seen as a strength, and can be difficult to distinguish from overconfidence until it is too late. Their massive sense of self-importance frees them from the doubt or caution that inhibits their colleagues. The narcissism will make sure everyone hears about their own achievements, and they have the tendency to attach themselves to others' achievements, creating an impressive image that masks their own failings.

Most people will have worked with a narcissist. The intelligent narcissist may be an expert at concealing their own failures, and masking the true depths of their self-interest and self-involvement. The less-intelligent narcissist is more likely to be constantly seeking attention, unsure why people tend to avoid them. Inevitably they believe they rightly deserve all sorts of markers of their specialness: bigger offices and salary; inflated job titles; a bigger budget dedicated to their needs; more support staff; and greater liberty to do as they wish. Sometimes their abilities are enough to get them what they want. Often their colleagues learn it is easier to give them what they want than unleash the consequences of a narcissist not getting what they think they deserve.

Narcissists are super-self-confident: they express considerable self-certainty. They are 'self-people' – self-asserting, self-possessed, self-aggrandizing, self-preoccupied, self-loving – and ultimately self-destructive. They seem to really believe in themselves: they are sure that they have been born lucky. At work they are outgoing, high energy, competitive and very 'political', depending of course on their normal (big five) trait profile. Thus the extraverted conscientious narcissist may be rather different from those who are more neurotic and open. They can make reasonable short-term leaders as long as they are not criticized, or made to share glory. They seem to have an insatiable need to be admired, loved and needed. This can appear amusing or pathetic to outside observers. They are often a model of the ambitious, driven, self-disciplined, successful leader or manager. The world, they believe and demand, is their stage.

But narcissism is a *disorder* of self-esteem (APA, 2013): it is essentially a cover-up. People with narcissistic personality disorder move themselves ever-closer to self-destruction because their aggressive self-promotion blinds their personal and business judgement. At work they exploit others to get ahead, yet they demand special treatment. Their reaction to any sort of criticism is extreme, including shame, rage, tantrums and theatrics. They aim to destroy that criticism, however well-intentioned and useful. They can be incredibly charming when others give them what they want, but are quick to turn on everyone else. They are poor empathizers who need other people to prop up their self-image. They are prone to manipulative, demanding and self-centred behaviours, but when charm fails they will resort to tears, aggression or whatever emotion helps them to get what they want.

What is most distinctive about the narcissists is their self-assurance, which often gives them charisma. They tend to be assertive and confident. They so completely expect to succeed, and take more credit for success than is warranted or fair, that they refuse to acknowledge failure, errors or mistakes. When things go right it is because of their efforts; when things go wrong, it is someone else's fault. This is a classic attribution error and leads to problems with truth telling because they always rationalize and reinterpret their failures and mistakes, usually by blaming them on others. It is difficult to know if a narcissist is dishonest, because they tend to believe their own hype.

Narcissists can be energetic, charismatic, leader-like, and willing to take the initiative to get projects moving. They can be relatively successful in management, sales and entrepreneurship, but usually only for short periods. However, they are arrogant, vain, overbearing, demanding, self-deceived and pompous – yet they are so colourful and engaging that they often attract followers. Their self-confidence is attractive. Naively, people believe that their confidence must be grounded in ability.

Narcissists handle stress and heavy workloads badly but can appear to do it effortlessly. They use their energy to look composed instead of doing the work. They delegate, assign and omit tasks. They beg, bully, plead and manipulate others into getting their work done. Their colleagues often find that doing their work for them is less stressful than facing the narcissist's emotional volatility. They are also quite persistent under pressure and they refuse to acknowledge failure. As a result of their inability to acknowledge failure or even mistakes, and the way they resist coaching and ignore negative feedback, they are unable to learn from experience. In a popular book Miller (2008) describes narcissistic bosses and employers as 'preeners'. For bosses, he suggests documenting your credentials, being realistic about what you can be proud of and to treat all employees with respect. He suggests to the potentially narcissistic employee to take an honest self-inventory (to gain insight); to emulate the successful and to present your ideas appropriately.

Yet narcissists can be a challenging beast to tame. They tend to be well-connected and charming. They know many people, but few people know them well enough to detect the true level of their self-interest. They move between jobs, companies and relationships quickly, making new friends and alliances, abandoning those who are no longer loyal supporters. They crave attention, and revel in conflict as much as praise. Try to fire or demote a narcissist and they will fight back with every tool at their disposal. Even the most severe consequences provide them with the opportunity to cast themselves as a martyr.

Some bosses find it easier to sideline their more narcissistic employees, remove them from situations where they can cause the most damage and hope they quit in search of greater glory somewhere else.

Narcissism is the need for recognition taken to obscene and unrealistic levels. But modest, realistic and fair levels of recognition are a healthy and effective motivator at work.

Recognition and recognition programmes

Recognition is important at work. Those who want to be recognized for a job well done are not necessarily raging narcissists, they just want to know their work is appreciated. Rewards of recognition at work are a very important but rather tricky business. Most employers want intrinsically motivated people who don't need too much extrinsic reward: read money. Hiring passion and independence is good, but surely there must be an easy way to hire the best without paying the most? But there is an easy way to describe someone who is intrinsically motivated, independent, intelligent and who doesn't need the company's money or recognition: leaving.

Often cynical employers will create fatuous recognition programmes. It is not unusual to find a billboard with lines of disillusioned faces labelled as 'Employee of the Month'. Supposedly this is the best employee in the company for that particular month. This may be encouraging for staff and customers, but the expressions worn by that 'Employee of the Month' often tell a far more discouraging story.

The idea is that the Employee of the Month programmes give well-deserved credit to the best-performing individuals, boosting morale through symbolic rewards and motivating excellence by providing positive examples for all other employees to emulate. But there are two important considerations. An important consideration brings up a host of questions about how that person was selected. Who nominates the employee of the month: peers, ie other serving staff; customers of the service; and/or supervisors and managers? Who is eligible? Who is considered? Based on what? A one-off encounter over a meal; a week-long interaction as a room steward, or what? A manager's hunch?

The effectiveness of recognition programmes is influenced mostly by five factors, but without the sixth factor it is doomed to failure (Furnham, 2012):

1 **Criteria.** The first issue is how one goes about becoming Employee of the Month. Particularly if it is accompanied by a large financial reward, some might use unsavoury or even illegal methods to get what they want. They might flatter and manipulate the decision maker, fake comment cards, bully or sabotage their competing colleagues. If these behaviours are tolerated, ignored or encouraged, recognition programmes can be a source of performance problems instead of an improvement. The criteria must be carefully considered and clearly communicated in order to promote good behaviour.

2 **Eligibility.** Often in the service industry, the division of labour limits recognition and creates a front-of-house/back-of-house problem. A tip in a restaurant is largely based on the performance of the server, while the invisible workers who prepared the meal can be forgotten. How would the laundry service manager of a hotel ever receive a commendation on a customer comment card? Limiting eligibility implicitly or explicitly can lead some departments to feel unappreciated and demotivated. Any employment recognition programmes must ensure those eligible have a realistic chance to qualify, based on criteria that are relevant to their job.

3 **Evaluation criteria.** A third problem is that the behavioural criteria are often unclear. If there are no clear requirements or evaluation criteria to receive recognition, it tends to become a popularity contest. A few of the most charming employees compete to win the evaluator's favour, and everyone else steers well clear of it. The cynical but ambitious worker may target particular customers likely to be docile, undemanding and happy to recommend them when the vote is made.

4 **Exclusivity.** An 'Employee of the Month' system can only have one winner. Of course, a system where *every* employee was recognized as 'Employee of the Month' would be equally fatuous. If the vast majority of employees are excluded, it can be a demotivating force. The vast majority of people do not get rewarded despite there being an almost

indistinguishable difference between their performance. Thus talented, hard-working, dedicated individuals may never be rewarded because there is always someone slightly better. This can lead to resentment, and some will decide it is easier to sabotage the top performer than to improve one's own performance.

5 **The Reigning Champion.** If the Employee of the Month programme is truly based on performance, it is likely that the same person will win most or all of the time. The top performer will probably be the top performer almost every month. And they already have the spotlight to showcase themselves as the top performer. In this situation, why not just make the company president Employee of the Month, every month?

6 **Sincerity.** It is not difficult to spot when recognition programmes are not sincere. Maybe the Employee of the Month board is mounted in the least desirable, poorly lit area of the office, just behind a plastic shrubbery. Perhaps the winner each month receives a formulaic e-mail from hr@company.com. Or the lactose-intolerant Employee of the Month is presented with a cheesecake in appreciation. Most people are quick to realize insincere thanks. Any recognition programme needs to represent genuine appreciation.

False appreciation is often more demotivating than nothing at all. Few things can inspire rage or disillusionment like the fiftieth time the mechanical voice says 'Thank you for waiting, your call is important to us' after an hour on hold. A quick e-mail response of 'Thanks, Pat, we really appreciate everything you do for this team' loses its lustre if the recipient's name is Matt.

Recognition for outcomes versus people

In the previous chapter we mentioned how failing to recognize and reward good ideas limits their spread. Whereas rewarding good ideas or outcomes promotes others in the organization to adopt those ideas or outcomes, ignoring them does not.

One of the most critical camps within the camp of generational differences doomsayers are those critical of ubiquitous rewards. They criticize the 'Everyone Gets a Trophy' culture, like Zadrozny's (2014) article titled 'My loser kid should get a trophy', which goes on to say, 'It's killed competition and produced a generation of young adults who can't get into college or even apply for a job without help from mum. If this madness isn't stopped, the children who win trophies for diddly today will be the leaders who capitulate to China (or Russia, or wherever) tomorrow.' However, she does go on to say that most participatory awards are given to young children or to reinforce other behaviours like 'sportsmanship, teamwork, losing with grace, and finding joy in an endeavour, even when you know you won't be the best. Leaving with a symbol of those things can't be so bad' (Zadrozny, 2014). Others offer constructive advice, 'We should teach kids to work for their rewards in life, because showing up is not enough to earn praise' (Jones, 2015). Some are concerned that the younger generations are rewarded for everything, even doing nothing. At competitive events, for example, every-one gets a 'participation' ribbon irrespective of their performance. The fear is that this creates an entitled generation who need constant praise and have no idea how to deal with failure.

Although generational prophets often take an alarmist tone, they do raise a valid point. Especially in the workplace, praise and recognition should be linked to performance, achievement and outcomes. Merryman (2013) explains this concisely, 'When children make mistakes, our job should not be to spin those losses into decorated victories. Instead, our job is to help kids overcome setbacks, to help them see that progress over time is more important than a particular win or loss, and to help them graciously congratulate the child who succeeded when they failed.' The same idea can be applied to employees. Company newsletters should avoid saying, 'this month we thought it was really nice to have Joe, Martha and Mahmoud in the company', in favour of identifying specific individuals or teams, their specific achievements, why they succeeded and the precise outcome of their work.

Consider the following five points for recognition:

- **Performance.** When possible, recognition should link the person (or team) to a specific behaviour or outcome. This offers the opportunity to elaborate on what was good, what was done well and what the desirable outcome was.

- **Individual development.** Recognition should align with individual goals, achievements and capacity. Don't recognize someone and lavishly praise them for their efforts if its a routine task they find boring, simple and unrewarding. Figure out what they have had difficulty with, what challenge they have overcome, or what their newest area of achievement is. Similarly, even lower performers or those with temporary performance issues deserve recognition when they improve or do something well. As we mentioned with mental illness in Chapter 4, about half of workers will struggle with mental illness at some point in their working life. For some people, just getting out of bed and getting to work in the morning is incredibly difficult and a huge achievement. Similarly, those with performance issues can be the most easily discouraged, focusing on what they are doing wrong is more likely than not to make their performance worse. Focus on what they are doing well, what they can do to improve.

- **Social context.** Recognition should be appropriate to the setting and the social context. If someone has been struggling with mental health issues, the company newsletter or blog is probably not the right place to announce and applaud their efforts. A quiet, private few words may be much more appropriate. Recognition of new and effective methods can be far more suited for public recognition.

- **Proper dissemination.** Is it better to recognize someone in person, in an e-mail, on the company newsletter, on the Employee of the Month wall, or in some other way? It depends what it is, and on the four other factors in this list. Take the example of a closely connected, small team who know each other well and communicate (internally) informally and conversationally. The team regularly recognizes each other by sending animated gifs, as reactions, in e-mail (we discussed animated gifs in Chapter 6). These might indicate surprise, excitement, being impressed or awed. They are often over-the-top silly images, extreme characterizations of emotions that are sent to be surprising and funny. This is appropriate within the group and is extremely effective because a brief note is strongly emphasized with humour and a private joke known only to the group. Of course, this example would not be appropriate for many workplaces and not necessarily for public dissemination.

- **Know the audience.** In organizational silos where departments work in isolation, team, departmental or personal rivalries should be considered. The audience should be receptive to the information (and in some cases, the audience is just the person being recognized). Recognizing one sort of achievement can increase resentment in others if favouritism is shown or recognition comes at the expense of another individual or group.

Motivating for quality versus quantity

As has been discussed throughout the previous chapters, extrinsic and intrinsic motivation are not mutually exclusive, nor is one more important than the other. Take a happy, motivated, high-performing employee who is very intrinsically motivated and tell them they love their job so much they are not going to get paid. Then tell them extrinsic rewards are less important than their love of the job. Their motivation will be swiftly directed towards the nearest exit.

The relationship is not always simple, but often the difference between intrinsic and extrinsic motivation can be attributed to the *quality* and *quantity* outcomes. In a 2014 meta-analysis of research across 40 years and including 183 different studies of over 200,000 participants Cerasoli, Nicklin and Ford (2014) confirmed that extrinsic motivation was most strongly related to quantity outcomes, while intrinsic motivation was more closely related to the quality of work produced.

We will revisit the example of the logistics worker who is paid a performance bonus based on the number of items that they ship out each day. If they exceed the requirement, their base salary is increased. Ship 120 per cent more items than the performance goal and receive 20 per cent more pay. The real challenge is that quantity is a straightforward way to measure performance and align with extrinsic rewards, but increasing quantity often leads to compromising quality. Reward call-centre employees for handling more complaints and completing the call becomes a greater priority than resolving the complaint.

This is a common model of compensation for performance, but it comes at an immediate cost when quantity is the only priority. What about errors? If 20 per cent more items are shipped out, but those additional 20 per cent are incorrect items, this is hardly an improvement in performance.

In the case of error rates in shipping, there is a clear way to account for human error in the performance management framework, and integrate it into the compensation framework. The employee gets a performance bonus based on the amount of items shipped ahead of performance goals, but to qualify for the bonuses, an accuracy rate must also be achieved.

This is one of the greatest challenges and opportunities for performance management: get motivation right and it is possible to improve quantity without sacrificing quality. Consider sales jobs that offer a commission as reward for each item (or service) sold. The salesperson receives, for example, 5 per cent of the profit as a bonus for their contribution. Individual profits are aligned with company profits. But what of quality? Does the salesperson have any interest in the suitability of the product for the customer? Or will they say anything to make their commission?

Enter intrinsic motivation. A salesperson who is not intrinsically motivated and gets no pleasure from their work is unlikely to have much interest in the end result. Why would an employee spend the time, energy and effort improving the quality of their work if they see no value in the product or service? In contrast, those who are motivated to make money and are also intrinsically motivated tend to have a different approach. A salesperson whose job and compensation framework covered all of these factors would be more likely to provide quality as well as quantity in their work.

In Chapter 7 we emphasized that intrinsic motivation involves *challenging work, recognition for one's achievement, being given responsibility, opportunity to do something meaningful, involvement in decision making,* and *a sense of importance to an organization.*

Intrinsic motivation imbues a sense of satisfaction and achievement from the nature and process of the work. The majority of people derive satisfaction from actions that have a positive impact on other people. Insurance brokers might report genuine satisfaction with helping their small-business client to get the best coverage for their situation. Many accountants will say that the pay, security and conditions of their job are important. But most report great satisfaction in their pro-bono work, helping lower-income clients to keep a bit more of their much-needed income. Seeing one's work have a positive impact can be incredibly motivating. Without any sense of purpose or personal involvement in the work, employees tend to maximize rewards with less regard for the consequences. Of course, motivation is not always selfless and valorous. In Chapter 13 we discuss what happens when motivation turns destructive.

Conclusion

There are two key messages to take from this chapter. The first is simple. Rewards are important. Second, rewards have the greatest effect when they are direct outcomes of desired behaviours or outcomes. In other words, reward good behaviour. Almost any behaviour can be encouraged with a sufficiently large reward. But, take away the reward and the behaviour is also likely to disappear.

Consider a variation of a common story told in psychology to explain intrinsic and extrinsic motivation. An employee has a habit of sending long e-mails to clients. These e-mails are not always necessary, but are often a method of procrastination combined with a way to 'look busy'. Their manager cannot convince the employee to stop, so decides instead to add 'communications' to their list of responsibilities, and include a performance bonus. Every e-mail to a client adds £1 to their pay cheque. Imagine this having two effects: first, because the performance bonus is paid by e-mail occurrence, not length, it promotes the quantity of e-mails while encouraging e-mails to be a shorter length. Second, because it is an added job responsibility instead of a method of procrastination, it becomes a task, and adding financial reward that is being conducted for the extrinsic motivation.

But what happens, later, if the financial compensation is taken away? A month later, take away the compensation, and a sense of dissatisfaction and unwillingness to do the task emerges. This illustrates how extrinsic rewards often can have obvious and straightforward effects, yet the longer-term implications and individual context can cause variation and complexity.

Chapter 10 explores motivators and culture at a company-wide level, building on individual differences in motivation. While most of the previous chapters have discussed how an individual's characteristics, especially their motivation, affects outcomes, the next chapter explores the effects that an organization's culture can have on motivation.

References

American Psychological Association [APA] (2013) *Diagnostic and Statistical Manual of Mental Disorders*, 5th edn, APA, Washington, DC

Argyle, M and Furnham, A (1998) *The Psychology of Money*, Routledge, Abingdon

Cerasoli, CP, Nicklin, JM and Ford, MT (2014) Intrinsic motivation and extrinsic incentives jointly predict performance: a 40-year meta-analysis, *Psychological Bulletin*, **140** (4)

Chen, MK, Lakshminarayanan, V and Santos, LR (2006) How basic are behavioral biases? Evidence from capuchin monkey trading behavior, *Journal of Political Economy*, **114** (3), pp 517–37

Darling, N (2011) [accessed 10 October 2016] Don't Kick that Pigeon! What Psychology Owes to the Dove, *Psychology Today* [Online] https://www.psychologytoday.com/blog/thinking-about-kids/201105/dont-kick-pigeon-what-psychology-owes-the-dove

Dubner, SJ and Levitt, SD (2005) Monkey business, *New York Times*, 5 June

Ferster, CB and Skinner, BF (1957) *Schedules of Reinforcement*, BF Skinner Foundation, Cambridge, MA

Furnham, A (2012) *The Talented Manager: 67 gems of business wisdom*, Palgrave Macmillan, Basingstoke

Jones, R (2015) Listen kids, not everyone is a winner, *CNN*, 18 August

Karimi, R and Alipour, F (2011) Reduce job stress in organizations: role of locus of control, *International Journal of Business and Social Science*, **2** (18), pp 232–36

Lakshminarayanan, VR, Chen, MK and Santos, LR (2011) The evolution of decision-making under risk: framing effects in monkey risk preferences, *Journal of Experimental Social Psychology*, **47**, pp 689–93

Lewis, AH (1908) Owners of America, *Cosmopolitan*, November

Magee, JC and Langer, CA (2008) How personalized and socialized power motivation facilitate antisocial and prosocial decision-making, *Journal of Research in Personality*, **42** (6), pp 1547–59

McClelland, DC (1970) The two faces of power, *Journal of International Affairs*, **24**, pp 29–47

Merryman, A (2013) Losing is good for you, *The New York Times*, 24 September

Miller, L (2008) *From Difficult to Disturbed: Understanding and managing the dysfunctional employee*, Amacom, New York

Spector, PE, Cooper, CL, Sanchez, JI, O'Driscoll, M and Sparks, K (2002) Locus of control and well-being at work: how generalizable are Western findings? *Academy of Management Journal*, **45** (2), pp 453–66

Writer, D (2005) Things I've learned about personality from studying political leaders at a distance, *Journal of Personality*, **73** (3), pp 557–82

Zadrozny, B (2014) My loser kid should get a trophy, *The Daily Beast*, 22 August

Culture and values

10

Introduction

The importance of financial and job security should not be underestimated. The importance of security is not equally important for everyone. Some prefer to ignore the importance of extrinsic motivators in favour of promoting motivation based on personal growth, development, opportunities or success. Graduates consistently rate 'personal growth' as their most important priority while career stability is rated consistently near the bottom of the list, alongside being seen with the wrong generation of an iPhone. Financial security, perks and a good company insurance plan are not the factors that most people wake up in the morning excited about. But they are still an important part of motivation in the workplace.

While intrinsic motivators can improve levels of optimal performance, extrinsic motivators can bring up the lower levels of performance. This chapter discusses the importance of job security, and the relationship with job demands in two case studies. It connects the concepts of organizational culture with individual motivation and values. Then we discuss an example of measuring values and motivation in a group, and conclude the chapter with succession planning. First, let's look at security in the context of culture change.

On culture and culture change

The concept of 'culture change' is a bit of an odd one. Nearly every company wants to change for the better, and everyone who has bothered to look realizes the times they are a-changing, as they always have been. It is trite but true to point out that the only consistent feature of business is that everything changes, always. But whether it is deliberate or unintentional change, whether it is managed well or poorly, can have a huge impact on profits and performance.

While many things can change, we also know from a great deal of psychological research that group or organizational cultures are surprisingly resistant to change. This is true not just of humans, but even groups of monkeys develop their own group culture. A study by Sapolsky (2004) describes how groups of monkeys have remarkably similar and enduring cultures. This can be observed by levels of aggression in the group. While some groups are highly aggressive, others are more cooperative and docile. These are enduring cultural attributes because in the wild the groups are dynamic, with members constantly changing. Much like the workplace, individuals change regularly and move between groups. The interesting finding is that aggressive and non-aggressive cultures are extremely persistent in the groups. Aggressive group cultures remain aggressive, even when no original members of the group remain (de Waal, 2004).

There are various explanations proposed for why group culture persists. One is that individuals self-select the group that fits their own attributes – aggressive monkeys choose to live in aggressive groups. Another is that the social context, the culture, of the group brings out or encourages behaviour in the individual. Social and personality psychologists love to argue these points, whether the environment influences the individual or the individual influences the environment. Both are correct. The most pertinent finding from Sapolsky (2004) was that culture does change in exceptional circumstances, using an example that sounds like a story created by the collective efforts of Margaret Atwood, Germaine Greer and David Attenborough. An outbreak of tuberculosis swept through a group of baboons. This particular strain of the disease hit hardest amongst the strongest in the group. The disease killed all of the largest, most aggressive, most autocratic and controlling males. Those killed off were aggressive enough to fight with neighbouring tribes over the rubbish from a nearby tourist camp and this had exposed them to beef riddled with bovine tuberculosis, which led to their demise.

Thus, Sapolsky (2004) reports how the rapid demise of all the most aggressive in the group led to the rapid emergence of a more warm and friendly culture, a relaxation of the previously strict baboon hierarchy. The group was much less likely to fight and bite. And they showed many more grooming behaviours that are considered prosocial and friendly among baboons, but antisocial for humans on public transport (context is important). This peaceful culture endured for decades afterwards, as the initial shock and rapid change became stable. Physiological tests from the baboons also showed that the lower-ranking baboons (who would be bullied in more aggressive groups) showed much lower levels of the stress hormone cortisol.

It is not too difficult to see how this example can parallel culture at work. It is not stealing tainted beef that destroyed Enron, but it is the same problem of a destructive culture eventually killing off its architects, as will be discussed in Chapter 14.

Leaving the obvious management jokes aside, what do baboons tell us about corporate culture? Anyone who has recently changed jobs will realize that different workplaces have different cultures. Many people wish their company culture would change, but leaving aside the fads, what can actually be changed and how can it actually be done? (We should be clear: the previous example is not meant to encourage serving tainted steaks at a board meeting.)

Consultants love to discuss corporate culture, because it is so clear to an outsider. Spend some time in the reception area, with the front-line staff, in the boardroom and in the break room and you will quickly get a sense of the culture within an organization. It can be much more difficult to see the culture when you are part of it, because spending any length of time in a group makes all of its behaviours, requirements and peculiarities seem 'normal'. That is because culture is the unspoken rules about 'the way things are done around here'.

There are different ways in which organizations can try to change their culture and seven classic ones are:

- **The friendly strategy.** This is rooted in interpersonal relationships and in-person sessions to change and discuss the processes. It is a warm and fuzzy approach that makes sure everyone is involved, heard and listened to. It is intended to create a feeling of 'we're all in this together'. If this strategy is used effectively with a clear message and direction it can be very powerful. If this approach, and those employing it, are averse to conflict and action it can waste time and ignore important issues.

- **The political strategy.** This strategy is a more Machiavellian approach to finding the key influencers, power brokers and informal leaders within the company. It is about winning the allegiance of a few key unofficial leaders who are liked and respected and can shape the opinions of those around them, and consequently the culture around them. The political strategists might convince, persuade, coerce, bribe, flatter or bully those key personnel. When it is done constructively and openly it can be effective. But when it is done covertly with shady tactics it can destabilize the organization and destroy the credibility and influence of those involved.

- **The economic strategy.** Money can be a powerful persuasion tool, and the more cynical might try to use economic motivators to change culture. If you are showing up to earn a pay cheque every day, we have already established what you are, now we're just haggling about price. As we have discussed extensively in previous chapters, money and rewards can change behaviour, but it often has unintended consequences. This strategy can be useful when it complements other initiatives but is often a costly, short-term gimmick that can seem coarse.

- **The academic strategy.** Some academics and professors assume that if you present people with enough information, they will come to the right conclusion on their own. The academic strategy involves presenting much data, commissioning studies and reports and may involve hiring experts and expensive consultants. While data and findings can be useful when they are presented palatably and are relevant to the company, they will not change anything in isolation. Overanalysis can often be symptomatic of inactive and cerebral cultures that avoid the problems at hand.

- **The technical strategy.** Technicians prefer to take a systematic and no-nonsense approach to change, fixing a company in the same mechanical way as fixing an engine. Find the problems, and fix or replace the structural components of the job like working environments, tools, resources and technology. Technical changes can be tactically helpful when they make minor improvements, but technocratic approaches can miss complexity, and create solutions that are worse than the problem.

- **The military strategy.** The military along with the police have their monopoly on using brute force, which many autocratic leaders envy. The emphasis is on finding the right weapon to address the problem. Physical force, agility and superiority are the means of making change. Any change requires a degree of forcefulness, determination and action. Yet, heavy-handed enforcers meet resistance, and change does not persist beyond their tenure.

- **The slacktivist strategy.** This is favoured by those who like a small dose of moral outrage with their morning coffee but want other people to fix the world's problems. Slacktivist approaches involve disseminating inspiring messages, rallying everyone to the chant of 'someone else needs to do something about this'. It can be helpful for identifying a problem, but identifying a problem is a very large and yawning chasm away from finding and implementing a solution. Raising anger or discontent without an effective behaviour to channel that emotion can polarize people and create a backlash. Creating a culture of outrage and dependency is an environment where destructive leaders thrive (see Chapter 13).

The seven examples each have their strengths and weaknesses, but it takes a knowledgeable and savvy leader to take the right amount from each strategy and develop a combined approach that actually works. Just enough camaraderie to make people receptive. Finding the right allies to get things done without being manipulative. Just the right amount of financial incentive to encourage the right behaviour. Informed decision making, based on evidence and a sound understanding. Tactical changes that complement the big-picture ideas. Just enough tenacity to make the change happen. And an inspiring message with an inspiring call to action.

It is probably easier to coax, bully or bribe behaviour change than it is to create lasting culture change. Behaviour can change, even when values do not, and that gap is where many problems arise, which is the topic of Chapter 11. But first, we look at two case studies of values in a particular type of work.

The following case studies are deliberately from two different people, representing different generations but with very similar values profiles. While reading these examples, consider the usefulness of comparing their profiles numerically as well as the value of understanding context and individual explanations of *why* they value particular things in the workplace.

Two case studies

The following two case studies show two very different people, from different generations, with almost identical motivating forces. The similarity, and their career path, are closely aligned with their values. Both are in teaching. Both report wanting job safety and security, along with stressing the importance of working conditions. Neither is very motivated by money (except having a liveable level of income, pension, and sufficient benefits; perks and bonuses are not rated as important). Interestingly, need for recognition is extremely low. Both individuals reported next to no desire to be recognized for their work.

These case studies are an excellent example of the findings by Moore, Grunberg and Krause (2015) that differences in values are much more pronounced between types of work and employment sectors than generations. That is, certain workplaces align well with specific values.

CASE STUDY 1 Cherie Mandoli

This first example directly contradicts generational stereotypes. Personal ambition, recognition and supportive management are not factors that Cherie even thinks about at work. She is a 28-year-old living in Canada who reports absolutely no need for recognition, fame, fortune or status. She has been working for two years, after completing a Bachelor's degree and Master's degree in education. She always worked part-time through secondary and post-secondary education. She has always been active in charitable and community organizations.

Her main focus, at the early stages of her career, is obtaining job security (see Figure 10.1). She works in a unionized environment with great perks and benefits for those within the union, but that comes with many barriers to joining the union and receiving the benefits. In discussion with Cherie, we discussed the union rules at length, which will be omitted because they are far more confusing and complex than any other subject covered in this book. She says all she wants to do is have regular, secure work. She wants to do her best, and have a job and career that will last a lifetime. To get into the union means many years with insecure, unpredictable amounts of work. She knows the system, the initial barriers that she is willing to overcome, and the benefits that will come with getting into the union.

As a teacher on call (supply teacher), she can work for weeks or months at a time, but may go for weeks or months with limited work. She does not see those

Figure 10.1 Motivators profile of Cherie Mandoli

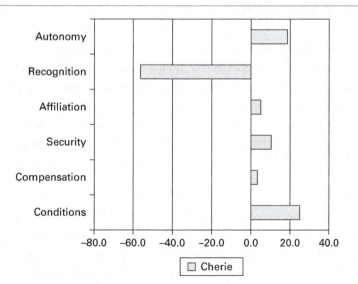

days off as a luxury because she wants to be working full time, and to be earning a self-sufficient income. That, however, is not a deterrent for Cherie. She knows what she wants to do, and she is determined to work in a job she loves. She is good at her work, she works hard and goes above and beyond what the job requires. She is more than willing to jump through the bureaucratic and administrative hoops to secure a lifelong teaching position.

She also reports a number of challenges in teaching, and in a newer generation of teaching. There are many complaints from students and parents, while teachers are under an increasing amount of scrutiny with very restricted ability to discipline students. She is undeterred by this, and shrugs it off by saying 'my only bad days are other people's bad days', meaning that angry or gloomy parents or students can be stressful. But she still loves the job.

This runs contrary to the typical stereotypes about younger generations who want quick promotions, recognition and development opportunities. Every aspect of the interview reinforces that this stereotype does not describe Cherie. Her motivators test results show that her recognition motivation is exceptionally low. Asking about her personal ambitions smoothly becomes a discussion about improving her students' education. Discussing her personal motivations begins with the need for job security and quickly moves into a discussion about how she motivates others. Towards the end of the interview I realize that talking about herself, her own motivations and what she wants from the job does not come naturally. For every question she talks about what she can put into the work, and what she would like others to get out of it.

A further challenge in this workplace is that her work requires a great deal of time spent compiling detailed records, making sure everything is clearly documented and always being cautious about social interactions. There is a great deal of scrutiny from many parents, as well as others, and she says she records times and dates and content of key conversations. She keeps daily records of attendance, and any action she took to follow up about the attendance (eg phone logs). She keeps student progress logs to monitor the performance of all students, particularly when there is a performance issue. She says, undeterred, that one mistake can be career-ending. Or one undocumented conversation behind closed doors, which appears to an external observer to be indecorous, and the consequences are extremely severe. She says she is even mindful to be cautious about closing a door or a window when talking individually with a student. She records precise times and locations of every individual conversation.

This is a great responsibility, and a time-consuming administrative and organizational burden. Many people, of any age, would balk at the responsibility and administrative burden. But Cherie, like many teachers, takes it on as part of the job. She focuses on the advantages: comprehensive records help her to keep track of progress and how to deal with performance issues, what has worked and what could be done better. She is doing her best, and she has found a way to make a difficult part of the job another strength.

In return she doesn't ask for an exceptionally high salary, bonuses or any formal recognition for her work. She is happy to spend time paying her dues, jumping through union hoops if necessary, along with investing in seven years of post-secondary education. She is resilient to the years of insecure and unpredictable hours and income for the first years it takes to get started.

In her day-to-day work Cherie is constantly dealing with performance issues. She says she has to learn how to work effectively with many different types of people. These are not employees based on selection criteria, her students are a cross-section of all children in the community. Any manager will see the parallels when she says the majority of her time is spent on a very small minority who have severe performance issues. But in some of the more difficult schools it is not uncommon for students to tell her, 'I didn't do it because I didn't care'.

There are two excellent lessons from Cherie's experience that apply to performance management:

- **Good documentation.** Consistently, well-documented performance reviews, particularly, are essential for good performance management systems. In Cherie's case, her student might say something like, 'You never told me I had to hand that in'. In a workplace, the same infantile excuses are given in different words. Someone 'didn't get the e-mail' for the third time. Or they 'weren't told about the deadline', or some similar excuse. Good documentation negates these excuses. Selecting high potential too, means identifying precisely what kind of potential one is looking for.

- **Constructive performance discussions.** School children can be overly sensitive, and as Cherie says, the age group she teaches is at a very important age for development. She watches her students go from being children to being young adults in a very short period of time. This means performance issues have to be addressed cautiously and constructively. Many people can remember a single experience of a teacher saying they were bad at maths or art, which has stuck with them for years or decades, and affected subsequent educational and career choices. That is not to say that confidence should be instilled where the talent is lacking (this also leads to problems and likely failure). Cherie says questions should be framed by asking what they were doing, and then asking what they were *supposed* to be doing. Lead them in the right direction, but emphasize that they *know* what they should be doing. Ask them why they haven't done their task and what they were supposed to do. Then ask what help they need to get it done. Guide them in the right direction, make it clear there is support, but reinforce they have the capacity to do it. The same guidelines are true when working with people of any age.

CASE STUDY 2 Michael Orwick

The second example is Michael Orwick, a professor at a Canadian college's business school. He is 59 years old from Western Canada and began teaching 18 years ago in 1998. He started teaching for a local chamber of commerce and found that he had a great deal of experience and knowledge that he could pass on, and he enjoyed working with others to see how 'stuff works'. He has been working as a college professor for nine years.

Mike's passion for teaching lies in finding new ways to help people learn, and to show how textbook examples look in the real world (see Figure 10.2). His experience and understanding from business provides him with the opportunity

Figure 10.2   Motivators profile of Mike Orwick

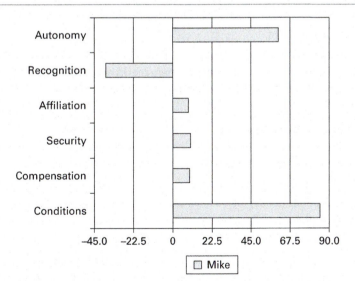

and the pleasure of combining real-world examples from his own experience to help others learn.

Similar to the previous example, he says bureaucracy, paperwork and a slower-moving organizational culture is one of the larger burdens in his work. Marking, in particular, is a slow, repetitive process that takes a large amount of time. Teachers who are passionate about their job often spend even more time marking in an effort to provide feedback and track performance. Repetitive and time-consuming tasks like marking can be a particular challenge for those who love their job and want to do it well. They are likely to put more time into these tasks, taking time away from other activities. Yet spending the extra time helps to track progress and ability, and informs other endeavours. The same is true of any performance management system. Taking the extra time to get it right is worthwhile.

Mike's autonomy score is high, and he says that although the organization is bureaucratic, he loves the freedom and autonomy he has in the classroom. He comes from a creative background, formerly working in radio broadcasting, so he is an excellent communicator and loves to find new and interesting ways to present information. Opportunities to be creative inspire and drive him and his work. He says he has always been creative, and wanted that autonomy in his work to be creative.

Another limitation on the creativity of his teaching is the common learning outcomes and common exams between classes. Mike makes an interesting point in relation to this, suggesting that the common learning outcomes are not a problem, but common exams are more limiting. Everyone should be learning the same thing, but standard tests limit the ways he can teach and test what his students have learned.

For example, instead of a standard multiple choice test Mike might ask a student True/False + Why questions, where marks are given not based on whether the True or False answer is correct, but on a 40-word justification of the answer. 'This replaces short answer questions (and the writing that goes with it), reduces the guessing, and best of all eliminates the student who just "writes the text back at you." Many of those students just write and write, hoping something will count for marks. The TF&W means they have to address the question directly.' Performance reviews could take a similar approach. Ask employees to rate their performance, then ask *why*. Top marks are given for those who can succinctly explain.

Our discussion of recognition was interesting because he said that unlike his need for autonomy, his need for recognition has changed substantially over the course of his career. Earlier in his career he said, 'I used to crave recognition because I worked against the odds most of my life and I always did very well.' He said that this also led to a degree of selfishness and arrogance, and he did work in a broadcasting career, which gave him a fair degree of publicity. In that job, self-promotion and need for recognition were probably assets. However, his need for recognition is now very low, much like Cherie. Mike says he thinks this was a gradual change in needing less recognition: 'I found the more I needed recognition, the more people withheld it.'

His answers also show a remarkable similarity to Cherie's in that success is consistently described in the results for other people. He says the greatest sense of satisfaction comes from seeing other people learn, seeing his students understand the concepts, and that the creativity and effort he puts into his work helps others.

One of his other, interesting points about recognition, was that he thought one of the consequences of teachers not getting recognized for their achievements is that this can slow progress. When good ideas are not recognized they are less likely to be more widely adopted. Interesting again that the discussion of recognition is sublimated into the greater good in this individual profile and type of work. But it also raises an interesting point about recognition in the workplace. Recognizing achievements and best practice can promote their spreading throughout the company.

Generational differences

Revisiting the discussion of generational differences, these two case studies illustrate how two people of different generations can be remarkably similar (see Figure 10.3). Although in these examples, Mike has higher autonomy and conditions scores, and Cherie has even lower recognition scores, consider the relative importance instead of the absolute numbers. Security and compensation are moderately important for both – but are still at a level where a minimum level is needed.

Conditions were rated as one of the most important factors by both, but greater discussion revealed the reason. They absolutely value clean, safe, secure, physically comfortable working conditions. This is not why they do the job, it is not what motivates, engages and excites them on a day-to-day basis. But they need a basic level of working conditions to do their job effectively. Their level of need for job conditions can be thought of as a potential demotivator, instead of a motivating tool. If the roof was crumbling they would probably both still love teaching people, but it would create some dissatisfaction.

Figure 10.3   Comparison of motivation profiles for Cherie and Mike

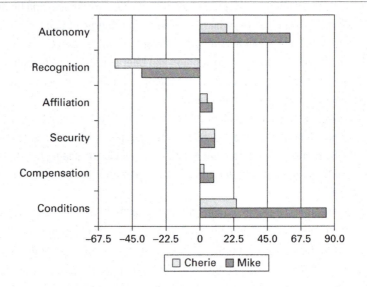

Recognition is by far the lowest score for both, and neither crave attention or praise for the work they do. This aligns with their work, as their achievement is channelled into the success of others, and they do not need to be recognized for their achievements. That is not to say they don't value the recognition when it is offered. As Mike said, 'the unsolicited thanks and recognition from students' mean more to him personally.

Linking organizational, team and individual values

As discussed in the example of teaching, motivation and values tend to differ in different occupations. So too can there be differences between departments, or teams, and within groups.

The previous case studies show that values can greatly influence career choices, and different types of motivations align better with different jobs. Moore, Grunberg and Krause (2015) confirmed this finding, and found that values differences were far more pronounced between employment sectors than between generations.

So how can we use the motivational test with groups? Table 10.1 shows a few simple ways, and in the final section of this chapter we provide an example of using it for succession planning with a group.

Table 10.1   Measuring individual, team and organizational motivation

	Averages	**Variance**
Individual	How are individual scores different from the team or organization average?	How wide is the variance between people?
Team	How do team averages compare with the organizational average?	How widely do the teams vary?
Organization	Is the organizational average different from the population average?	What is the average variance across the organization?

Asking the questions in Table 10.1 leads to an analysis of how common or universal the values are within teams or at the organization. Are there individual outliers? Are there particular teams that are different? Does the company have a culture of varying motivation, or are most/all motivated by the same thing, working for the same reasons? Do these differences work with or against the different roles and responsibilities and the type of work?

There are different applications of these measures, and succession planning is an excellent application – the final section in this chapter provides a real-world example of the motivational test used within an organization's succession plan.

Succession planning

As implied but not endorsed earlier in this chapter, what would happen if the leadership team was suddenly poisoned? Would the share price rise or fall? Would employees mourn or celebrate? Who is poised to take over – and do they have a training in pharmaceuticals and/or sabotage?

Most organizations say that they think about succession planning, but many do little or nothing about it. It is a relatively simple concept. Who will take on future job openings? This is not just an issue of skills and abilities, but who has the capacity and potential to successfully take over different positions. A good succession plan covers how future potential will be developed in-house. Lazy succession planning relies on recruiters or chance to hope someone outside the company can be found to plug a talent gap.

The rationale is to avoid unnecessary difficulties and to solve HR difficulties before they become a problem. Plan for succession and make sure that roles, departments and jobs can be seamlessly filled by new employees. This minimizes disruption, and hopefully keeps performance at optimal levels.

Some organizations speak disingenuously or behind veils about careers. The lifetime career is a thing of the past. Lifetime employees are sad or unambitious. Employees alone are responsible for their career future. Yet, the lucky are included in the succession plan. This plan sends messages about the anointed and the chosen to the whole organization. The individuals recognized as 'high potentials' or the 'future leaders' set an example of optimal behaviour and performance in the company.

One underhanded trick is to try to keep the succession plan secret. But this often backfires because things always get out. Once word gets out that there is a plan, then however vague and/or lacking in detail, the rumours spread and can be more damaging than revealing the actual plan.

Another problem with succession plans is the same challenge faced by strategic planners. The plan can go out of date rather quickly, but it is extraordinarily difficult to predict when its usefulness will expire. Factors within and without the organization can change. A 10-year succession plan is no good if the company has a 90 per cent annual employee turnover. Or, a 10-year succession plan where 10 per cent of the promotional opportunities that are spoken for can be the cause of 90 per cent annual turnover.

The top talent is also the most mobile talent. Headhunters and recruiting companies will look to the succession planning to find the most valuable and vulnerable people to poach. Thus, the plan needs to be kept up to date. It also needs to produce desirable outcomes and promote good behaviour. Consider what can be learned from exit interviews, and understand who and why people are leaving as well as who is in the succession plan and why.

Then, how to manage the succession. People learn from experience and there is no one better to prepare the next candidate than the person who has previously done the job well. One way to do this is to have an 'acting' role, where the new person learns on the job while the previous person stays in the job. This allows the new 'acting' person to learn the key responsibilities as well as developing relationships and learning about the culture. Parachuting people into a vacant role is a much greater challenge, and a steeper learning curve that is much more likely to lead to failure.

But succession planning should also have a 'failure management' portion that is often completely absent from performance management systems. Every organization will have some underperformers who never pull their weight, cause conflict or are simply unqualified. Similarly, a poorly planned and implemented succession plan can sour attitudes and alienate those who are good performers, but are unrecognized as part of the 'talent'.

Some organizations are dominated by these types, whereas healthier organizations probably have far fewer. But they can also be difficult to get rid of. A voluntary severance package has no appeal to them. They cross their arms and scowl through any motivational seminar. They do not want to be retrained, or troubled with any sort of stretch assignment. The surprising thing is that everyone knows who these people are in their organization. When asked to list these people, nearly every list identifies the same name. So why do these problems so often go unaddressed?

The first, common reason, is management failure. Performance issues are difficult to deal with, and some managers avoid the problem instead of dealing with it. But at the heart of the issue is often that there is no plan for failure. Companies love a 'framework for success', but 'frameworks for failure' are few and far between. Necessary, though.

Embracing failure and its management is a lost opportunity, and there are different types of failure. Opportunity failure is inherent in stretch assignments, job shadowing and 'acting' positions. This is a format where failure has built-in backups, or the cost of failure is low. In these opportunity failure positions, there is a chance to learn from the experience of failure and, equally important, learn how one reacts to failure. Improvement failure can describe someone who has the potential to perform well, but their current behaviour is failing. The right resources, motivation or support can turn this failure into good performance. The other type is intractable failure, which cannot be resolved or improved. When it cannot be changed or improved, this type of failure needs to be removed.

Planning for failure is an opportunity to minimize problems before they become catastrophic. Succession planning should involve planning for failure as well as success. In the meantime, never book more than half of the senior management team on the same flight.

A concluding case study: practical example

Recently, one of the authors used the motivator test as part of a project where an organization reviewed the employment relationship with a segment of their employees.

The group of about two dozen employees were advisors who conduct audits and advised businesses in their industry on compliance with environmental regulations. All worked as independent contractors. The contracts were essentially 'zero hours' contracts (these contracts and similar arrangements are discussed in Chapter 12). One of the challenges for this group was that they were distributed across a very large and diverse geographic area of about 1 million square kilometres. That is about four times the size of the United Kingdom.

Performance also widely varied in the group, with a minority of contractors completing a majority of the work. Not necessarily problematic in itself, given that some contractors were working in small geographic regions with high concentration of clients, while others were working in very rural and remote regions.

As is true of many contracts, this organization was conducting a full review of the employment relationship and its HR systems, primarily to address the performance issues with a few, specific contractors. This is extremely common in organizations, like when managers conduct a thorough performance review of the entire department when they have one problematic person in mind. Often independent contractors are called in to outsource the problem. Politicians, too, love to order an inquiry into a problem, procrastinating on an issue where the problem is clear, but no one wants to deal with it.

The group completed the motivational test alongside other questionnaires. The initial results showed this group was substantially different from the population average on a few dimensions. As shown in Figure 10.4, average need for autonomy and affiliation was substantially higher; need for security was much lower.

The least variation between advisors was also in autonomy items, suggesting this was a common theme across everyone in the industry. Interestingly, advisors, as a group, indicated they were not getting sufficient autonomy.

Figure 10.4   Example of population average and group motivators scores

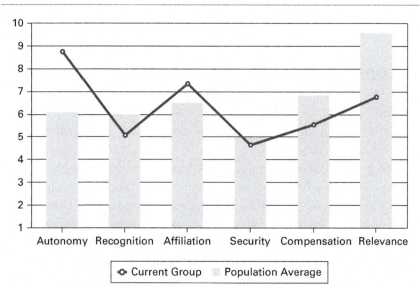

This was also the greatest source of dissatisfaction, which will be discussed further in Chapter 11.

Two interesting findings from this work can be generalized across all workplaces. First, even though this is a type of work that is constrained by very black-and-white regulations and guidelines, advisors want autonomy to work within that framework. They liked working as contractors and liked the flexibility it offered. There were some concerns with ambiguity and mixed information, so they wanted autonomy *within a clear framework*.

The implication of this was to develop a very clear HR manual with performance management criteria. This was a document to keep the contractual obligations clear, along with a clear performance management framework. It created the structure and framework needed to do their job, with freedom in their approach to the work.

Second, advisors clearly indicated that security was not a priority for them. And while their need for security was low, they indicated that the level of job security was sufficient. Many suggested they liked the flexibility and low minimum requirements; some had other work, others were semi-retired and all indicated no desire for greater job security.

The implication of this was that the decision was taken to continue the employment relationship with advisors as independent contractors. This model fitted better than an employee relationship. Low minimum targets were set, so those who wanted to work less would not have excessive targets. But targets were developed to address the previous performance issues. Regional targets were also set, so those in rural and remote regions were not unfairly measured in the performance management framework.

Clear evidence from testing motivation, understanding the employment relationship and the organizational culture provided clear information that could be acted on. Considering this information is useful for developing organizational policy and learning about those within it. Testing also provides a baseline of data, against which future data can be compared.

References

de Waal, FBM (2004) Peace lessons from an unlikely source, *PLoS Biology*, 2(4), pp 434–36

Moore, S, Grunberg, L and Krause, AJ (2015) Generational differences in workplace expectations: a comparison of production and professional workers, *Current Psychology*, **34**, pp 346–62

Sapolsky, R (2004) Emergence of a peaceful culture in wild baboons, *PLoS Biology*, 2 (4), e.124

The importance 11
of motivation gaps

Introduction

An individual's motivators are important and necessary to understand, but it is possible to go further and obtain more nuanced information about motivation and its consequent effects at work. Consider what effects a large pay rise would have for an individual who is not at all motivated by compensation. It may have little to no effect. It is not just the level of the motivator that matters, it is also useful to measure the difference between what individuals *want* and what they perceive they *receive*. If compensation is extremely important to one person, but what they are receiving in compensation is far below what they desire, that is a direct path to dissatisfaction and a raft of other problems.

But there are no implicitly 'right' or 'wrong' values. They are inherently personal. The reason why you value something is probably more important than *what* you value in the sense of motivation, career satisfaction and productivity. The match (or mismatch) between desired motivators and the rewards actually received explain a lot. Preliminary research with the HPMI (Thomson, 2016) indicated that values gaps could be used to predict up to 44 per cent of the variance in work engagement. This research also found that the values gaps predicted between 15 per cent and 57 per cent of an individual's commitment to their organization.

This chapter will discuss the concept of a motivation gap, primarily using case studies to demonstrate how motivation gaps look in real-world contexts. This is one of the concepts that is most important to understand in context because the reasons behind the motivation gap and its effects can look very different qualitatively, even if the numerical profiles are similar.

Mind the motivation gap

What happens when an employee values one thing, but they are given another? If one is buying a gift for a partner to make up for previously bad behaviour, a bottle of champagne is not good compensation for drunken behaviour the night before. If the remedy does not align with the problem, it is not likely to solve it. When an employee feels they are not being given enough flexibility, no amount of money will change their dissatisfaction with the flexibility of their working environment. Likewise, employees who feel underpaid or undervalued probably don't care if they are given more autonomy in their work.

There are two different approaches to address this, because the values gap works differently for intrinsic compared with extrinsic motivators.

Extrinsic

Extrinsic motivators are factors that cause dissatisfaction when they are not met (see Chapters 9 and 10). So the gap between the required level of a motivator desired, and the level at which it is provided or fulfilled at work, explains dissatisfaction. That means the extrinsic gap is very closely tied to negative outcomes such as disengagement, low commitment and turnover intention.

The focus should be meeting the basic levels of these extrinsic needs without excessively overcompensating with extrinsic rewards. The consistent findings from research show that excessive extrinsic rewards, such as pay and compensation, increases the basic level of desire for that type of reward (Lepper, Greene and Nisbett, 1973; Gerhart, Rynes and Fulmer, 2009). That is not to say that people should be paid at subsistence levels. Pay should be commensurate to minimum levels and appropriate to the nature of the work. But flagrant excess normalizes itself and creates greater base-levels of perceived need. This is expensive and counter-productive.

Intrinsic

There is a hugely profitable and rapidly expanding happiness industry. Blame the 'Everyone gets a trophy youth culture', or chronically upbeat attitudes in some sectors – the slick consultants who sell off-the-shelf happiness packages in a half-day workshop for four easy payments of just-within-your-budget. But there are any number of inspirational products that are intended to intrinsically motivate people. Inspirational speakers really can get people excited, but their effects are temporary.

The HPMI three facets of intrinsic motivation are about autonomy, affiliation and accomplishment. Intrinsic motivation is about doing a good job, doing it independently, or is derived from a sense of meaning and purpose in the work. Unlike extrinsic motivators, these should absolutely exceed the basic minimum levels whenever feasible. Without meeting the basic levels employees are likely to be demotivated. But exceeding in these factors increases performance, work engagement and a host of other desirable factors (as described in Chapters 7 and 8).

Remember, the basic 'needed' levels can vary widely between individuals as well. This floor and ceiling consideration (Figure 11.1) was introduced in Chapter 2. There is no baseline, universal level that applies to everyone, and we would not expect there to be unless everyone was identical. On average, physicians expect greater financial rewards for their work than sales clerks. Consultants typically expect greater autonomy than accountants. And even within these groups there is great variation.

Figure 11.1 Motivation floor and ceiling: meeting extrinsic motivation needs, exceeding intrinsic motivation needs

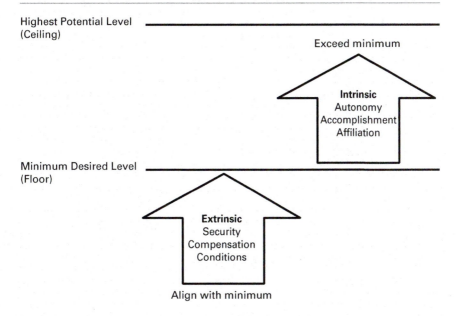

Two spy stories

To illustrate the values gap in a more unique and interesting setting, we talked to an ex-MI6 agent who was active throughout much of the Cold War and has very extensive experience with disgruntled and dissatisfied workers, often exploiting the motivation gap to pursue the objectives of the organization. For obvious reasons, this person will remain anonymous. Where the information is in the public domain, references are included for further reading.

The values gap is important because it often explains why people quit, defect, sabotage their employers or become whistle-blowers. Our ex-spy had two examples he said best illustrate the motivation gap and defections, told from personal experience, one from either side of the Cold War.

Aldrich Ames, CIA defector

Aldrich Ames defected from the CIA to the KGB in 1985, only a few years before the demise of the Soviet Union and the fall of the Berlin Wall. Money was a strong motivator in Ames's defection: he took millions of dollars from the KGB for his work. News reports from the period suggest money was his main motivation for defecting. Superficially this looks true, and his background does not indicate other motivations. He was from a middle-class background, his father was part of the CIA and he never showed any interest in communist ideology or economic models. He certainly didn't 'need' the money.

His work history was less than sterling. He failed at university. His early career with the CIA was mixed with a range of performance reviews from good reports to poor ones. He did become an expert on the KGB through his work. He was overlooked for promotion in 1985 and seems to have resented it, and he developed a reputation for being combative and disgruntled (Furnham and Taylor, 2011).

Instead of any ideological reason, Ames said he defected to the Russians simply because he ceased to respect the United States or his employer. Ames said that he believed the CIA was a morally corrupt and dangerous institution while believing the Soviets did not pose a threat to anyone else. He said, 'I personally felt totally alienated from my own culture... I did not feel part of our society' and that 'The truth is there was only one barrier left, and that was one of personal loyalty to the people I knew and, unfortunately, it was not a very strong one' (Earley, 1997).

Money was a motivating factor for Ames, which he openly admits. He was US $45,000 in debt at the time and his first request to the KGB was for

US $50,000. But he did not stop working for the Russians once he was out of debt, indicating money was not the only motivating factor. Many suggest that his love affair and marriage with second wife Rosario was another driving motivation. He wanted money, and the security it provided to pursue his relationship with her, and use the money to impress her. This means that although the major motivation gap would be financial, the story is not that simple. This example highlights a few important points.

First, the extrinsic motivators, particularly money and security, can have significant effects when they are not met. Individual levels may vary, and individual circumstances can affect their variation. But people who feel they do not make enough money and that their job cannot provide them with the required financial resources or job security are likely to find other means of supplementing their income. When they have a negative attitude towards their employer, their tactics are more likely to be destructive towards their employer.

Second, this demonstrates how the levels are important, but the quantitative piece, the reason why the person is motivated at a certain level, is equally important. Knowing there is a motivation gap in the compensation factor is the first step, and the first sign there might be a problem. Understanding why allows one to take steps to deal with the issue.

Third, the example shows why monitoring performance and measuring motivation is so important. Ames was not ideologically motivated to work for the KGB, and there is no indication in his early life that this was an unavoidable path. If his employers were aware of his motivation gap in compensation and security, as well as taking more notice when he became obviously disaffected, the situation could have been avoided. Perhaps the working relationship within the CIA could have been saved, but if unsalvageable his termination would have prevented a serious defection.

Finally, it illustrates a point about oversight that will be discussed further in Chapter 13. Strong personal and family connections often help to prevent derailment. Many effective leaders and CEOs report that a strong connection with an honest and constructive spouse keeps them grounded and gives them perspective that their colleagues may be too diplomatic to put across. This is discussed further in Chapter 13 as a method for preventing derailment.

Oleg Gordievsky, Soviet colonel and KGB defector

Oleg Gordievsky joined the KGB in 1963 and worked as a double agent for the British at MI6 from 1974 to 1985. He initially was a strong believer in communism and the planned economy. But his support for the Soviet Union began to wane from his first international posting in Denmark, and declined sharply after the Soviets invaded Czechoslovakia in 1968 (National Security Archive, 2013).

The story takes a more exciting turn when he was discovered by the Soviets and on 22 May 1985 Gordievsky was ordered to return to Moscow. On his return he was taken prisoner, then drugged and interrogated by Soviet counter-intelligence. There are suggestions he was arrested on information from Aldrich Ames, but it has never been officially confirmed (Wise, 2015).

The MI6 contact we spoke to was part of the team that exfiltrated Gordievsky (helped him escape). After hours of intensive questioning Gordievsky was released, told he would never have another overseas assignment and was suspected of spying for a foreign power. But Soviet officials stalled and he was allowed to rejoin his family in Moscow by June.

MI6 and Gordievsky had arranged a series of subtle signals that would set in motion an escape plan for him and his family – a detailed plan, ready to be set in motion if the Soviets discovered or suspected his defection. In late July, while his wife and children were on holiday in Azerbaijan, Gordievsky evaded the KGB officers monitoring him during a regular jog and, with help, was smuggled across the border to Finland. He was then flown back to England, as was his family.

The motivation for Gordievsky's defection is markedly different from Ames's. The financial motivation was completely absent, and throughout his entire career he demonstrated constructive and prosocial intentions, which he eventually realized were being channelled into destructive means. When he began to see the destructive effects of Soviet policy he decided to defect, to put his efforts towards what he believed to be a more worthy cause and a more constructive use of his abilities. For Gordievsky, the values gap would likely have registered in autonomy and affiliation.

Motivating factors

The examples highlight a few points. First, different motivation gaps can have much the same effect. Whether the gap is in extrinsic or intrinsic motivation, the large gap can lead to problems. In the cases of Ames and Gordievsky, both were prime targets to become double agents, but motivated by very different things. Second, the process and the appeal are different, based on the different motivation. If the gap is financial, then it may be relatively easy and straightforward to motivate that person towards any behaviours. Whereas if it is, like Gordievsky's case, dependent on an ethical judgement and motivation to do the right thing, recruitment methods may be very different.

Third, a values gap may not always be salvageable for the organization. Gordievsky became fundamentally opposed to the ideology of the Soviet Union and became motivated to work against instead of for it. This made him a prime target for MI6 recruiters, but there may have been nothing the Soviets could have done to win him over. Not all companies have such extreme consequences when there are motivation gaps with employees, but this example does show that it is not always possible to address the gap. Sometimes compensation plans or similar can be adjusted to motivate employees. Sometimes the motivation gap is just something that demonstrates the individual would be more motivated and fulfilled at another company.

Finally, look at both cases in the perspective of extrinsic and intrinsic motivation. When minimum levels of extrinsic motivators are not met, dissatisfaction quickly occurs. When greater intrinsic fulfilment is possible in a different organization or role, commitment and allegiances can change. Ames was motivated by money, and probably could have been bought by anyone (although his expertise was related to the KGB, making it an obvious target) whereas Gordievsky sought an organization that would align with his beliefs and allow autonomy and affiliation with the side he believed in.

Millennial motivation: a unique case study

Let's move to a more relatable, but no less remarkable case study. This is another case study of a 'millennial' who defies many of the negative millennial stereotypes, but is similar to some.

CASE STUDY

Damita is a 23-year-old Austrian woman whose father was Iranian and mother Austrian.

She is one of the most intensely motivated people I have ever met. However, she has no interest in climbing a greasy pole or putting her talents and ambition towards furthering a career that does not contribute to the well-being of others. She is immensely employable, and has done well in various private sector positions but has not felt the work was motivating (we will discuss why a bit later). She is a prime example of having all the indicators of high potential (MacRae and Furnham, 2014).

Her background had a strong influence on shaping her current motivation. She grew up in a working-class family who lived in social housing, Austria's equivalent of a British council estate. She had a very challenging childhood, a difficult home life and she often experienced physical discipline while growing up. None of the barriers stopped her though, and she was a high achiever from an early age.

Excelling in school gave her more opportunities, but came with further challenges. Her mother worked extremely hard to pay for her private-school tuition and she excelled in school. She says: 'I was treated like a child prodigy by my teachers, which meant everyone had enormous expectations, but everyone else bullied me pretty badly because of it.' At 15 she won second place in the Concours Général, an award created in 1744 to recognize achievement at a young age. Previous winners include names like Victor Hugo, Louis Pasteur and Georges Pompidou. At 19 she completed a Bachelor of Sciences at Goldsmiths, University of London, winning the Gold Award, which recognizes undergraduates for participation in activities above and beyond their academic studies and that demonstrate initiative and personal development. By 20 she had completed a master's degree in Research Methods in Psychology from University College London, one of the world's top research universities.

She says her background made success more important because unlike most people she does not have a 'home base' that she can return to if necessary, like many others her age do. This, she says, probably heightens her need for stability. Her profile (Figure 11.2) shows very high need for conditions. Her average levels

Figure 11.2 Damita's motivation profile

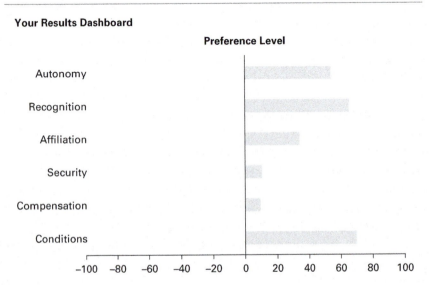

Your Results Dashboard

of compensation and security motivators are consistent with this – she needs basic levels, but they are not a priority.

She is extraordinarily employable and has a strong work ethic. She speaks three languages fluently and is learning another three. Her first language is German, but she speaks English with a flawless American accent. Just talking with her about what motivates her you can see passion and ambition almost bubbling over. She is incredibly keen to work hard, build a career and succeed within it. This type of enthusiasm can be incredibly desirable in the workplace, because the enthusiasm spreads throughout the workplace. However, this enthusiasm can also be a weakness for Damita. She is passionately interested in so many things, more than competent of doing anything she sets her mind to, but it is clear she sometimes has trouble channelling that passion into focused efforts. She wants to do so much, and while she has a big-picture direction in mind she is not yet focused on some of the concrete elements of planning. This is not necessarily a problem; most people spend their early twenties, and often longer, exploring different types of work before they discover what direction they want their career to take.

Although her motivation and independence defy the common misconceptions about millennials, she does fit the common image about wanting development opportunities, wanting to progress quickly, wanting to make a difference and for her contributions to be acknowledged and appreciated. And her passion is for social entrepreneurship. She wants her work to have some meaning, and to improve things for others. She is ambitious, but as so often is the case, the important question is *ambition to do what*? She is highly motivated by autonomy, but became demotivated and eventually quit companies that fell short in fulfilling her need for autonomy.

She has worked at for-profit companies, like market research where she did very well, but she didn't stay at any of these jobs for very long. She tutors students part-time, and loves that work and the positive impact it can have for students. She has been involved in various charities, with one example that illustrates she is certainly not an idealistic, but out-of-touch millennial. For example, she worked for a market research company doing work that was not enough of an intellectual challenge and was not making full use of her potential. Not that she wouldn't complete some of the less exciting tasks that are required in any job, but the prospect of doing it for years with no prospect of work she found meaningful meant she eventually left. Recognition is also very important to her, but how she is recognized is an important consideration. She wants to be recognized for contributing to a group or another person's well-being instead of for individual achievement.

She helped to found a charitable organization whose mission was to teach refugees in Austria, particularly Syrian refugees, to speak German. The objective was practical, clear and considered based on potential outcomes. She thought the best thing she could do for refugees was to provide them with the necessary language skills to find work, build a new life and integrate into society. She wanted to make sure that refugees would have the same opportunities she had in Austria to succeed. She left after about a year because the organization took a more idealistic than practical direction. And as happens in many organizations, the organization was dominated by people with great intentions but not implementation. In her words, 'their idea of teaching people is sitting in parks and having picnics and singing songs' and 'making friends'. 'The point of the organization wasn't just to make friends with a bunch of boys around my age, I wanted to have productive classes and I can't do that if grammar doesn't seem to matter to anyone as long as we're all together having fun.' There is no better example than this to show there is as much difference within any generation, as between. This also demonstrates how the values gap can appear. Everyone may have the same overall objective, but higher levels of motivators can make some individuals in any organization more susceptible to motivation gaps.

Damita is firm in her dedication to 'giving back' and being involved in a career that involves doing good for others. But she is still practical about the prospects about that. 'Any profession can add value and then there are a lot of professions that can be actively harmful, and some in the middle, but it always depends on what exactly you're doing. It really depends on the individual position. If you're a doctor you could be a neurosurgeon or work with Doctors Without Borders, or you could have a TV show and sell dubious stuff to vulnerable people, like Dr Oz.'

Many organizations could (and some do) harness this type of energy. There is nothing implicitly wrong with hierarchies, and organizations cannot function without a structure and accountability. But one cut-throat career path up a greasy pole can alienate a section of the talent pool, and leave them feeling untalented.

The point of this case study is that Damita is extraordinarily motivated, has high potential to do almost anything she sets her mind to, and a track record of success. Not everyone has it, and not everyone has the same level of ambition but it is often overlooked, particularly when it is not channelled directly into career progression within that company. Her motivation certainly is unlikely to register as what is commonly seen as career 'ambition', because her motivation is directed more towards outcomes and helping others than her own personal advancement. Of course, if an employer could channel this motivation effectively, it would be a huge opportunity to gain a highly effective, motivated and committed employee. Understanding this gap would give an employer the tools to develop and retain high-potential talent like Damita.

This also reinforces the important point that a 'generation' does not necessarily imply shared experience. Much is made of young people today who are likely to stay at home, or return home (so-called the Boomerang generation), of 'families with so-called "kidults" cluttering up the sofa and eating all the cereal. They either never left or have scuttled back as soon as the ink was dry on their graduation certificate' (Borg, 2016). The alarmists say things like, 'Grown-up children who are still in their family home are living the "life of Riley" while unknowingly pushing their parents into debt, research shows. The so-called "boomerang generation" are placing their parents under serious financial pressure by living at home even in their twenties and thirties' (Eccles, 2015). For Damita, and many others, this is simply not an option. Not everyone within a generation has a shared cultural experience – and this is what employers must not forget.

I asked Damita if she had any advice for her six-year-old self and she said, 'Honestly, I'd probably just give her a really big hug and tell her it's not fair the way her family treats her and that it's not normal and it has nothing to do with who she is. And to keep reading.' Good advice for anyone.

Conclusion

Understanding motivation is the first step, but understanding the gap between individual motivation and motivators provided at work provides a much more nuanced explanation of a person's motivation, and potential occurrence of related behaviours. Motivation gaps are strongly related to other concepts such as work engagement and organizational commitment. Large motivation gaps are demotivating and make burnout more likely.

The two spy stories were used in this chapter as more extreme examples of consequences that can result from motivation gaps at work. However, these examples are not fundamentally different from HR challenges in any other organization. Like the examples in the intelligence services, every organization faces challenges with employee demands for compensation and issues such as mismatches in organizational and individual ideologies about work.

Finally, the case study featuring Damita should be an optimistic example of the next generation entering the workforce. As mentioned in Chapter 3 there is a broad diversity of motivation in any generation and the younger generation(s) are no different. Understand employees individually in order to identify opportunities based on what motivates them and what they may (or may not) be receiving from their work. Consider the individual case and the reason behind that person's motivation and motivation gaps in order to fully develop their potential.

References

Borg, L (2016) Boomerang generation: how to cope when your kids won't leave home, *The Telegraph*, 14 May

Earley, P (1997) *Confessions of a Spy: Real story of Aldrich Ames*, Coronet Books, London

Eccles, L (2015) The boomerang generation forcing their parents into debt: experts say they should not be afraid to ask children for rent and money towards bills, *Mail Online*, 17 April

Furnham, A and Taylor, J (2011) *Bad Apples: Identify, prevent & manage negative behavior at work*, Palgrave Macmillan, Basingstoke

Gerhart, B, Rynes, SL and Fulmer, IS (2009) Pay and performance: individuals, groups, and executives, *The Academy of Management Annals*, 3 (1), pp 251–315

Lepper, MP, Greene, D and Nisbett, RE (1973) Undermining children's intrinsic interest with extrinsic reward: a test of the 'overjustification hypothesis', *Journal of Personality and Social Psychology*, 28 (1), pp 129–37

MacRae, IS and Furnham, A (2014) *High Potential: How to spot, manage and develop talented people at work*, Bloomsbury, London

National Security Archive (2013) The 1983 War Scare: 'The Last Paroxysm' of the Cold War, National Security Archive Electronic Briefing Book No. 426

Thomson, I (2016) Mind the values gap – the impact of a motivation values gap on three key work related outcomes, master's dissertation, University College London

Wise, D (2015) [accessed 10 October 2016] Thirty Years Later, We Still Don't Truly Know Who Betrayed These Spies, *Smithsonian Magazine*, November [Online] http://www.smithsonianmag.com/history/still-unexplained-cold-war-fbi-cia-180956969/?no-ist

Outsourcing motivation

12

Introduction

The nature of work, and employment relationships, are changing. More people are working remotely, working independently as consultants and there are increasing options for 'flexible' employment terms. This can be a great opportunity for employers and employees. However, every change has positive and negative consequences. Flexibility for some may be insecurity for others. Outsourcing can have very positive or negative effects on motivation.

Outsourcing production and services is nothing new and has been a prominent feature of company expansion since the British textile industry outsourcing textile production and labour to India in the 19th century. It really started to take off later in the 20th century and continues. Critics would argue it can exploit cheap labour, and be used to get around national labour laws and the rights of workers. Nelson Mandela's (2000) criticism was, 'Where globalization means, as it so often does, that the rich and powerful now have new means to further enrich and empower themselves at the cost of the poorer and weaker, we have a responsibility to protest in the name of universal freedom.' Proponents would argue that it makes the entire world a smaller and more accessible market. Milton Friedman said, 'In Globalization 1.0, which began around 1492, the world went from size large to size medium. In Globalization 2.0, the era that introduced us to multinational companies, it went from size medium to size small. And then around 2000 came Globalization 3.0, in which the world went from being small to tiny' (Pink, 2005).

The reality of outsourcing is that it is often lower-skilled and the least intrinsically motivating types of work that are the simplest to outsource. This can be appealing for improving workplaces because the least-motivating types of work can simply be moved overseas at a lower cost. Call centres are notorious for their low engagement, employee dissatisfaction and high turn-over. They are a prime target for outsourcing. Work can also be outsourced by subcontracting it to another company. It may still be in the same country, but the work is conducted outside the company. Costs need to be cut in a department? Outsource the whole thing and let consultants compete on providing the required services for the lowest fee.

Outsourcing is not just a large-scale, production-type movement of labour to cheaper regions. Subcontracting is a better term to use in this chapter, which covers all possible methods of moving work outside of the organization.

An example of subcontracting

The largest and most profitable companies make extensive use of overseas labour forces. Apple products are proudly emblazoned with the words 'designed in California' (leaving out the 'Made in China'). But with tens of millions of Apple products sold every year, consumers want ever-newer models at affordable prices. An estimate from *Forbes* (Worstall, 2013) suggested that moving Apple's iPhone production to the United States would cost the company about $4 per phone, but interestingly notes that it would be impossible to assemble the hundreds of thousands of labourers required for production. The example of Apple is apt, because stories have regularly surfaced over the years criticizing Apple's working conditions in China, such as 'excessive overtime and problems with overtime compensa-tion; several health and safety risks; and crucial communication gaps that have led to a widespread sense of unsafe working conditions among work-ers' (Guglielmo, 2012). In cases such as these, subcontracting overseas can create two problems with regards to motivation:

- **Internal.** Some employees and some corporate cultures may not care very much about the conditions of overseas workers. But one of the intrinsic motivators in the HPMI is affiliation, which has strong components of social responsibility and giving back. A strong intrinsic motivator for many people is the desire to improve the lot of others – to use their skills for the betterment of their team, their workplace, clients, customers or society as a whole. If an environmental charity holds investments in fossil fuel shares, it looks bad. If a children's charity relies on child labour from a supplier it is not very motivating for staff. Whereas, outsourcing or moving pieces of the business to constructive endeavours, or ventures with philanthropic components, can be incredibly motivating. This aligns with the discussions in Chapter 10: all parts of the business must be aligned to create the desired culture and to make sure the culture is lived.

- **External.** Stories of the maltreatment of an overseas workforce can be a public relations disaster for any company. Even though there might be different labour laws, minimum wages and different 'organizational cultures' where the workforce is based, hearing that the shiny new device was made by an 11-year-old working a 16-hour day is not something that endears most customers to a product. The cost savings of outsourcing parts of the business may be significant, but consider the potential costs. Online activists love a good story of business hypocrisy, and exploitation is likely to come out in one way or another.

The potential problems, along with the consequences, highlight the importance of effective oversight. One of the appeals of outsourcing and subcontracting is that required deliverables can be specified, but one need not handle the administration, project management, etc. The provider of the services or goods is being paid to save the hiring organization the headache of this, right?

Perhaps, but proper oversight is still important. Let's look at some of the considerations that should be made when subcontracting.

Zero hours contracts

Zero hours contracts are a type of contract that outlines the working relationship between an employer and employee. The main feature, as the name implies, is that the employer does not guarantee any hours. There is a formal relationship, but no guarantee of the work. It is equivalent to hiring someone as an independent contractor.

Zero hours contracts represent a large and growing sector of the workforce. In the UK, in 2015 nearly 750,000 employees, 2.4 per cent of the workforce, were on zero hours contracts (Office for National Statistics, 2015). Generational differences are pronounced in this type of work, with 6.7 per cent of younger (16–24) workers and 3.6 per cent of older workers (65+) having zero hours contracts.

Opinion is strongly divided on zero hours contracts, with some suggesting that they give employers the flexibility they need to meet fluctuating demands. Others complain that zero hours contracts are exploitative of people who need the work but have no other option. Both are correct to an extent, but the issue highlights how the employment relationship can have significant effects on motivation.

There is a heated debate about zero hours contracts. Just as with the generational issue, both sides of the argument raise valid points. And while zero hours contracts are a good fit for some people and their work, it is challenging for others. The majority of workers on zero hours contracts in the UK report they do not want any more hours. A large proportion (24 per cent) want more hours in their current job, 12 per cent want a new job with more hours and 5 per cent want an additional job; 5 per cent of workers on zero hours contracts worked no hours (ONS, 2015). This might suggest that the arrangement works for some, but is still unsatisfactory for many workers.

Pennycock, Cory and Alakeson (2013) found that zero hours contract workers were less likely to have a degree (21 per cent compared with 31 per cent of the workforce), they are more likely to be from outside the UK (48 per cent compared with 25 per cent). Research from the Chartered Institute for Personnel and Development (CIPD, 2013) suggested that 14 per cent of zero hours contract workers reported insufficient hours each week and, of those working part time, 38 per cent would like to work more hours. Across all workers, 14 per cent said their employer often provides them with less working hours than necessary to have a basic standard of living; 18 per cent said this happens, but not often; 20 per cent said they have being penalized for not being available for work; 50 per cent of zero hours contract workers earn less than £15,000 per year (compared with 6 per cent of the workforce). A study by the union Unite (2013), of its own members, found that only 13 per cent of workers on zero hours contracts said they wanted to stay on a zero hours contract.

Clearly zero hours contracts are difficult for some people, while conversely the majority are making enough for a basic standard of living, are not penalized when unavailable for work, and some are satisfied with the arrangement. We are not going to say whether zero hours contracts are right or wrong; clearly they are good for some, but not for all. However, it does raise important issues. The first is a more general discussion related to job security (we have gone into more detail on how job security can impact motivation in Chapter 10). The second issue concerns implementation. Given below are two examples to contrast the extreme differences that could exist in a type of zero hours contract.

First, let's say that a high-paid, highly skilled professional retires at 60. After six months of retirement they decide they would like to work, but don't want to go back to their full-time job. They meet with their previous employer who cannot promise a salary or regular hours, but could use support from time to time on projects. Both agree on an arrangement that is beneficial for both parties. They sign a zero hours contract, which specifies a formal employment relationship with an hourly rate, but no guarantee of work. This person then acts as support on a project-by-project basis. The employer has greater capacity, without having to pay someone a salary. The employee can agree to work on specific projects, but is not required to accept any work. Sounds like an ideal situation, and is a fair arrangement for both.

Second, take the example of a worker in a distribution centre earning the minimum wage. They have a zero hours contract that asks them to call in every morning at 7.30 am to see if there is work for them that day. They may not be invited to work. If they do get offered work, their shift could be from a few hours to 12 hours; if something changes during the shift, they may be asked to leave early. There may be some people for whom this arrangement works well, but the problem is when it creates a substantial imbalance of power. If the work does not pay enough for the worker to live on then it can trap people in a cycle of dependency. Varying and unpredictable shifts make it difficult to find additional work. Some zero hours contracts do not allow the employee to work for any other employer. This can be more challenging.

The most obvious argument, of course, is that in both examples employees are not required to work. They can turn down shifts, or choose days or weeks not to work. This simple argument is, of course, valid but may raise concerns when the employee relies on that job for a basic standard of living. One could argue that insecure work and income is better than none at all. Others would argue that low-income jobs that will not pay the bills are unfair. Henry Rollins ironically notes, 'If you paid Americans a living wage, they would be able to pay for products made by Americans in America' (Rollins, 2010).

The skills argument

There is also a more general argument about developing skills within a company and creating a talent pipeline for high-potential employees to be trained and promoted within the company. We have discussed this experience trap, where entry-level positions require previous experience, and the implications of this are profound for insecure, low-paid work. This type of work is rarely a position that comes with learning or development opportunities. The whole purpose of getting low-paid, unskilled workers in high-turnover occupations is that they are quick and cheap to replace. Not worth investing in, right?

The problem that this approach can create is that a large section of the workforce with little job opportunity, few prospects, and little chance of any improvement, creates challenging situations for those workers. Of course it is not the individual responsibility of any one employer to develop and train people across the labour market – that is supposed to be what the public education system is for. But it can create a situation where no one takes responsibility, so the collective costs affect everyone.

Much is made of the war for talent, and future labour shortages: 38 per cent of businesses around the world already report difficulty filling jobs, the highest level since the 2008 financial crash (Manpower Group, 2015). The potential effects of this on business are shown in Figure 12.1. Randstad estimates that the UK will have a 3.1 million shortfall of workers (9 per cent of the total workforce) by 2050 (Randstad, n.d.). The McKinsey Institute (Dobbs *et al*, 2012) estimates that by 2020, globally there will be a short-age of 2 million workers with post-secondary education, 45 million with secondary education and, in developed economies, even 90 million less workers than needed for low-skilled jobs.

The severity of the problem is most pronounced in the skills gap, not just the net number of entrants to the workforce. Many will complain that the state educational system and even university does not prepare graduates

Figure 12.1   Employer ratings of how talent shortages will affect their business

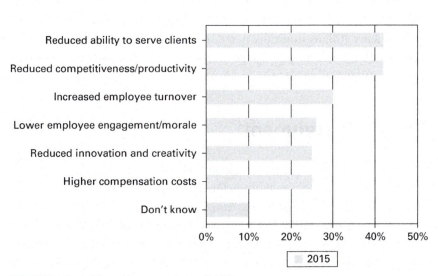

SOURCE Adapted from Manpower Group (2015)

for the workplace. For example, an article in *Fortune* suggests: 'In other words, they lack on the job training. Universities teach students how to think, but they don't provide real-world experience, so people leave school unprepared for the workplace' (Smith, 2015). Fair, and generally true. The problem can be seen as a 'tragedy of the commons' situation.

The term 'tragedy of the commons' is a theory in economics that originally comes from the 1833 Victorian economist William Forster Lloyd, and which was popularized in the 1960s by ecologist Garrett Hardin (1968). The example comes from unregulated 'commons' grazing land in Britain that was shared by multiple farmers. The potential benefits were available to all farmers equally. There are potential benefits of cheating the system, for any individual farmer to overgraze their cattle, but the whole group shares the damages that result from this. Every farmer has an incentive to cheat the system, so most have a tendency to overgraze a little. Short-term self-interest often wins while there are long-term consequences.

A similar scenario occurs in the labour market. Many companies use headhunters to poach top talent from other companies instead of training their own potential talent internally. The short-term benefits are clear: poaching top talent is faster than training internally. But this approach can only go so far. If every company is trying to recruit externally instead of training internally, the potential talent pool remains small or dwindles. An individual company can benefit from hiring employees their competitors have developed, but if everyone does it then it creates serious problems for the system. It is not always possible to promote from within but there are clear benefits to creating high-potential pathways that start from the very front line of the organization.

There is a story about President Kennedy's visit to NASA in 1962 that business journalists and motivational speakers always love to drag out. During his tour of NASA Kennedy struck up a conversation with someone in a hallway saying, 'Hi, I'm Jack Kennedy, what do you do here?' The reply, from the janitor, was 'Well, Mr President, I'm helping put a man on the moon' (Nemo, 2014). Many love this story because it illustrates the idea that anyone in the company, no matter their position, can feel like they are contributing to the collective mission and vision of the company.

This is possible. But achieving that level of engagement and creating that kind of company culture is much more difficult if their employment relationship is inconsistent or without mutual responsibilities between the employer and employee. It is unlikely that the janitor in the NASA story was a contract worker from a temporary staffing company on a zero hours contract. It is much harder to feel like part of a big picture when one's employer cannot promise any sort of security, long-term future or even day-to-day inclusion in the company.

The best high-potential models (discussed extensively in MacRae and Furnham, 2014) involve spotting the foundational components of high potential that will predict success in the future. Knowledge can be learned and taught. Experience can be gained. An intelligent, conscientious employee can have huge potential, even an employee in a position that might otherwise be overlooked. But the opportunity is obvious: if they are already in the company and have potential to advance, *someone* should be able to spot them.

An illustration from succession planning

As is true of the different methods of subcontracting, zero hours contracts do meet certain needs for certain types of work. They can be a good arrangement for some employers and some employees, but are also open to abuse. A cautionary, true example from a government department highlights a common problem and potential opportunity. The employees within the department are largely older workers and are very experienced, but the majority of the workforce is at, or nearing, retirement age. Their capacity is stretched, but they need to deliver results within tight time frames. One of the workers retires, taking out a full government pension. In a desperate attempt to fill the role, the department offers this person part-time work (as much or as little as desired) as a stop-gap to ensure everything gets done. They are now, essentially, paying double (full retirement and wages) for this work. It is a short-term solution that exacerbates the long-term problem. There is no succession planning, and no long-term training and development strategy.

The solution is obvious: instead of contracting the retiree to do the same work as before, hire them to train someone new. Better yet, get them training and mentoring their own replacement. It is a question of foresight. It is also a potentially strong motivator (affiliation). Of course getting paid to do one's previous job while also receiving a pension can be financially, extrinsically motivating. But it is demotivating to see such a foolish waste of resource. It is also unfortunate and demotivating in a situation and workplace like this when a lifetime of skills, knowledge and experience are accumulated over a lifetime of working for this department and are then lost through retirement.

Hire the retiree to train their own replacement. Focus on the value of the role and what it adds to the company, not just the skills needed to do the job. Along with the skills required to do the job, the seasoned expert can pass along their insider knowledge and expertise to the new person. Not just an overview of the job, but how to get it done effectively. This is a remarkably common and extraordinarily costly problem that should be easy to avoid. Why not build 'training one's successor' into a retirement plan? What could be more motivating towards the end of a career than an opportunity to pass on one's knowledge and ensure that every tip and trick learned over a lifetime of work can be valuable to someone else and to the company – that is, assuming the soon-to-be retiree is not disengaged, demotivated and eager to leave as soon as possible.

This can also be incredibly motivating for the new employee, or new person in the position. What better way to start a job than learning how to do it with a seasoned insider? This is a more sophisticated type of onboarding than simple orientation sessions, it is a fast track into being an insider. Cultivating that sense of belonging, being privileged to insider, unique or specialized information and providing a trainer or mentor as a model of the benefits of being in that workplace – over the long term this is a powerful way to kick-start employee motivation early, create a sense of connection with the company, instil a sense of capability early on, improve organizational commitment and reduce turnover intention. Many people do not see themselves working for any company for long, because often the company has not demonstrated that this is a possibility.

As we discussed in Chapter 3, it is not just younger generations who are discriminated against. But instead of being loudly criticized, older generations of workers are often quietly forgotten. And like any discrimination, the potential value that older workers have (and may be keen to offer) can be lost if it is overlooked.

Conclusion

The nature of work and employment relationships between organizations and individuals is changing and will continue to change. There are opportunities along with challenges that arise from subcontracting arrangements and outsourcing work. The short-term benefits must always balance potential long-term consequences. Ensure that employment relationships and contracts align with the overall vision and strategy of the company. If there is a mismatch, it will be disengaging and ultimately lead to problems with profitability and productivity.

This chapter discussed some of the potential challenges in outsourcing and subcontracting work. There are potentially negative effects on employee (or contractor) motivation and performance if the employment relationship is not carefully considered. Yet new systems and arrangements offer opportunities that may have been difficult or impossible in more rigid systems and employment relationships. Flexibility offers opportunities as well as challenges. Chapter 5 discussed the importance and usefulness of measuring motivation, and that lesson should be applied to understanding the effects of traditional and contemporary employment relationships on motivation and performance – measure it to understand it.

References

Chartered Institute for Personnel and Development [CIPD] (2013) [accessed 10 October 2016] Zero-Hours Contracts: Myth and reality [Online] http://www.cipd.co.uk/hr-resources/research/zero-hours-contracts-myth-reality.aspx

Dobbs, R, Madgavkar, A, Barton, D, Labaye, E, Manyika, J, Roxburgh, C, Lund, S and Madhav, S (2012) *The World at Work: Jobs pay, and skills for 3.5 billion people*, McKinsey Global Institute

Guglielmo, C (2012) Nightline goes inside Apple factories in China, *Forbes*, 22 February

Hardin, G (1968) The tragedy of the commons, *Science*, **162** (3859), pp 1243–48

Lloyd, WF (1833) *Two Lectures on the Checks to Population*, Collingwood, Oxford

MacRae, IS and Furnham, A (2014) *High Potential: How to spot, manage and develop talented people at work*, Bloomsbury, London

Mandela, N (2000) Speech on receiving the Freedom Award from the National Civil Rights Museum

Manpower Group (2015) 2015 Talent Shortage Survey

Nemo, S (2014) [accessed 10 October 2016] What a NASA Janitor Can Teach Us About Living a Bigger Life, *The Business Journals* [Online] http://www.bizjournals.com/bizjournals/how-to/growth-strategies/2014/12/what-a-nasa-janitor-can-teach-us.html

Office for National Statistics [ONS] (2015), Labour Force Survey

Pennycock, M, Cory, G and Alakeson, V (2013) *A Matter of Time: The rise of zero-hours contracts*, Resolution Foundation

Pink, DH (2005) Why the world is flat, *Wired Magazine*, 1 May

Randstad (n.d.) UK faces 3.1 million shortfall in workforce by 2050, Press Release, Randstad

Rollins, H (2010) The simple solution to America's unemployment problem, *Vanity Fair*, 14 December

Smith, R (2015) College doesn't prepare students for full-time jobs – internships do, *Fortune*, 16 June

Unite (2013) [accessed 10 October 2016] Zero Hours Contracts Brief [Online] http://www.unitetheunion.org/uploaded/documents/001-Zero%20hours%20contracts%20brief-v211-12576.pdf

Worstall, T (2013) If Apple brought iPhone manufacturing to the US it would cost them $4.2 billion, *Forbes*, 25 September

The dark side and derailed motivation

13

Introduction

It is a common conversational expression to say someone is 'motivated' or 'ambitious'. It conveys a sense of personal achievement and drive, someone who is determined to 'go places'. The often overlooked but essential question is '*motivated to do what?*', '*ambitious to achieve what goals?*'

We generally think about motivation as a positive thing: the internal drive that fuels behaviour. But what happens when someone is highly motivated to do something unsavoury or downright destructive?

In Chapter 9 we discussed how excessive self-esteem and desire for fame can be toxic and destructive in the extreme. Upon further examination, we should not automatically assume that a disgruntled employee is *demotivated*. That employee may still have high need for autonomy and desire to make a difference. Yet, when they cannot exercise their autonomy within their job description, some nimble fingers or loose lips belie their motivation to sabotage. Motivate people in the right direction and they build bridges; motivate them in the wrong direction and they would rather blow them up.

Gangs, cults and terrorist organizations

People join groups, organizations, political parties and community organizations and churches because they give them a sense of belonging. But what about toxic and destructive organizations? What kind of people are drawn to organizations like Islamic State, the Ku Klux Klan, Al-Shabaab or the Irish Republican Army?

Typically we assume that the most strange and deviant people are attracted to the most destructive groups. This is a common mistake and is referred to by psychologists as the attribution bias. Everyone has a tendency to attribute their own success to their own positive characteristics and blame failure on circumstances, chance or fate; whereas we tend to see other people's flaws as inherent and their successes caused by external factors. Yet many people who get caught up in destructive, criminal and other types of bad behaviour have more in common with everyone else than you would expect.

Applying blame and condemnation is a moralistic argument. An evil organization clearly attracts evil people, of an entirely different type than normal, law-abiding and upstanding citizens, right? Actually it is not. Rather than blaming extremists or bad corporate behaviour for being different, it is just as important to understand the appeal of cults, extremists and criminal activity.

Studies of cults and extremist groups show there are five techniques that most have in common. These trends can apply to toxic organizations – albeit in less extreme forms – that motivate employees to bad behaviour, often within the realms of legal behaviour but pushing the boundaries on what is ethical or moral. This often happens in financial services companies where the unethical behaviour of 'rogue' traders is ignored, while their activities are profitable and, in some cases, their behaviour is tacitly condoned. The example of Enron in Chapter 14 is a prime example of this.

Any group can offer friendship, shared identity, values, respect and stability. These can be powerful incentives for people seeking them. Like cults, organizations can offer structure, the ability to learn new skills and to work with others. Toxic organizations have three main elements in common – conducive environment, colluding followers and destructive leaders – which toxic leaders will take advantage of (MacRae and Furnham, 2014).

Conducive environment

Environments that are threatening and unstable can encourage destructive and toxic behaviours across the organization, including in the leadership. Unstable environments, like economic and social dislocation, often allow leaders to seize more authority and power when people demand quick and decisive action. Closed or complex decision-making systems can also create conducive environments when systems are so complex that it makes accountability difficult or impossible to assign.

Perceptions of threats, especially external threats, is a common feature of conducive environments. Feelings of threat, mistreatment, desperation or financial difficulties make people more likely to condone aggressive leadership, and more susceptible to populist messages in favour of rational solutions (Solomon, Greenberg and Pyszczynski, 1991).

Lack of checks, balances and oversight is a key feature of environments conducive to toxic leadership. These are environments where destructive behaviour goes unchecked and unregulated, allowing toxic situations to get out of control. Organizations that do not have systems for limiting power – or have Byzantine administrative and governance structures that allow improper uses of power to go unchallenged – are ripe for exploitation.

In the context of motivation, conducive environments are likely to increase the need for motivators like security and conditions, when people seek safety in the face of threatening environments.

Colluding followers

Colluding followers are an essential part of toxic leadership: leaders can do very little without a group of supporters, reports or colleagues to help. While some followers may also be deliberately destructive and seek to benefit from a toxic leader, many colluding followers are supportive for less deliberate reasons. Often people follow toxic leaders because they feel the need for social order, fitting in with the group, obedience to authority, or imitating those with higher status (Padilla, Hogan and Kaiser, 2007).

One of the most common reasons that followers collude with toxic leaders is rooted in motivation. Employees strive to meet previously unmet basic needs (extrinsic motivators) through any means necessary. Those worried about having sufficient resources, security or conditions are most likely to be vulnerable to toxic leaders. This is likely one of the reasons that the most economically unstable or improvised countries in the world have the most corrupt governments (Transparency International, 2005).

Ambition is another reason that followers might collude with toxic leaders, which again raises the question: ambition to do what? Those who have the largest motivation gap, whether they feel underpaid, underappreciated or micromanaged, can be more susceptible to toxic leaders who offer solutions. Those who are ambitious for personal gain, irrespective of group or organizational consequences, are easier to exploit by toxic leaders. Examples such as the Enron scandal – when ambitious people are motivated to make huge financial gains irrespective of the consequences – demonstrate the destructive power of ambitious, colluding followers (McLean and Elkind, 2005). The example of Enron is discussed in detail in Chapter 14.

Destructive leaders

There are five main components of destructive leadership, as described by Padilla and colleagues (2007): charisma, personalized use of power, narcissism, negative life themes and an ideology of hate.

First, destructive leaders have charisma and charm. While not all charismatic leaders are destructive, most destructive leaders are charismatic. They are able to communicate a strong and clear vision of a desirable future. They also have the ability to present themselves well and appear to have strong personal energy. Second, narcissism, strong personal self-belief, is a regular feature of destructive leaders that comes with entitled attitudes and grandiose fantasies about themselves. It is often related to overconfidence, which leads to serious mistakes in business.

Third, destructive leaders use power and influence for their own purposes. Ethical leaders tend to use power for the greater good, and to improve things for the organization and others within it; destructive leaders use power for personal gain, irrespective of the effects on others. Fourth, destructive leaders often have a history of problems in their early life including traumatic childhood events, difficult upbringing or experiences of powerlessness that can predispose them to becoming destructive leaders later in life. Finally, destructive leaders have an ideology of hate. They tend to see the world in terms of external enemies to be destroyed. Often scapegoats are identified as the major source of all problems, which can also be used as a distraction from the real problems.

Most destructive leaders have a combination of these five characteristics that often make them effective at gaining power in the short term, particularly when they see opportunities presented by conducive environments and colluding followers, but this also tends to lead them to derailment in the longer term.

Techniques of toxic organizations

There are five techniques that toxic organizations often use to manipulate their followers:

- **Severing ties.** Cults often make people sever their ties with family and friends. The new recruit is insulated from reality and external opinions, allowing whatever behaviour occurs within the cult to become normalized. Organizations can do this with long working hours, careful monitoring of behaviour and other methods to ensure their employees are isolated from public opinion or common ethics.

- **Unquestioning obedience.** Extremist organizations do not tolerate dissent, and they often have long lists of rules that are to be obeyed no matter what. Often arbitrary or petty rules are introduced to reinforce and condition unquestioning obedience to any and all rules. Organizations can implement similar rules and regulations. The idea is to 'break in' all new recruits and instil unquestioning obedience early on.

- **Monotonous work.** Group members are required to work long hours and spend most of their time on monotonous, sometimes pointless, and often physically exhausting tasks. Recruits become physically and mentally exhausted, and are unable to resist or think for themselves. Organizations, too, can exhaust people with mindless, petty and unnecessary tasks, normalizing cultures of presenteeism even if counter-productive.

- **Illicitly obtaining money.** All groups need money to exist and thrive. Some organizations are more focused on money than others, but the recruits are involved in the process of raising funds. Recruits themselves may be exploited for financial gain.

- **High exit costs.** Leaving the organization or failure to comply is met with extreme consequences or retribution. The costs of punishment for leaving the organization are seen to be even more extreme than the difficulties associated with staying. For example, an employer could withdraw a bonus or ask for it to be returned. Other techniques could include threats to prevent future employment by providing negative references or harmful information.

Some individuals are more susceptive to these toxic techniques and destructive leaders, and motivation is a strong component of this, particularly motivation gaps (as discussed in Chapter 11). Personal characteristics can make people more resilient, but motivation gaps, particularly in extrinsic motivators, can make people more vulnerable to destructive leaders. Destructive leaders, too, may create extrinsic values gaps with the promise of a resolution in exchange for loyalty.

Misdirected motivation

Let's look at our six motivational factors. As we discussed in Chapters 2 and 5, the rationale behind motivation is equally as important as the type of motivation. So let's revisit the six motivational components and see how the strongest motivations can become destructive. Each has examples of how individual versus environmental factors can turn toxic.

Autonomy

Employees value their independence at work. They want to be in control of their work and how they do it. They value independence in their job.

When ambitious people want to be independent, it is always important to ask the question: independent to do what? If they are motivated to improve profitability and performance, that is incredibly desirable. But what of the people who want the freedom to embezzle funds, abuse their power in the company or hurt others?

Autonomy is a powerful motivator in the workplace, and strong independent performance should be rewarded with the flexibility to exercise one's own judgement. But not without oversight. Freedom and flexibility to get the job done should not include independence from accountability or oversight.

Accomplishment

Accomplishment and recognition are important, and all employees want to be recognized for their hard work and effort. But excessive attention seeking can be incredibly destructive when the person takes credit for the work of others and demands undeserved praise.

Also be cautious of those who demand attention at all costs. Some attention seeking and need for recognition goes beyond caring what the attention is for. The most dramatic revel in conflict and chaos, and demand the starring role. Most people conform to social pressures and want to be liked. But a few thrive on destruction. They would rather be loathed than be anonymous. Some people have an incredible knack for creating trouble irrespective of the personal consequences.

Affiliation

Contribution to the team, being part of something greater and helping others are all admirable motivators.

But those who value the quality of their relationships, seek harmony and want to contribute to a greater cause can be easy to manipulate. Passive followers are the ideal recruiting grounds for manipulative leaders. Followers can quickly become collaborators in threatening environments.

Security

Some people value having a safe and secure workplace. They want or need the security of the job, and are prepared to make sacrifices to achieve that security.

Need for security is not a problem when those needs are met, but when that security is lost, that person becomes vulnerable. Worry creeps into every aspect of their work and their stress is spread around the office liberally.

They may also be vulnerable to promises of safety and security at any cost. Again, the autocratic leader will be quick to promise security in exchange for loyalty at any cost. Those who value their job security can more easily be convinced to make sacrifices for the return to stability.

Compensation

Work pays, and most people work to get paid. There is nothing inherently wrong in going to work in order to get a pay cheque. The desire for compensation becomes problematic when it is pursued to the detriment of other areas. When greater payouts are pursued to the detriment of legal and ethical guidelines, or to the detriment of the company as a whole.

Company theft is also tied to the need for compensation. Employees who feel undervalued are more likely to steal company resources. The severity of this ranges from stealing office pencils in an act of petty revenge to embezzling company or client funds for personal use.

Relevance

The job conditions and environment that employees want can vary quite drastically. There is nothing inherently destructive about wanting clean, secure and comfortable working conditions. However, these can turn destructive when not met, or when being comfortable and wanting effortless work exceeds the motivation to perform well in the job.

Organizational defence mechanisms

Misdirected motivation can often lead to defence mechanisms. Being alert and aware of these potential defence mechanisms in the workplace can indicate potential problems and potential for derailment. Defence mechanisms are often used to describe individuals but could also be adapted to describe organizations.

Sigmund Freud introduced the concept of defence mechanisms to psychology, and his daughter Anna Freud continued to develop and expand upon the concept (Freud, 1937). One of her most well-known ideas is that anxiety or stress is triggered by some sort of event and threat. Negative emotions trigger a need to react to potential threats. These concepts continue to be used as ways of explaining how people react to organizational change (Bovey and Hede, 2001; Walsh and Moss, 2010).

The idea is simple. Over time, everyone experiences different types of setbacks, failures and mistakes. Stress of one form or another is part of everyone's life in varying degrees over time. Thus, we develop ways of managing and reacting to stressful situations. Failure, humiliation, shame and disappointment are bound to crop up. We cannot always get what we want at work, and no career path is free from challenges.

Stress tends to induce an automatic fight or flight response. Yet, running away from problems or fighting with colleagues is rarely a productive activity. The part of the brain that evolved to deal with dangerous predators, the primitive lizard part of the brain, wants to make a split-second decision either to run away or fight head on. This is rarely productive in life or at work, so we develop different ways of reacting: these are defence mechanisms.

Different individuals develop different ways of coping with stress. They have different reactions that may have been learned or they may have been the most effective reactions in the past. Some are more infantile than others, and some tend to be quite effective. As with any behaviour, there are always advantages and disadvantages. Rigid, authoritarian managers may find that exerting total control over their employees produces the desired results, to the detriment of employee morale. The namby-pamby flip-flopping manager may be able to ingratiate themselves and have a generic set of platitudes to wave around the office, but they can never commit to a decision.

But, defence mechanisms can also be used to describe organizations and groups. Corporate culture is the often unspoken approach to getting the job done. Organizational culture was introduced in Chapter 8, and now we look at some of the typical defence mechanisms that organizations use. When the organization is threatened, how are they and the people in it likely to react? Typical responses are:

- **Repression.** Out of sight, out of mind. Repressing problems is a common way of combating the stress that the problem creates. Increasingly complex organizations with Byzantine structures of management and accounting find it easier to hide problems. Problematic behaviour is moved, hidden and forgotten in order to avoid the consequences.

The problem with repression is, of course, hidden problems have a way of growing even larger when out of sight. Eventually the skeletons in the closet pile up to such an explosive degree that they are no longer possible to hide. But in a culture of repression, almost everyone is complicit and the fear of consequences triggers further repression.

- **Denial.** This is a deliberate refusal to acknowledge reality. Signs of trouble, once seen, are ignored. Troubling reports are met with disdain: the numbers and the findings couldn't possibly be accurate; everything is fine, and the alternative is unthinkable.

  Denial is great fuel for company bubbles. If a company is rapidly growing, reporting great profits and one is invested in the outcomes, the inevitable crash becomes unthinkable.

- **Projection.** This involves putting the blame on others. One's own shortcomings, failures and mistakes are the fault of another. At work, the boss is often a handy vessel for projection. Organizations tend to place the blame on external parties: economic conditions and labour market conditions are a favourite. The regulator is a handy target for blame when things go wrong and governments and regulations are a useful source for projection. The company *could* be making a lot of money, but the regulation does not allow for it.

  Generational differences tend to be a go-to target for projection. Some managers say they just cannot find reliable workers any more. The new generation is apparently lazy and feckless, unsuitable for the modern workplace. But a business with a 50 per cent employee turnover rate is clearly projecting their own inadequacies when their competitor only has a 10 per cent employee turnover rate.

- **Reaction-formation.** Unacceptable or unwanted feelings are turned into the opposite emotion. This is a common reaction to authoritarian and abusive leaders. Aggression and power consolidation are interpreted as a 'strong leader' who is admired for taking the strong and tough approach.

  The employee who hates their boss may become excessively compliant in response to their feelings; companies that swindle their customers develop the approach that if their customers are stupid enough to buy it, they deserve the consequences.

- **Sublimation.** This is when inappropriate desires (often sex and aggression) are channelled into more productive activities. Anger at a colleague or one's manager is channelled into a healthy reaction such as exercise. Stress in one's personal life is channelled into working harder.

Sublimation may or may not be a healthy organizational outlet, depending on the resultant behaviour. It can be healthy when directed towards positive or prosocial outcomes. Logging companies, for example, use some of their profits to replant trees; oil companies support environmental charities; banks support artistic, cultural and humanitarian organizations.

- **Rationalization.** Fast-talkers and the well-educated tend to favour rationalization. It involves explaining away the troubling emotions with complex legal, intellectual or ethical arguments. Incompetence is rationalized with complex and often imaginary reasoning. Talking endlessly about the inevitability of the problem is favoured instead of attempting to solve the problem.

  Companies do the same. Every time governments raise the minimum wage many companies commission and construct complex economic analyses explaining why paying their employees a slightly higher wage would result in the imminent collapse of the capitalist and democratic West.

- **Displacement.** This involves targeting an innocent victim instead of the actual source of the problem. The angry worker comes home and kicks the cat. The uneducated and unemployed have a tendency to blame immigrants. Politicians, when made to seem powerless, try to project their power outwardly, into other parts of the world. Those who report bullying or harassment may themselves become the target of displaced anger.

  Displacement is common in authoritarian organizations where bullying is rife. The president insults his direct reports – then the leadership team, unable to fight back, pass the aggression and abuse down the chain of command. Bullies always learn who is the most vulnerable person to target. When aggression or abuse are an acceptable means to an end within the company culture, it spreads like an infectious disease.

  Neglect, too, can be a common method of displacement. The disillusioned call-centre worker cannot be aggressive or openly rude to a customer. Yet, they can be passive, unhelpful and evasive, which is equally problematic.

- **Regression.** This involves reverting to childlike or immature behaviours. The overall plan falls aside in favour of sulking. The problem is, regression is often an effective tactic because it involves inappropriate and attention-seeking behaviours that create a feeling of urgency. Slamming doors, shouting and sulking do attract attention.

Negotiations between union leaders and governments have a tendency to descend into childish name-calling and accusations. Complex negotiations can descend to the level of a petty sibling rivalry where hurting the opposing party becomes more important than resolving the issue.

All these defence mechanisms can be warning signs if they are prevalent in a company culture. Even sublimation should be understood in order to ensure that the root cause of the defence mechanism is not ignored. How does the company react to a warning? Blame the messenger? Ignore the warning? Explain away the problem? Or deal with the issue?

Three dark-side factors and motivation

While there are various ways of conceptualizing dark-side and derailment factors, we propose three major factors that are most relevant to motivation and behaviour in the workplace. These three factors – naughty, withdrawn and influencing – are not necessarily destructive, but are fairly good warning signs. Also, they are not necessarily scales of badness, that is, there can be 'optimal' levels, where they are useful but not destructive if taken too far. This will be discussed in the next section.

The three major factors can be described as:

- **Naughty.** This is a general tendency towards bad behaviour. Jokes and pranks may be harmless outcomes of this factor at the moderate levels. At higher levels it can be more destructive, with sabotaging colleagues or creating chaos in the workplace. At lower levels it is more rigid, rule-oriented and less risk taking. This may be desirable in some workplaces, but can lead to avoidant or overly cautious behaviour.

  Some evolutionary psychologists have even suggested that extreme risk-taking behaviour, decried in the media following the 2008–09 economic collapse, is often reinforced in organizational leaders in spite of potential dangers, because under benevolent circumstances or in the face of weak opposition it can be associated with success (Johnson, Wrangham and Rosen, 2002).

  Individuals higher on this factor are more motivated by pay and accomplishment while being less motivated by conditions (Table 13.1).

Table 13.1   Naughtiness correlated with motivation

Motivator	Correlation
Pay	0.17
Conditions	−0.11
Accomplishment	0.27

Table 13.2   Withdrawn correlated with motivation

Motivator	Correlation
Conditions	0.23
Affiliation	−0.20

Table 13.3   Instrumentality correlated with motivation

Motivator	Correlation
Autonomy	0.48
Accomplishment	0.26
Affiliation	0.44

- **Withdrawn.** This is how outgoing and social a person is. At moderate levels this is much like extraversion, whereas at more extremely high levels it can be attention-seeking, demanding and narcissistic or histrionic behaviours. At lower levels it can be nervous, avoidant or socially withdrawn.

  Individuals higher on this factor are less motivated by their job conditions or comfort and are more motivated by affiliation motivators such as passing on information and working with others.

- **Influencing.** This is a focus on outcomes, getting things done (possibly at any cost). At moderate levels, this is a positive attribute, being outcome-oriented and prioritizing implementation. At the more extreme levels this may turn into Machiavellian or manipulative behaviours, getting things done at all costs. At the lower levels it can appear as indecision, inability to get things done, and no capacity to make difficult decisions or necessary sacrifices.

There is a relationship between high instrumentality and unethical decision making in the workplace but moderate levels can be related to improved creativity, while very high levels of narcissistic self-confidence are related to self-reported creativity, but no better creative performance (Spain, Harms and Lebreton, 2013). In a study of 39 US presidents, ratings of instrumentality were positively associated with not only charisma but also rated performance (Deluga, 2001). Leaders with high instrumentality also tended to serve more years in elected office and have a greater number of legislative achievements (Simonton, 1986). Moreover, the success of instrumental leaders was significantly enhanced when paired with higher levels of intelligence.

Those at higher levels of influencing are much more motivated by all three intrinsic factors: autonomy, achievement and affiliation. This is not necessarily problematic, but can turn destructive when the focus on objectives becomes too intense and leads to neglecting possible effects on colleagues or the organization as a whole.

An examination of 237 people's dark-side traits and HPMI motivators showed strong correlations between these dark-side traits and motivation. Figure 13.1 is a flow diagram that shows relationships between the three dark-side traits and correlated motivators. The size of each bar shows the strength of the relationship.

Figure 13.1   Flow diagram of relationships between dark-side traits and motivators

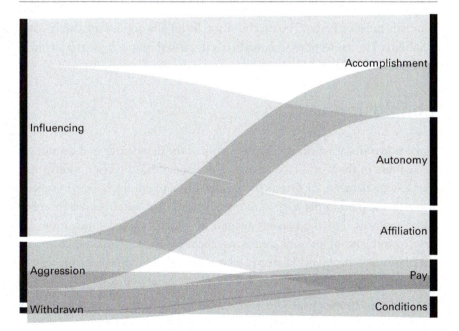

Optimality and the adaptive dark side

There are some indications that modest levels of 'dark-side' traits can be useful in the workplace, just as extreme personality traits have advantages as well as negative or undesirable features (MacRae and Furnham, 2014). Even on the dark-side traits, the majority of people fall within the statistically 'average' range that psychologists would refer to as 'normal'. Nearly all individual difference traits are normally distributed. Most people (68 per cent) fall within one standard deviation of the average range. Very few people have the most extreme traits, which is equally true of dark-side traits. They are rare by definition and exist at the extreme ends of the spectrum. There are strengths and weaknesses at every level of any particular trait and these can become more pronounced at the extreme ends.

Even characteristics that are often considered beneficial and healthy can occur at extremes. Healthy, high self-esteem in the extremes can manifest as narcissism. Creative thinking can become schizotypal or paranoid at the extreme end of the scale. An assertive approach to conflict can be taken too far and become aggressive or bullying behaviour. There may be an optimal range for dark-side traits, and the optimal ranges for these three dark-side factors are currently under investigation (for example: Doherty, 2016; Kotobi, 2016; Thornton, 2016). Selection errors can occur when arbitrary cut-off points think in a linear way that more (or less) of a particular characteristic must be better. Too much (or too little) of a good thing can become a liability. This concept of maximality is discussed in much greater detail in MacRae and Furnham (2014).

Conclusion

Dark-side traits at work can explain many of the destructive and derailment behaviours in the workplace. It is also an issue of misdirection motivation, along with elements of destructive leadership and conducive environment. It is often rooted in the *why* of motivation, not just what people are motivated towards, but the reasons behind it. Understanding motivation can help to mitigate or prevent destructive behaviours and individuals before they become a problem. There are four essential components of preventing dark-side potential from becoming destructive behaviour:

- **Oversight.** Proper oversight is the most essential tool any organization has to manage potential dark side and derailment. The difference between destructive urges and destructive behaviours is partly motivation – but it is also opportunity. Good corporate governance is essential to make sure the leadership and the entire organization have the proper level of oversight to make sure destructive potential does not turn into destructive behaviours. People need the autonomy to do their job, but also need the support and guidance to make sure they do not derail. Understanding the warning signs and having the tools and knowledge to spot them is an asset.

- **Sophisticated measurement.** Derailment potential can often be spotted before it becomes a problem. Tools to measure dark-side traits are one method of spotting derailment potential. Assessors must understand the potential derailment behaviours. Motivation can be a strong indicator of potentially dangerous and destructive behaviours. Just as the two previous examples of defectors from the intelligence services (Chapter 11) show the potentially serious consequences of unmet motivation gaps, understanding and measuring motivation gaps in the organization can help to identify potential derailment and prevent or mitigate the consequences before they become severe.

- **Personal support.** Derailment is often sparked or begins to grow in isolation. Those who become frustrated or disillusioned at work may feel isolated in the organization. Close, constructive relationships with others inside and outside of the organization can mitigate this, and potential consequences. Trusted friends, spouses, trusted coaches or mentors can mitigate or prevent derailment. Good advice, a grounded opinion or close social ties to help a person make informed and constructive decisions can prevent derailment. Unfortunately, those who need the honest opinion of a friend or colleague most can be the most resistant, least willing to listen or have lost friends to bad behaviour. Destructive behaviours are often socially isolating and can contribute to the spiral of derailment.

- **Self-awareness.** Understanding and awareness of oneself and personal characteristics, peculiarities and situation can help to prevent derailment. For example, being aware of what kind of situations are likely to incite one's own destructive behaviours can lead that person to take steps to avoid derailment.

In *The Lucifer Effect*, Philip Zimbardo (2008) describes how individuals can become corrupted by 'the toxic triangle' and describes how personal awareness as well as knowledge of psychological factors that lead to derailment can help 'inoculate' people against derailment. This book is highly recommended for anyone who wants to understand the dark-side traits, how environments can be conducive to destructive behaviours and what to do about it.

In the final chapter, we conclude the book with three examples from real organizations: one example of organizational failure and two examples of best practice.

References

Bovey, WH and Hede, A (2001) Resistance to organisational change: the role of defense mechanisms, *Journal of Managerial Psychology*, **16** (7), pp 534–48

Deluga, R (2001) American presidential Machiavellianism: implications for charismatic leadership and rated performance, *The Leadership Quarterly*, **12**, pp 339–63

Doherty, S (2016) *Validation of a Dark Side Model of Personality in the Workplace*, unpublished master's dissertation, University College London: London & Maastrict University: Maastrict

Freud, A (1937) *The Ego and the Mechanisms of Defence*, Hogarth Press and Institute of Psycho-Analysis, London

Johnson, D, Wrangham, R and Rosen, S (2002) Is military incompetence adaptive? An empirical test with risk-taking behavior in modern warfare, *Evolution and Human Behavior*, **23**, pp 245–64

Kotobi, L (2016) *The Evil Power: Validation of a new measure of dark side traits in the workplace*, unpublished master's dissertation, University College London: London & Maastrict University: Maastrict

MacRae, I and Furnham, A (2014) *High Potential: How to spot, manage and develop talented people at work*, Bloomsbury, London

McLean, B and Elkind, P (2005) *The Smartest Guys in the Room*, Penguin, New York

Padilla, A, Hogan, R and Kaiser, RB (2007) The toxic triangle: destructive leaders, susceptible followers, and conducive environments, *The Leadership Quarterly*, **18**, pp 176–94

Simonton, D (1986) Presidential personality: biographical use of the Gough Adjective Checklist, *Journal of Personality and Social Psychology*, **51**, pp 149–60

Solomon, S, Greenberg, J and Pyszczynski, T (1991) A terror management theory of social behavior: the psychological functions of self-esteem and cultural worldviews, *Advances in Experimental Social Psychology*, **24**, pp 93–159

Spain, SM, Harms, P and Lebreton, JM (2013) The dark side of personality at work, *Journal of Organizational Behavior*, DOI: 10.1002/job.1894

Thornton, K (2016) Validation of a dark side model of personality in the workplace, unpublished master's dissertation, University College London

Transparency International (2005) Transparency International Corruptions Perception Index

Walsh, KD and Moss, C (2010) Psychodynamic perspectives on organizational change and their relevance to transformational practice development, *International Journal of Nursing Practice*, **10**, pp 205–12

Zimbardo, P (2008) *The Lucifer Effect: How good people turn evil*, Rider, London

Best and worst practice from real companies 14

Introduction

This final chapter will conclude the book with three case studies from real companies. Two of the companies have been remarkably successful in recent years, and their success is used to highlight best practice of the ideas discussed in previous chapters. They provide models of best practice and demonstrate the profound effects of getting it right in the world of business. The third case study is an example of spectacular company failure that is also illustrative of what can happen when things go wrong, and illustrates many of the points made in previous chapters.

Successful companies learn from their own successes and failures, as well as the success and failure of others. Every company, like every person, will make mistakes at some point. The challenge (and opportunity) is identifying and resolving problems before they become too serious to face or too large to resolve.

The first cautionary tale is that of Enron, a company that, for a long time, commentators believed to be wildly successful – until everything unravelled. The company was believed to have the best, most intelligent people responsible for their almost unbelievable success. In the end, it collapsed – as a model of leadership teams with nearly all the right attributes but which were motivated towards ultimately destructive behaviours. The second tale is best-practice example G Adventures, a young and thriving travel company. It is a perfect example of motivation channelled constructively and effectively to make it a profitable company as well as a great company for its employees. The third case study, building on what was introduced in Chapter 8 with Ryan LLC, shows how creating a strong and constructive organizational culture and using measurement tools effectively can make great improvements within a company.

In these final three case studies, remember the key messages of previous chapters. The two positive case studies demonstrate how companies can substantially improve profitability and productivity and that improving employee well-being is complementary (if not necessary) to corporate success. Each of the case studies demonstrate that things *can* get better, although the cautionary tale serves as a warning that companies do not automatically move in that direction – it takes care and effort, and destructive or conflicting values can have terrible consequences.

Consider the context of each example. The case studies are all from very different industries, across different countries with very different types of work and different business models. What worked in one may not work in another; employees motivated in one company may be very different from some or many other companies. To be successful, the successes of one company can and must be adapted to suit the people and the culture of another company. There is no black-and-white template for profitability or for motivating people. It requires a strong knowledge of the strengths and weaknesses within one's own company (at all levels) in order to apply the lessons learned from the success and failure of others.

Cautionary tale 1: Enron and destructive culture

Enron only lasted 16 years, between 1985 and 2001, and initially appeared to be one of the most fantastically successful companies of its time. It turned out to be built on creative accounting and brilliant (but completely unethical and unsustainable) accounting processes. In its short history, with meteoric rise followed by swift and brutal collapse, it achieved notoriety as one of the most spectacular cases of accounting fraud in a company.

The growth of Enron was almost unimaginably rapid. By 2000 the company's annual revenue had reached US $100 billion. Its stock price peaked at US $90 and it was the sixth largest energy company in the world (CBC, 2006). The company was lauded as a model of entrepreneurship, and in 2000 the *New York Times* quoted their president, Jeffrey Skilling, saying two words to sum up the management philosophy at Enron: 'Loose and tight. Loose on everything related to creativity' (Salpukas, 1999). This apparently included the accounting practices. But, like any story built on lies, eventually – in 2001 – it all came toppling down. In October 2001 they posted their first quarterly loss in four years – of US $618 million. When the US Securities and Exchange Commission began an investigation they found a huge and complex system arranged to hide Enron's massive debt. The books had not just been cooked, they had been marinating.

The mechanics of Enron's accounting are not important, but for anyone interested in the details, McLean and Elkind's (2004) book *The Smartest Guys in the Room* and the subsequent film of the same name (Gibney *et al*, 2005) are highly recommended. The main point to consider in Enron's case is that their story is not one of incompetence, it is a story of extremely intelligent leadership and experts whose motivation and talents were directed towards destructive ends and dogged pursuit of money.

They used complex financial mechanisms to make risky bets and grow the company. Intelligence was highly valued in the company as much as (if not more) than bringing in money to the company. Enron President Jeffrey Skilling, when he was in business school and was asked by a professor at Harvard if he was smart, said, 'I'm [expletive]ing smart'. One of his favourite books was *The Selfish Gene* by Richard Dawkins (1976), which shaped a Darwinian view of the world and business (Gibney *et al*, 2005). Everything about the way Enron operated encouraged a culture of cut-throat competition, survival of the strongest and unrelenting focus on making money at all costs. An ex-trader at Enron said of the culture, 'If I'm on the way to my boss's office talking about compensation and if I can stomp on someone's throat on the way and that doubles it, well then I'll stomp on the guy's throat.' This behaviour was not just an undercurrent in company culture, it was explicitly and lavishly rewarded. A US $5 million bonus would not be uncommon for top performers.

This is a perfect example of motivation being channelled towards dark-side and destructive behaviours (Chapter 13). Aggression and destruction were encouraged when they were seen to be profitable, whether the consequences were borne by other employees or even their clients. They did not stop at dodgy accounting and making risky financial bets, but used their size and near-monopoly on industries such as energy to rig markets and essentially blackmail governments and their customers. In the California Energy Crisis of 2000 and 2001, Enron manipulated with strategies such as artificially interfering with energy lines, creating fake energy trades to inflate the price of energy, and moving energy to different regions to inflate the price and overcharge. They were significant political donors, the largest donors to George Bush and the Republican Party at the time, while they lobbied for deregulation and limiting corporate liability to lawsuits (Broder and van Natta, 2000). They also took advantage of subsequent deregulation to use strategies such as buying power capped at US $250 per megawatt and reselling it in other regions for US $1,200 per megawatt. This energy crisis that Enron was involved in inflated the price of energy by about 10 times the normal price and led to rolling power blackouts across California (BBC, 2002).

For the sake of argument, we could ask the question of whether this is actually a bad thing. If a company is profitable, growing, returns strong earnings to its shareholders and compensates its employees well, does it matter how they do business? Do the ends justify the means? This might be a question worth entertaining if Enron was a success story to this day, but everything that brought their short-term appearance of success was all that became their downfall in the end.

The lies, the fraud, the cooked books all came collapsing down, around accusations that senior leadership ransacked the company of earnings for their own gain while secretly the company was rotting away from within. Even while their share price soared, their profits collapsed, bad investments were written off and they aggressively pursued expansion even when there was no good financial reason to do so – but many received bonuses through the process of these bad deals. Employees, buoyed by the company's appearance of success, put their life savings and pensions into Enron stocks, fuelling the boom of an ultimately unsustainable stock. Executives got away with millions while their regular employees lost everything.

On 29 January 2001, Nancy Lay, the wife of Enron's president, said: 'It's gone. There's nothing left. Everything we had was mostly in Enron stock' (Stanley and Yardley, 2001). When news began to get out, Enron's share price fell from its peak of over US $90 to below US $1. This cost investors billions, many of whom were employees of the company. Enron filed for bankruptcy in December 2001 and over 5,000 employees lost their jobs.

There are lessons to learn from this that are still relevant today. Disgraced and convicted former Enron boss Andrew Fastow warned in 2015 that companies now have even more scope to bend the rules than existed during his time at Enron. He said: 'It is easy to find examples of companies causing misrepresentations while following the rules, and they are using those tools to do it. Most companies do not do it to the extent that I did it at Enron, so they don't suffer the consequences like we suffered, but companies do it to varying degrees' (Naidu-Ghelani, 2015).

When companies misdirect motivation towards destructive and even illegal activities, they ultimately fail and the consequences spread to many others, including their employees, shareholders, clients and even sometimes the wider economy. When financial motivations are priorities and rewarded at the expense of everything else, there will be a heavy price to pay in the long term.

There is much to be learned from this example though, and a thorough analysis by da Silveira (2013) suggests key lessons to be taken from the Enron debacle about corporate governance:

- **Gap between stated policies on paper and actual practice.** Although Enron had auditing practices, a governance checklist and various documents setting out rules of how things 'should' be done, in practice none of these occurred. The culture of the organization (Chapter 8) created a workplace where financial success was rewarded irrespective of the method, and poor performance was punished. A close-knit circle ensured that the stated rules were easily circumvented and those set to receive the greatest financial rewards also were responsible for oversight and governance.

- **Illusion of success.** Extensive media coverage and widespread commendations of Enron's performance created an image of success along with pressure to continually increase performance and make more money. The widespread discourse about Enron's success created a feeling of invincibility within the company, which helped its leaders to neglect the real problems within the company. Communication (Chapter 6) within the company was structured to centralize power and convey curated misinformation, and not to let the necessary information circulate within the company.

- **Incentivizing counter-productive behaviour.** Rewards based on deals closed, with little thought of long-term cash flow. Many pocketed large bonuses for loss-making deals. Publicly, the executives were under a great deal of pressure to continue to post profits, and indeed, their continued survival in the end depended on hiding the catastrophic state of company finances. It was doomed to failure because of systemic problems but the leadership had a huge stake in prolonging its downfall, which ultimately made the eventual fall even worse. This aligns closely with the discussion of performance reviews in Chapter 5 and intrinsic motivators in Chapter 7.

- **Relying on reputation instead of substance.** The company relied on famous business names and institutions to prop up and enhance their image. They hired big-name legal firms and investment banks for advice. They made a great deal of noise about respected institutions like Harvard Business School and used media representations of their success as an actual measure of success. Investors, along with most observers and commentators, failed to sufficiently question or investigate the real source of the apparent success. As discussed in Chapter 13 about the dark side, oversight and accountability are essential components to stave off and prevent this type of behaviour.

- **Blind trust and greed.** There is no question that those within the company as well as investors were not just too trusting, they were too greedy. Enron quickly became a get-rich-quick scheme that was making people almost unbelievable amounts of money. As we discussed in Chapter 9, there are parts of the human brain that still act in a similar way to our close primate cousins such as macaques. The investors were not just victims in a swindle, they actively participated in fuelling an artificial rise based on image and stoked by their own greed. Get-rich-quick schemes never stop being attractive, but they often end in tears.

- **System susceptible to fraud.** The changes of deregulation and the way the market worked at the time was extremely susceptible to fraud. Enron took advantage, but the structure was in place to allow them and others to take advantage of the system. Unethical and criminal behaviour is ultimately the responsibility of the perpetrators but, as discussed in Chapter 13, toxic environments breed toxic behaviour. Systems without proper regulation and oversight will attract unscrupulous characters and groups who are willing and able to take advantage for their own benefit.

The case of Enron, although tragic for many involved, can be taken as a lesson for companies about what to do to prevent derailment, and the role and importance of proper oversight – and it is helpful for viewing motivation as a driving force that can either be constructive or destructive. It must be harnessed and channelled effectively, or the consequences can be severe.

Next, let's look at a very different company with a very different organizational culture.

Best-practice example 1: G Adventures

G Adventures is an adventure tourism company founded in Toronto, Canada in 1990 by Bruce Poon Tip, which has grown from a single-person company to an international company with over 1,300 employees. They have experienced extraordinary growth and success in past decades, for which they credit their employees around the globe.

G Adventures has a very different attitude to human resources and company culture. We spoke with Sean Graham at G Adventures to discuss why the company is a great place to work and what they do differently. It is apparent from the beginning of the conversation that Sean is passionate about working at G Adventures, loves working there and what the company values. He emphasizes how important people are to the company, how their success means success to the company. Most companies will say something similar, that their most important asset is their people, but Sean and G Adventures clearly demonstrate that this company is different.

G Adventures takes training and development to a new level. Development activities take place in different countries all over the world, and employees from around the globe are sent to these events at locations where G Adventures does business. For example, a retreat for emerging leaders might be a week or two in Costa Rica. There are development activities, team competitions, and great opportunities to get to know the team from around the world. This is not just fun though, as Sean goes into greater detail about the programme it is clear that it is not just for 'fun'.

Even while Sean is talking informally, but animatedly, about these development sessions, leadership events and company policies it becomes clear this is a well-crafted and cohesive talent management policy bundled into activities that reinforce company culture and provide a great deal of real development opportunities. Without any need for management speak or jargon, this is a company that is doing everything that would be described in any talent management textbook. But they go further and are doing it in a way that reflects the company values and culture, and in a way that the employees enjoy the process.

There are a few things that initially strike me as less serious approaches, such as everyone in the company being allowed to choose their own title (some current titles include Professor of Culture, The Happy Maker, The Happy Little Vegemite, Thinkanaut, Solutionator, and Viking God). It would be easy to be priggish about the job titles, but the reason it works is because it fits within the company culture. Chapter 8 discussed how policies should fit with the culture of the organization, and this reinforces it.

G Adventures has been a successful company because everything they do seems to be well-thought out, cohesive and designed to improve the work for those who work there as well as company performance. It is not compromise; their success clearly is built on engaged and motivated employees who like working there. The youth and energy that the company almost exudes is not a consequence of the industry they are in, it is a core component of their business model that has clearly been successful.

Another impressive event is their annual company retreat called G Stock. The company flies over 200 staff from all around the world and sends another 200+ staff from 'Base Camp'. All travel and expenses are covered by the company and many more prizes and gifts are given to employees during the retreat. This is a great reward, and a chance for the company to recognize individual contributions as well as team success. Awards that have been earned over the previous year are presented and this is an excellent forum to promote best practice in the company and recognize achievement (as discussed in Chapter 9). The retreat extends beyond, for example into the city of Toronto with a company talent show, cultural fair and scavenger hunt.

The purpose of this event is to make connections within the company. In a global company with locations around the world, it is the ideal forum to make connections across the company, particularly when other locations are also products that the company is selling to its travel customers. Representatives from around the world get a chance to describe what is so great about their own destination, and those within the company who would be selling that destination can hear about it first hand. This may seem to be an extravagant and expensive way of promoting communication across the company and recognizing employees, but it works. It is particularly well-suited to this industry. The efforts at raising the ceiling of intrinsic motivation (Chapter 2) have worked extraordinarily well in this case.

There is actually a simple genius in this approach, which should be clear from their leadership development programmes. Bringing together all the emerging leaders in the company to one location, to work together, have friendly competition and learn from each other greatly strengthens the development programme. The future leaders of the company are not just sitting in a classroom through a half-hearted leadership development course. They are working together, learning teamwork and leadership skills first hand, and building relationships with the company's future leaders from around the world. The fact that it is fun, engaging and at an exciting destination is not just a bonus, it is inherent to the process. Sean tells me there is a Maya Angelou quote that explains it best, 'I've learned that people will forget what you said, people will forget what you did, but people will never forget how you made them feel.' That is the heart of motivation and engagement that G Adventures has got so right.

The growth and continued success of the company demonstrates its success. In 25 years it has grown from a one-person company to a global company with US \$350 million revenue. Their customer satisfaction ratings are consistently around 99 per cent. The travel industry is notorious for high employee turnover rates, averaging about 35 per cent (Noland, 2015). G Adventures has an employee turnover rate of only 5 per cent. The company's growth speaks for itself, while in 2016 it was rated by Great Places to Work as one of the 10 best multinational workplaces in Canada. The president of G Adventures, Poon Tip (Tip, 2014), sums up the heart of their success, 'I want people to love coming to work each day, [I want to] create a place where people don't just come to work, but where they feel that they are contributing to something greater. Do that and their work, no matter what it is they do, becomes a calling.' That is the heart of motivation and engagement.

Best-practice example 2: Ryan LLC

The example of Ryan LLC was briefly introduced in Chapter 8, as an example of flexible working schedules and a performance management system based entirely on outcomes that substantially increased the autonomy given to employees.

Ryan LLC is also a prime example of a company that effectively uses measurement along with excellent systems and software to complement their business and unique approach to motivating employees. They are exemplars of measuring motivation (as discussed in Chapter 5). They have developed a completely flexible work environment where employees are evaluated purely on objective performance. Employees are given complete autonomy to work when, where and how they want.

Ryan, a tax services company, had been incredibly successful when measured by profit. Revenue steadily increased since its inception in 1991, and employees were very well paid. In 1991, the first year of operating, Ryan's revenues were US $156,000 and rose steadily, with revenues now exceeding US $400 million. Working conditions, however, became increasingly tough as the company began to grow. In the late 1990s and early 2000s employees were expected to be in the office at least eight hours per day and at least 50 hours per week. Salaried employees had their vacation policies rescinded. The company was developing a reputation for being a sweatshop. It was a well-paid sweatshop, but consequently employee turnover was at 20 per cent. Turnover is expensive for any company, but for a highly skilled sector like tax services 20 per cent turnover, even in a profitable and growing company, is a significant cost.

Ryan is a prime example of a successful company using measurement to understand what is going on in their organization, learning from their mistakes, and using problems as a catalyst to make their workplace better for their employees as well as increasing profits. In 2008 they changed the gruelling 50-hour week and changed benefits to a completely flexible system. Employees were no longer required to put in 50 office hours, instead there were no required office hours. Benefits were extended to all employees, including paid maternity, paternity and medical leave (in the United States, this leave is not required to be paid). The vacation and time-off policy was completely transformed. Employees were given full control of their own vacation schedules and time off. Employee performance was only to be measured based on actual performance: when and how each person worked was left up to their own autonomy.

They were collecting data, and they made use of this. For example, in 2005 their employee survey showed a concerning trend (Kowske, 2013):

- Management involves people in decisions that affect their jobs or work environment: 62 per cent.
- People are encouraged to balance their work life and their personal life: 42 per cent.
- Taking everything into account, I would say this is a great place to work: 67 per cent.
- People look forward to coming to work here: 58 per cent.
- I want to work here for a long time: 56 per cent.
- I feel good about the way we contribute to the community: 55 per cent.

After bringing in the flexible work policy with the systems to support it, they noticed a remarkable difference in employee attitudes, shown in Figure 14.1.

The precise wording of the employee survey questions in Figure 14.1 were:

- Management involves people in decisions that affect their jobs or work environment.
- I feel good about the way we contribute to the community.
- People look forward to coming to work here.
- People are encouraged to balance their work life and personal life.
- I want to work here for a long time.
- Taking everything into account, I would say this is a great place to work.

This translated immediately into improved client outcomes as well as happier employees. The year the system was implemented, 2008, shows an immediate increase in client service quality, rising steadily in subsequent years (Figure 14.2). Their employee turnover, too, dropped to nearly half in the first year of the new system. This demonstrates the potential effect of filling in the motivation gap (Chapter 11). The motivation gap leads to demotivation, disengagement and ultimately higher turnover.

Figure 14.1 Ryan Employee Survey results 2005 and 2012

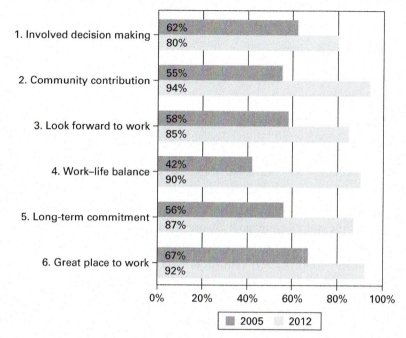

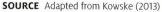
SOURCE Adapted from Kowske (2013)

Figure 14.2 Client service quality, 2004–12

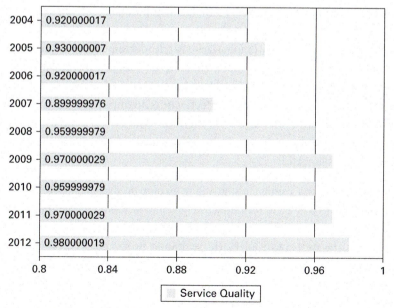

SOURCE Adapted from Kowske (2013)

The flexibility was extremely effective, but it required a good system for monitoring performance. They set up the 'myRyan' system and expanded their measurement system to include:

- client satisfaction scores;
- financial targets;
- project evaluation goals;
- 360-degree evaluation scores;
- individual performance evaluation scores.

Then performance was evaluated using the criteria shown in Table 14.1. The main performance criteria are given the majority of the weight in the evaluation, with financial targets and client service quality emphasized. Less important, but still relevant goals, were tracked under Tier 2, which only counts for 20 per cent of the overall performance review weight. However, their inclusion confirms and reinforces that they are still important and necessary criteria.

There are four interesting points about this to consider. First, there are different tiers of metrics. These have different weightings that emphasize their relative importance. Exceeding financial targets can have a very large boost on the overall score. Second, benchmarking, allows the company to assess minimum levels of performance, as well as those above average. Third, progress can be tracked relatively and absolutely over time for any individual employee. Fourth, notice that leadership and management potential is evaluated, but has a 0 per cent weight on the overall score performance. This helps to identify potential leaders, but also emphasizes that leadership ability is not a core competency, or a required component of most people's work. This type of performance delusion (MacRae and Furnham, 2014) is discussed in Chapter 8.

Identifying leaders, when done effectively, is an important activity for any organization. Ryan's system allows them to identify those with leadership potential, and employees who are interested in a leadership career path. One employee at Ryan said:

> Last year I expressed an interest in taking on more leadership responsibilities.
> I was quickly included in the hiring, training and mentoring processes related to
> new business development hires. [A leader] provided constructive feedback and
> helped me be aware of Ryan's extensive training programmes that could better
> develop my leadership skills. In addition, I learned through working closely
> with senior leadership how to understand government funding programmes and
> how best to integrate a new acquisition into the business development group.
> The opportunity to learn about a new service line was very rewarding.

Table 14.1 myRyan performance evaluation framework

	Scale	Benchmark	Minimum	Actual	% of Benchmark	Weight	Score
			Tier 1 (80%)				
Financial Goal	$	US$8,000	US$0	US$16,000	200%	40%	80.0%
Client Service	6	5.8	5.2	4.9	94.2%	40%	37.68%
			Tier 2 (20%)				
Firm-wide Initiatives	5	4	3	3.5	125%	5%	6.25%
Leadership and Management	5	4	3	4	100%	0%	
Core Competencies	5	4	3	2.5	62.5%	5%	3.13%
TOTAL							127.06%

The performance evaluation system also shows how an individual can be meeting or exceeding a particular goal – such as their financial targets, which is an important part of performance – but still be underperforming in other areas. For example, the financial targets are exceeded, which has a dramatic effect on their performance score, but client services are below the benchmark as well as the minimum score. This identifies potential areas for improvement. It may also highlight discussions about performance that are important to have. Why are sales high but client satisfaction is relatively low? What can be done to change this?

At Ryan, flexibility is implemented at an individual and team level. General guidelines are agreed at a team level about performance management feedback, communication, use of technology, protocols such as core office hours, scheduled meetings, etc, and team-level performance measures and benchmarks within that particular team. The flexibility of this system allows managers to use the overall performance management framework and adapt and add to it to suit the context and responsibilities of a particular team. This is important because regions as well as teams can vary within any company.

In Chapter 4, we discussed how a 'family-oriented' approach to designing HR policy worked well. That was for a company with mainly shift work with a large proportion of employees working in factories. Obviously manufacturing jobs have less flexibility than professional services. However, the example of Ryan shows how there are different types of workplaces and approaches to work that improve the experience of work for those with families. Two examples from Ryan employees are given below:

'myRyan has allowed me to take part in my children's extracurricular activities without being made to feel guilty when having to occasionally leave a little earlier in the work day. This past year my son had made the rep baseball team in our town. With some of the games being a far distance, leaving work early is sometimes the only option to get him to the game on time, but when sitting in the stands and he looks into the crowd and smiles at you, you know there is no other place you would rather be. myRyan has alleviated some of the stress involved in being a full-time working mother with young children.

In Spring, 2013, I had a dilemma on my hands. My sister who was nine months pregnant with her first baby (and my first nephew or niece) had asked me to be her labour coach months before. It was 10 am and she called to say she was in labour. I was at the office and scheduled to be on the TaxDirect line until 1 pm, but also part of the team that would analyse the federal budget that afternoon. I had mentioned to my manager, months before, that I was 'on call', but I was now trying to figure out how late I could leave without the risk of missing this amazing event! I approached my manager to let him know my sister had called and that I might try to stay until 1 pm, as I expected a long labour since this was her first baby. He insisted I leave right away and assured me the team would manage just fine. It was a great example of putting the person before the work they do, when there is a chance to do so.

The impact on the business has been profoundly positive in all respects. Not only did employee satisfaction improve greatly (as shown in Figure 14.1), after implementing the change in 2008 the company continued to grow rapidly. Revenues in 2012 exceeded 2008 revenues by 52 per cent (up to US $350 million) and grew further, to over US $400 million in 2013. Employee headcount more than doubled in the same period, from 677 employees to 1,582 employees, growing to over 2,100 employees in 2015. The organization continues to be recognized as an excellent workplace. In 2016 Great Places to Work rated them number one as the best workplace for flexibility in the United States, number four on the list of best places to work in the Netherlands, number five on the list in Canada of best workplaces for women, and number 17 on the list of best large and multinational workplaces in Canada.

Management also sees the value in these tools:

I love the Engagement Pulse. I appreciate knowing the mood of my team. I hate to see a sad face on my dashboard, so the pulse comments give me the opportunity to resolve concerns and better manage my team on a consistent basis. The check-in questions also help keep me accountable to recognizing my team and being clear on my expectations, so they can be clear on their daily goals.

Like all case studies, Ryan is just one example of a company that has transformed its culture. The company has profited, and employees are much happier in their work. The two are complementary, not exclusive. It is also an excellent example of some of the problems that many small companies experience when they grow. For example, the expanding company is getting the job done, profits keep coming in and revenues keep increasing. But, in the expansion, the small company is focused on expansion and forgets to take care of the people in it. The consequences of demotivated, unhappy employees is expensive for the company and bad for the people inside it. As with all case studies, different types of organization may need to use measurement systems in different ways or different purposes. However, there are a few lessons that can be learned for any organization. Delta Emerson (President, Global Shared Services) says that Ryan learned three essential lessons from the process, which apply universally:

1 **Find what works for you**: 'What worked for us won't work for everyone. We're happy to tell people our story and what we learned, but we can't say, "Do exactly like we did, and you'll be fine."'

2 **Involve your employees**: 'You have to have everybody involved so they have a piece of it. That way, when you encounter a pothole, they are more likely to work with you than point at you and say, "Hey, you screwed up."'

3 **Anticipate growing pains**: 'Not everybody is going to be thrilled with the concept of flexibility, and you are going to have to manage that and anticipate it.'

Ryan is a perfect illustration of our main point. Even successful, profitable and growing companies have significant opportunities to improve. They found that improving work for employees increased their company effectiveness. At Ryan, they measured and understood the problem, came up with a solution and promptly and effectively implemented a new and better system. They saw results and went from good to better.

Conclusion

The science and research of motivation and performance at work teaches us a great deal about what can be done to motivate people at work, and how to improve profitability, productivity and make work a better place for those who do it. The encouraging and exciting message is that practitioners have a long way to go to implement the messages from research into practice.

This is a great opportunity for those who are prepared to seize it, and have the potential to create huge competitive advantages for those who make improvements.

The encouraging message, both from science and practice in organizations, clearly shows that work is not a battle between organizational performance and employee well-being. Health and happiness do not need to be sacrificed for productivity and profit. Motivated, engaged employees are more effective, more creative, more productive and have more to offer in the workplace. The best workplaces create a culture and environment where employees have the capacity and opportunity to contribute their full potential to the company.

The lesson from generational differences should also make it apparent that there are still a great deal of myths and misinformation about the world of work. Stereotyping can lead to poor management decisions, prejudices that lead to conscious or unconscious biases in selection, and retention and development that may get the wrong person, for the wrong reasons and demotivate a large segment of the workforce. Generational differences are a myth that can be counter-productive in the same way that discrimination based on gender, sexuality, ethnicity and other factors do not predict workplace performance in any meaningful way. A great deal is made about the war on talent, but equitable practices (such as those discussed in Chapter 2) create opportunities to broaden the talent pool and get the right people for the job while engaging and motivating the entire workforce. Those in first have the competitive advantage, and first choice over their competitors.

The world of work is changing, always has been changing, and will continue to change. Chapter 12 discussed outsourcing, contracting and employment agreements such as zero hours contracts. These trends will continue and are likely to be amplified in the coming years. Just like there is no 'right' type of motivation, there is no simple answer to whether these arrangements are ultimately beneficial or harmful. The truth probably lies somewhere in the middle. More importantly, the answer lies more in the *how* than the *what*. Different organizational models, cultures and employment relationships suit different organizations and individuals in different ways in different times. It should not be a matter of guesswork; measuring motivation and other factors like engagement will inform decision making and tell a great deal about the organization.

As the three case studies in this chapter demonstrate, along with the content throughout this book, motivation is as complex as it is an essential component of productivity, profitability and well-being in the workplace.

References

BBC (2002) Enron 'manipulated energy crisis', BBC News, 7 May

Broder, JM and van Natta, D Jr (2000) The 2000 campaign: the money; perks for the biggest donors, and pleas for more cash, *The New York Times*, 30 July

CBC (2006) The rise and fall of Enron: a brief history, CBC News, 25 May

da Silveira, AM (2013) The Enron scandal a decade later: lessons learned? working paper, Corporate Governance at the School of Economics, Management and Accounting at the University of São Paulo

Gibney, A, Elkind, P, McLean, B and Coyote, P (2005) Enron: the smartest guys in the room (video file)

Kowske, B (2013) [accessed 10 October 2016] The Flexible Workplace Delivers Results, *Bersin by Deloitte* [Online] http://www.bestcompaniesaz.com/pdf/ryans-eight-year-journey.pdf

MacRae, IS and Furnham, A (2014) *High Potential: How to spot, manage and develop talented people at work*, Bloomsbury, London

McLean, B and Elkind, P (2004) *The Smartest Guys in the Room: The amazing rise and scandalous fall of Enron*, Penguin, London

Naidu-Ghelani, R (2015) Companies still bending financial rules, Enron boss warns, BBC, 6 November

Noland, T (2015) G Adventures: the company that runs on happiness, *TriplePundit*, 6 October

Salpukas, A (1999) Firing up an idea machine; Enron is encouraging the entrepreneurs within, *The New York Times*, 27 June

Stanley, A and Yardley, J (2001) Enron's many strands: the ex-chairman; Lay's wife defends him and says that they're ruined, *The New York Times*, 29 January

Tip, TP (2014) *Looptail: How one company changed the world by reinventing business*, Piaktus, London

GOING FURTHER

Although the book ends here, we would like to continue the discussion about motivation and performance in the workplace and would like to hear from you, dear readers, about your own experiences with motivation and performance at work. We will be including the best comments and examples in future publications (either online articles or even in future books).

We would also like to invite you to complete a free version of the HPMI, to test your own motivators in the workplace. We are offering this at no cost so that you can compare your results with the case studies and examples included in this book and the supplementary articles online. Feel free to share this with friends or colleagues and compare your scores. If your colleagues, your manager or employees are interested, share your results and use the test to start a discussion of what motivates you at work and why.

We are also open to questions about any of the content in this book. You can submit your questions at **www.highpotentialpsych.co.uk/motivperformance**, and the best questions will be featured in Q&A articles. Get in touch with us on social media to continue the discussion and stay up-to-date about future events, resources and publications:

https://twitter.com/IanSMacRae

https://twitter.com/ProfAdrianFurnh

https://www.facebook.com/ianmacrae.highpotential/

We would like this book to be more than just the text within it; we want this to spark conversations about motivation and performance at work and to work with you, dear readers, to continue to advance what is such an exciting field of research and practice: making work better and making work better for those who do it.

INDEX

Note: The index is filed in alphabetical, word-by-word order. 'Mc' and numbers are filed as spelt out in full and acronyms filed as presented. Page locators in *italics* denote information contained within a Figure or Table.

CPSIA information can be obtained
at www.ICGtesting.com
Printed in the USA
LVOW13s1449190417
531395LV00017B/210/P